AVENUES OF HISTORY

CONTENTS

PART ONE

PART TWO

PART THREE

v

AUTHOR'S NOTE

I HAVE to thank the editors and owners of *The Times Literary Supplement* and of *The Times*, of *Commentary*, the *Listener*, *History Today*, the *Manchester Guardian*, the *National Review*, the *New Statesman and Nation*, the *Quarterly Review*, and *Time and Tide* for permission to reprint essays, or parts of essays, which appeared in their columns.

I have further to thank the Accademia Nazionale dei Lincei in Rome for permission to reprint my essay on 'Liberty and Nationality' which in 1948 was presented as a paper to the Tenth Conference 'Volta' of that Academy, and appeared in the Proceedings of the Conference.

L. B. NAMIER

60 *The Grampians*
London, W.6
15 *February* 1952

Avenues of History

PART I

HISTORY

THE SUBJECT matter of history is human affairs, men in action, things which have happened and how they happened; concrete events fixed in time and space, and their grounding in the thoughts and feelings of men—not things universal and generalized; events as complex and diversified as the men who wrought them, those rational beings whose knowledge is seldom sufficient, whose ideas are but distantly related to reality, and who are never moved by reason alone. Yet in all intelligent historical quest there is, underneath, a discreet, tentative search for the typical and recurrent in the psyche and actions of man (even in his unreason), and a search for a morphology of human affairs, curbed though that search be by the recognition that absent from the life of communities is the integration peculiar to living organisms: "fifty men do not make a centipede". On the practical side history should help man to master the past immanent both in his person and in his social setting, and induce in him a fuller understanding of the present through a heightened awareness of what is, or is not, peculiar to his own age. Knowledge and understanding are required before any reasonable endeavour can be made to direct and control; and man, despite a thousand dismal failures and though more and more oppressed by his own creations, can never abandon the attempt to navigate the seas of destiny, and resign himself to drifting in them: he therefore tries to gain a better comprehension of the circumstances in which he is set and of his own ways of acting. History further provides a mental discipline and, as 'case history', supplies materials for training in specific professions.

And last but not least, it is written and read for its own sake: it answers a need in human nature and a curiosity; it pleases and inspires; and as all the works of man are historically conditioned, knowledge of history is required for the full enjoyment of man's cultural heritage in literature, in painting and sculpture, architecture, or music.

Even animals have inherited habits and preconceived ideas which may, or may not, answer the exigencies of reality. Man is born into a world which swaddles him in the material and spiritual inheritance of society. Primitive man is probably even more the captive of custom and tradition, and is certainly less capable of conceiving and contriving change. But has constant and rapid change, now the law of our lives, set man free? Man-generated, it is seldom man-controlled; it has acquired a momentum of its own, while the vastly extended and infinitely complex social setting adds enormously to the mass of human actions determined neither by vital instinct nor by reason, but by a routine inherent in that setting. Thus the past is on top of us and with us all the time; and there is only one way of mastering it even remotely in any one sector: by knowing how these things have come to be, which helps to understand their nature, character, and their correlation, or lack of correlation, to the present realities of life.

Maladjustment in human affairs is a concomitant of change. Forms, procedure, and ideas outlive the conditions which gave them rise: disbodied they continue an independent existence. Thus the 'separation of powers' once supplied a rough delimitation and working compromise between separate centres of power— the Crown and Parliament, or the British Government and Colonial Assemblies; but next, enshrined in a doctrine or in systems based on that doctrine, the separation was continued even in undivided sovereignty; it has weighed on the constitutional development of France and shaped that of the United States. Or again, nations fight ghosts: for about two generations after 1815 the new France passionately defended herself against the return of an *ancien régime* which nothing could have resurrected, while conservative France, old and new, dreaded the repetition of a political revolution which had run its course and was extinct—a semblance of flames that could neither warm nor scorch. In this country the fear of Spain survived deep into the seventeenth, and of France deep into the nineteenth century, after either had ceased to be a danger to Britain: and each time those out-dated fears favoured the rise of the nation which, in turn, was to become a menace. The *cri de cœur* of a member of the Long Parliament, 'You will shout, "Fire, fire", be it in Noah's flood', describes one aspect of the ever-recurring divergence between fixed ideas and a changing reality. From such examples some people will readily draw the lesson that a similar situation has now arisen with regard to Germany and Russia: which may, or may not, be the case, but must not be adjudged on the force of historical analogy.

While ideas outlive reality, names and words outlast both. The nature and meaning of what they serve to denote or express, change often by wellnigh imperceptible deflection: a gentle, reassuring process which in practice preserves continuity and fosters an illusion of stability; but which is apt to give rise to wrong inferences. Take two examples: there were bishops in the fourth century, and party names were in use in eighteenth-century England; yet conclusions must not be drawn from either fact without a thorough understanding of what those terms then covered. On the other hand there are permanent elements in the lives of communities which, refracted through the prism of ages, reappear in different colours. In the sixteenth century religion was the primary conscious bond of communities, in the nineteenth it was supplanted as such by nationality: the emphasis has changed and the terms in which certain things are expressed or disputed; much less the underlying reality—there always was a strong national element in religion, and there is a religious element in nationality. Caught in the perennial tangle of names, ideas, and reality, man plays with them, and they play with him.

At times, when the burden of the past becomes unbearable, men stand forth determined to brush 'the clouds away of precedent and custom', and to live by 'the great beacon light God set in all'; the Puritans called it conscience, the French of 1789 called it reason. But even conscience and reason move in the grooves of inherited, historically conditioned ideas and words; and when man has wiped the slate clean and tries to write his own message, the past which lives in him and has moulded him will bring back the very things he has tried to obliterate. The French Revolution, on its ideological side, set out with Rousseau's dictum: 'Man is born free, yet everywhere he is in chains'—a historical statement equally incorrect with regard to the individual as to mankind; but though the men of 1789 thought themselves omnipotent by force of reason, in order to feel assured that liberty was possible they had to believe that once it had been: they appealed to history while consciously trying to break with the past. And when under pressure of war an efficient government had to be found, 'in the chaos of pure reason', writes Albert Sorel, 'men brutally fell back on past practice: instinct made them revert to habits, routine, and precedents: and of these there were none to favour liberty, but plenty for despotism'.

The way of life of a nation, *les mœurs*, cannot be transformed by an act of will or an edict; attempts to do so, expressive of intellectual *hubris* (*eritis sicut Deus* . . .), invariably lead to confusion. Planned change can envisage only a narrow sector of life, while the wider repercussions can seldom be forecast. Hence the admitted superiority of 'organic change': of empiric practice advancing by slow, tentative steps. Yet human society is not an organism capable of unconscious growth: at every stage thought and theory intervene, more often impeding than promoting readjustments imposed by circumstances and achieved in practice. No one ever planned the role of the British Prime Minister or of the Cabinet: theory and sentiment alike were averse to them in the early, formative stages; and as for political parties, no sooner had they appeared than men started praying for their extinction.

A dilettante is one who takes himself more seriously than his work; and doctrinaires enamoured of their theories or ingenious ideas are dilettanti in public affairs. On the contrary, the historical approach is intellectually humble; the aim is to comprehend situations, to study trends, to discover how things work: and the crowning attainment of historical study is a historical sense—an intuitive understanding of how things do not happen (how they did happen is a matter of specific knowledge). Yet study unsupported by practical experience will seldom produce a historian: hence the poverty of a great deal of history written by cloistered generations. We have been brought up on the tale that the King 'left the Cabinet' because George I did not know English (an occurrence and explanation unknown to contemporaries, or to eighteenth-century authors); what did happen was that business gradually passed from the large and dignified Cabinet presided over by the King to a much smaller body of working Ministers: a characteristically English process. Or again, the German historian, Professor Dahlmann, probably the most eminent intellectual in the Frankfurt Parliament, having in April 1848 completed his first draft of a constitution for Germany—the product of a week's intensive labours—hoped thus 'with a few incisive paragraphs to heal the ills of a thousand years'. Would anyone now think that possible? Even the scepticism of the masses with regard to election promises derives probably from a greater maturity; though often consciously turned against the 'politicians', it expresses subconscious doubts concerning the feasibility of vast programmatic action.

A neurotic, according to Freud, is a man dominated by unconscious memories, fixated on the past, and incapable of overcoming it: the regular condition of human communities. Yet the dead festering past cannot be eliminated by violent action any more than an obsession can be cured by beating the patient. History has therein a 'psycho-analytic' function; and it further resembles psycho-analysis in being better able to diagnose than to cure: the beneficial therapeutic effects of history have so far been small; and it is in the nature of things that it should be so. Science can construct apparatus which the user need not understand: a child can switch on the electric light. Nor does surgery depend for its success on being understood by the patient. But psycho-analysis works, if at all, through the emotions and the psyche of the individual; and history, to be effective, would have to work through those of the masses. It would have to educate them. But how can it? what can it give them? The study of history—of human affairs —has to go deep and remain uncontaminated to be of value; and then the value is not in its factual contents—'education is that which remains after one has forgotten all one has learnt'. Wisdom does not spring from remembered events, and the mind is cluttered up by an excess of recollections. 'One is apt to perish in politics from too much memory', wrote Tocqueville. But ways of thinking—'an intellectual climate'—can apparently be transmitted without traversing the experiences which went to shape them.

Popularized history is mostly dull and valueless; 'popular' history, that which grips and sways the masses, is mostly a figment. To popularize usually means to oversimplify: fine shades and distinctions disappear, the tree is stripped of its foliage and branches, there remains a dead stump. On the other hand, to affect the masses history has to work on their passions and emotions, projecting them through a distorted, mythical past into a coveted future: it is then the product of imagination and fervour, and not of accurate perception and critical understanding. Such pseudo-history, in which the Germans excel but which is known also in other countries, has been supplied in profusion during the last 150 years: *la trahison des clercs* Jules Benda has called it; and Paul Valéry indicts all history as 'the most dangerous product distilled in the laboratory of the human mind'. But articulate speech and articulate thought do endow man with a cognizance and a conscious memory of things not of his own experience, which is history; and this will inevitably influence his conscious actions: he will talk and think in terms of historical experience however small and uncertain his factual knowledge. The choice therefore lies between an attempt at critical inquiry and thought, and the mere babble of blurred reminiscences and fanciful interpretations. The foremost task of honest history is to discredit and drive out its futile or dishonest varieties.

'Does history repeat itself?' No two events or chains of events are identical any more than two individuals or their lives. Yet the lives of all men can be summed up, as in Anatole France's story, in eight words: 'They were born, they suffered, and they died.' The elimination of individual variants, which tend to cancel out each other where large numbers are involved, is likely to disclose certain basic regularities. There may be cycles in history and a rhythm: but if there are, the range of our experience and knowledge is insufficient to establish them; and if there are not, the turn of our minds will still incline us to assume their existence and to invent them. 'Is there a thing whereof men say, See, this is new? it hath been already, in the ages which were before us.'

Man is a repetitive, aping animal; and to basic regularities and individual variations he adds the element of imitation and of expected repetition. The memory of the sudden German collapse in 1918, after a long series of conquests, helped to sustain our morale in 1940, and was the skeleton at the German feast of victories. A German soldier who had been in Warsaw in 1918, and returned there with the conquering German armies in 1939, said to a friend: 'Last time a washer-woman disarmed me. I wonder who will this time.' When the Russian revolution broke out in March 1917, there were people who expected that the Russian armies would now fight with a new *élan*, forgetting that in 1792 war broke out in the third year of revolution, while in 1917 revolution broke out in the third year of war; the French peasant-soldier—to mention but one factor—went to the front to retain the land he had seized, while the Russian peasant-soldier

went home to seize it. One of the aims of sound historical education must be to wean men from expecting automatic repetition
and from juggling with uncorrelated precedents and analogies;
they must be trained to fit things into long-range historical processes, and not to think in isolated word-concepts working in a
void: for it is possible to believe anything so long as the question
is not asked how it could come to be, or how it could work. When
in 1938 Chamberlain and Halifax signified their readiness to admit
territorial changes in Central Europe provided these were effected
'by reasonable agreements and not by force', they were using
a-historical concepts; had ever a European continental nation
ceded territory except under extreme duress, or if possessed of
crushing superiority used it with moderation? There was escapism
in that sham-expectation but also a lack of historical thinking.
Or again, in the 1,250 large pages of British pre-Munich diplomatic documents, Czechoslovakia is treated throughout as an
untenable creation but the question is never asked what the political and strategic configuration of Europe would be after Czechoslovakia had been obliterated: an escapist reticence favoured by
man's innate reluctance to think out the long-range consequences
of his actions.

   In certain disciplines, such as diplomacy, military art, politics,
or finance, individual experience is obviously and necessarily
inadequate: men have to draw on history, which is vicarious
experience, less vivid and formative but much wider. Can men
learn from it? That depends on the quality and accuracy of the
historian's perceptions and conclusions, and on the critical facul-
ties of the reader—on the 'argument', and on the 'intellects' to
comprehend it. When erudition exceeds intelligence, past results
are rigidly applied to radically changed situations and preparations
are completed for fighting the previous war. Conclusions drawn
primarily from experience in the narrow theatre of the Crimean
War gave rise to Frossard's doctrine of systematic defence; next,
the German victories of 1870 made military opinion swing back
in favour of relentless attack; the price paid for it in the trench-
warfare of 1914–18 produced in turn the Maginot mentality
among the French public and politicians, though much less among
the soldiers who continued to plan offensive action: but in the
slow-motion style of 1918. The Germans in 1914 neglected
Clausewitz's injunction, if there is one enemy to go for his capital,
but if two, for their line of communication. In 1940 they correctly

went first for the Channel ports, and only next for Paris; but in 1941 they perhaps unduly neglected a new factor in warfare: had their main initial offensive been directed against the Caucasus, they might have cut off Russia's oil supply and immobilized her armies. The time lag in disciplined military thought is aggravated on the victorious side by the glory which attaches to past successes and by the prestige of their ageing artificers. Yet in all spheres alike, even in the freest, false analogies, the product of superficial knowledge and reasoning, are the pitfall of history as *magistra vitae*.

Human affairs being the subject matter of history, all human pursuits and disciplines in their social aspects enter into it. But as no human mind can master more than a fraction of what would be required for a wide and balanced understanding of human affairs, limitation and selection are essential in the historian's craft. Analytic insight into the tangle of human affairs coupled with a consciousness of his own limitations is the mark of the real historian, and maturity is attained perhaps later in his work than in any other discipline.

As history deals with concrete events fixed in time and space, narrative is its basic medium—but guided by analytic selection of what to narrate. The function of the historian is akin to that of the painter and not of the photographic camera: to discover and set forth, to single out and stress that which is of the nature of the thing, and not to reproduce indiscriminately all that meets the eye. To distinguish a tree you look at its shape, its bark and leaf; counting and measuring its branches would get you nowhere. Similarly what matters in history is the great outline and the significant detail; what must be avoided is the deadly morass of irrelevant narrative.

History is therefore necessarily subjective and individual, conditioned by the interest and vision of the historian. His interest if intense and sincere is contagious, and the test of his originality is whether it is convincing; once stated, his discoveries should appear obvious. The discussion whether history is an art or a science seems futile: it is like medical diagnosis; a great deal of previous experience and knowledge, and the scientific approach of the trained mind, are required, yet the final conclusions (to be re-examined in the light of evidence) are intuitive: an art. The great historian is like the great artist or doctor: after he has done his work, others should not be able to practise within its sphere in the terms of the preceding era. Yet the great mass of the work even of the masters of the craft is devoted to studies of a preparatory character and primarily for the use of the profession. One must plough and sow before one can reap; and it is in such studies that the historian receives his training and keeps up his proficiency. The hackneyed witticism about 'dry-as-dust' historians who 'know more and more about less and less' comes mostly from people who write and read history without real thought or intellectual purpose—as a senseless ritual.

Biographies have become the ritualist form of English historiography; they predominate as much as portraits do in English oil-painting: both answer a custom and a demand, and pay homage to the importance ascribed to individuals; but they may also be due to fear of unbounded fields or to a lack of creative imagination. A biography has a beginning and an end, and a track to follow between the two points; and even great historians sometimes use its framework for studies of wider transactions and problems. But the typical political biography mixes up three different functions, and in that mixture finds an excuse for doing each badly. It uses the papers and correspondence of the biographee; an editor would have to annotate them carefully, collate them with other material, explain obscure transactions, and deal with problems on their own ground; the biographer can select whatever he chooses—'the human being' is his subject. But to deal with the human being would require knowledge of ancillary disciplines, foremost of psychology, both normal and pathological, and insight into the human mind and character; while most biographers if asked for their qualifications could only answer more or less like the girl who applied for the post of nurse to children: that she herself was once a child. Lastly, the 'background' can be compiled from elementary text-books—'after all', the biographer will protest, 'I do not claim to write an original history of the time'. Even 'and his Time' in the title is often treated as a mere excuse for sticking in anything, however irrelevant, found among the papers of the person concerned. True biography is a great and exacting art; but even biographies written on the assumption that this is the easiest form of history, find a much wider public than works of an impersonal character: they seem more human, and are therefore supposed to be 'easy reading'.

In each period the subject of history is determined by the interest of its authors and readers. When clerics formed the bulk of the reading public, religious history was the dominant subject; in Courts the interest shifted to princes and their reigns, their diplomacy and wars; in the Parliamentary era statesmen and their careers became the standard theme; and with the rise of the middle classes, economic history moved to the foreground, but through a certain inertia long remained a mere history of economic policy, dealing in this country with enclosures, the repeal of the Corn Laws, factory legislation, etc. Even the advent of Everyman has so far failed to add demographic history to the older well-established branches—but how could historians working in isolation successfully tackle the task? No one would expect a contemporary survey of the life and work of the people or of political behaviour to be undertaken otherwise than by teams. Why then for a past period? The low productivity of historical research in this, and even in many another, direction, is due to antiquated concepts and methods—'always scribble, scribble, scribble! eh, Mr. Gibbon?' —but the questions now asked and the materials to be mastered would have baffled even that greatest and most industrious of eighteenth-century historians. Unless there is concerted research, history cannot deal with aggregates otherwise than in vague generalizations: to treat them as entities in which each person retains his individuality requires a new technique.

A beginning in that direction is being made in the new, officially sponsored, History of Parliament based on the biographies of all the Members who sat in the House of Commons up to 1901: a demographic study of the most significant group-formation in the life of this country. Are we then going back to 'biographies' after all? Criticism of inept biography does not imply that history can ever deal with anything but 'men in action'. But it is a new pattern of an aggregate character, and based on materials much richer than were ever tapped in the past, that we are trying to delineate.

CIVILIZATION ON TRIAL

'By "the age in which we are living" I mean the last five or six thousand years within which mankind, after having been human for at least six hundred thousand years before that, attained the modest level of social and moral achievement that we call "civilization." ' This sentence supplies the key to Dr. Toynbee's historical thinking.[1] That age, which on the cosmic time scale is 'of such infinitesimal brevity' that it could hardly be shown 'on any chart of the whole history of this planet,' has seen nineteen distinct civilizations, of which five survive. 'I mean by a civilization the smallest unit of historical study at which one arrives when one tries to understand the history of one's own country.' Thus, for instance, that of the United States could not be understood by itself, but to render it intelligible 'you need not look beyond Western Europe into Eastern Europe or the Islamic world, nor behind the origins of our Western European civilization to the decline and fall of the Graeco-Roman civilization.' And vice versa: 'The smallest intelligible fields of historical study' are to Toynbee 'whole societies and not arbitrarily insulated fragments of them like the nation-states of the modern West or the city-states of the Graeco-Roman world.' His work is a protest against what he calls 'our own unconscionable parochial-mindedness,' 'the parish-pump politics of our Western society as inscribed on triumphal arches in a half-dozen parochial capitals or recorded in the national and municipal archives of ephemeral "Great Powers" '; and he himself tries to envisage the history of the last five or six thousand years as one whole, within which 'the histories of all societies of the species called civilizations' are 'in some sense parallel and contemporary.' Indeed, 'the philosophical

[1] Arnold J. Toynbee, *Civilization on Trial* (Oxford University Press).

contemporaneity of all civilizations' is a basic tenet of his historical outlook.

Arnold Toynbee studied, and next taught, *Literae Humaniores* at Oxford, a discipline based almost entirely on the Greek and Latin classics. 'As a training-ground,' he writes, 'the history of the Graeco-Roman world has its conspicuous merits.' It is visible in perspective and can be seen as a whole; its surviving materials are manageable in quantity and 'well-balanced in their character'— 'statues, poems, and works of philosophy count here for more than the texts of laws and treaties'; and 'its outlook is oecumenical rather than parochial'—Athens educated all Hellas, while Rome made the whole Graeco-Roman world into a single common-wealth. Here then was his starting-point: a thorough knowledge of a civilization, distant and 'ancient' according to our usual norms, and dead, which none the less lives in us, and in that sense, too, is 'contemporaneous.' But Toynbee did not stop at that, or at the Byzantine world. To certain reminiscences which he quotes in his book from the time, more than forty years ago, when we both were undergraduates at Balliol, I shall add two. I think of a night when we sat on the floor in his room, poring over a large map, he tracing the journeys of Marco Polo, and I the *Itinerary* of Benjamin of Tudela: we were comparing the two—his reading already extended to Central Asia and Old Cathay. And next I remember how he staggered me when, towards the end of our time at Oxford, he told me that he had worked an average of ten hours a day: no mean feat while all that Oxford offers and claims invades the undergraduate's time-table. It is the range of his interests combined with a supreme capacity for sustained work which have enabled him effectively to extend his vision and knowledge beyond what even the most widely read historians have attempted.

The First World War made Toynbee study the problems of Europe as a unit, and in the Political Intelligence Department of the Foreign Office, in which we two again worked together, his thorough acquaintance with Greece, a by-product of his classical studies, caused his being put in charge of Near Eastern affairs, which then meant fighting the 'unspeakable Turk.' But soon after the war, Toynbee changed from a pro-Greek into a pro-Turk and, fascinated by Islam, became an eager student of its history and culture: a third 'civilization' swam into his ken, and carried him far into those regions of Central Asia which already at an earlier stage had excited his imagination. He tried to jump clear of his 'native Western standing-ground,' that remote corner 'at the extreme western tip of one of the many peninsulas of the Continent of Asia,' and survey the world from its centre, the old meeting-place 'of the religions and philosophies of India, China, Iran, Syria, and Greece.' 'Our first task is to perceive . . . all the known civilizations, surviving or extinct, as a unity,' as so many 'essays in a single great common human enterprise,' which is 'to transcend the level of primitive human life.'

Toynbee was born and bred in Victorian England, at 'the noon of a halcyon day' which was 'fatuously expected to endure to eternity.' But to him the mood of Kipling's 'Recessional' appealed more than that of Kipling's self-confident imperialism: he did not expect (perhaps hardly wished) the British Empire to endure, nor the supremacy of Europe, nor the ascendency of the West— possibly not even man's rule on the globe. There is a marked strand of pessimism in him, even of defeatism; and he was to witness historical developments which seem fully to justify his misgivings: if now he tries to reassure himself and others, at least concerning the future of the human race as a whole, his attempts seem rather strained, are emotionally less accentuated than his forebodings of doom, and on the whole fail to carry conviction. His 'morphology of the species of society called civilizations' concerns itself with the 'recurring pattern in the process of their breakdowns, declines, and falls' much rather than with their rise —for which preference there is also a valid objective reason: while the unfathomable mystery of life and creation attaches to origins, 'breakdown means loss of control' and a consequent lapse into automatism; and 'automatic processes are apt to be uniform and regular,' and are therefore more amenable to systemization. And here is Toynbee's diagnosis: the cause of death of civilizations has invariably been 'either War or Class or some combination of the two'; and 'the regular pattern of social disintegration is a schism of the disintegrating society into a recalcitrant proletariat and a less efficient dominant minority.' Man who 'is relatively good at dealing with non-human nature,' is bad at dealing 'with human nature in himself and in his fellow human beings': 'a dazzling success in the field of intellect . . . and a dismal failure in the things of the spirit.' 'There is no warrant for supposing that, within "historical times," there has been any progress in . . . human nature . . . either physical or spiritual.' The outstanding achievement of Western civilization is to have unified mankind which previously inhabited many mansions but now is gathered under one roof: 'it looks almost as though a radical Westernization of the entire world were now inevitable.' In that unification technology is 'the most obvious ingredient'—but 'man cannot live by technology alone.' 'Our Western "know-how" has unified the whole world . . . and it has inflamed the institutions of War and Class, which are the two congenital diseases of civilization, into utterly fatal maladies.' In the past their ravages 'have not yet ever been all-embracing.' The lower strata of society usually survived, and when one society collapsed, it did not necessarily drag down others with it. But now class has 'become capable of irrevocably disintegrating society, and war of annihilating the entire human race'; and if disintegration sets in, it will probably be final. Perhaps the achievements of the ten thousand years of attempts at civilization will be wiped out; perhaps even the million years of human existence on the globe. But the globe has been in existence some five to eight hundred million years; winged insects some two hundred and fifty million years; and the now extinct giant reptiles reigned on it about eighty million years. Moreover astronomy has reduced to wellnigh laughable dimensions the cosmic importance of our globe, which at one time was looked upon as the centre, and indeed the purpose, of the universe. Such is the deeper, emotional trend of Toynbee's thought. Yet when faced by the question whether our civilization is doomed, he answers emphatically in the negative. 'What shall we do to be saved? In politics, establish a constitutional co-operative system of world government. In economics, find working compromises . . . between free enterprise and socialism. In the life of the spirit, put the secular super-structure back onto religious foundations.'

'War or class or some combination of the two' as the cause of death of civilization—this is a formula which, like many a wide generalization of that kind, can be imposed on history, but seems hardly to exhaust even the major factors, and is defective in structure. War is an armed conflict between nations or States, or between parties within them, while class is an order of stratification of society: two disparate concepts co-ordinated as causes. But class is only one among the elements generating strife, rather overemphasized as such in our time; and Toynbee's formula, reduced to a single denominator, predicates no more than that conflicts between human aggregates have invariably been the cause of the downfall of civilizations; and naturally the more powerful the material and technical means at man's disposal, the more devastating become such conflicts.

Ultimately the problem is psychological (but psychology hardly enters into Toynbee's study of mankind, not even group psychology): why does that social animal, man, who progresses by working in groups, periodically wipe out his achievements in inter-group conflicts? Psychologists explain that communal life is based on suppression of hostile impulses within the group, and that these seek release outside it: if such conflicts are, indeed, mere occasions for the unloading of destructive human passions—and history seems to bear out this view—rational advice is beside the point. To fill what might be described as 'a hollow place' within his own system, Toynbee seems to turn, more and more, towards religion, but with a strained optimism and Victorian utilitarianism which deprive both his old system and his new beliefs of validity. You have just to see, he seems to say, how useful co-operation, compromises, and a religious faith can be, and you can't go wrong. *Deus ex machina?*

Toynbee's conscious views on the place of religion in the life of mankind have undergone a change, and were this not mainly intellectual and pragmatic, it would be bound to transform his entire concept of history; but so far it seems to have produced only chaos. Hitherto religion was placed by him on one level with other cultural or social phenomena. In the diffusion of civilizations, 'spiritual waves of radiation . . . weaken as they travel outwards,' but gain new life when they collide and coalesce with other such waves. 'The coalescence of a Greek wave with an Indian wave has generated the Buddhist civilization of the Far East. . . . The same Greek wave has also coalesced with a Syrian wave, and it is this union that has generated the Christian civilization of our Western world' ('Syrian' is significant). In another passage he speaks of religion as the weak spot in the Greek's armour 'at which the Oriental counter-stroke went home and made history.' Here religion appears as a historically determined phenomenon.

But now in the essay on 'Christianity and Civilization,' he thus analyses the various views about their mutual relation. 'One of the oldest and most persistent views is that Christianity was the destroyer of the civilization within whose framework it grew up'

—this he rejects, as the decay of the Graeco-Roman civilization had set in at a much earlier stage: 'The rise of the philosophies, and *a fortiori* that of the religions, was not a cause; it was a consequence.' According to a second view, 'Christianity is, as it were, the egg, grub, and chrysalis between butterfly and butterfly. Christianity is a transitional thing which bridges the gap between one civilization and another, and I confess that I myself held this rather patronizing view for many years.' A similar part can be ascribed to Islam, Hinduism, and Buddhism within their own spheres. A third possible view is 'the exact inverse of the second': that so far from religion being a 'subsidiary to the reproduction of secular civilizations . . . the successive rises and falls of civilizations may be subsidiary to the growth of religion.' Then, 'if our secular Western civilization perishes, Christianity may be expected not only to endure but to grow in wisdom and stature as the result of a fresh experience of secular catastrophe.' And in another essay Toynbee enjoins on us 'to relegate economic and political history to a subordinate place and give religious history the primacy.' But then he himself must make up his mind whether to treat religion as revealed truth or as a historically conditioned phenomenon; and if he writes as a believing Christian, it is incongruous to say as he does on page 24: '. . . about A.D. 1500 to reckon in terms of our Western parochial era . . .'

If truth is the core of religion, origins matter more than subsequent developments; the question of 'evolution' and 'growth' hardly arise for it; and Sinai and Calvary assume a transcendent character. Then the history of the Jewish people, so closely bound up with these two events, acquires peculiar significance; so does perhaps what that fervent Catholic, Léon Bloy, calls 'the Jewish Mystery,' and refuses to call 'the Jewish Question'; and so does the Return. But Toynbee, when surveying world history through a telescope, does not perceive the Jewish people: it simply does not enter into his purview, or is submerged in 'a Syrian wave.'

Towards Zionism his attitude has been negative, not to say hostile; though, to my knowledge, no anti-Jewish feeling ever entered into it. What did count for a great deal was his pro-Islamism, which is marked even in this collection of essays, and which sometimes results in surprising statements. Thus, according to him, as late as the sixteenth century, 'Islam inspired . . . hysteria in Western hearts' because 'it wielded a sword of the spirit against which there was no defence in material armaments,' and Westerners were in danger of 'turning Turk.' Is he not projecting on to others a phase in his own development? For who were these potential converts to Islam? He can hardly generalize from the exceptional case of the Bosnian Bogumils, who were not even sincere converts.[1] On page 76, he makes a Moslem claim that Islam has retrieved 'the revelation of the One True God' from 'polytheism and idolatory.' But when on page 87 he writes that 'Islam's creative gift to mankind is monotheism, and we surely dare not throw this gift away,' it is by no means clear that he is merely reproducing a Moslem claim. On page 88 he declares that Islam has 'a mighty spiritual mission still to carry out.' But in the essay on 'Islam, the West, and the Future,' he admits that 'nationalism, and not Pan-Islamism is the formation into which the Islamic peoples are falling; and for the majority of Muslims the inevitable, though undesired, outcome of nationalism will be submergence in the cosmopolitan proletariat of the Western world.' None the less, Toynbee still discerns a mission for Islam. 'Two conspicuous sources of danger . . . in the present relations of this cosmopolitan proletariat with the dominant element in our modern Western society are race consciousness and alcohol; and in the struggle with each of these evils the Islamic spirit has a service to render which might prove, if it were accepted, to be of high moral and social value.' The pro-Moslems in Britain are legion; but few there are who will join Toynbee in setting up their Moslem hero as a 'dry' John Brown.

Whatever the weaknesses of Toynbee's work, his ability to survey continents and ages in one great sweep is impressive, and so is the freshness and creative quality of his imagination. Among

[1] Toynbee subsequently altered his contention, and in an article published in the American review, *Commentary*, in February 1949, wrote: 'The Moslem missionary never had much success in still unconquered Christian countries. Islam gradually converted those Christians who were conquered by the Moslems, and, in the Ottoman Empire, down to the seventeenth century of our era, Christian converts were mostly found among Western Christian deserters or prisoners, and subject Eastern Christians who had been conscripted in childhood as public slaves and been brought up by the Turks.' This is a very different story which says little for 'the sword of the spirit' wielded by Islam. But even this new version alters as it proceeds. Islam is first said to have 'gradually converted those Christians who were conquered by the Moslems,' which is not correct; but by the end of the sentence the process tapers down to deserters and prisoners, and to children carried off by the Turks.

the thirteen essays which compose this volume, the one that best
illustrates his style of thought is perhaps 'The Unification of the
World and the Change in Historical Perspective.' It deals with the
way in which the Western voyages of discovery transformed
'man's human environment' and the historical outlook at least
of the non-Western peoples.

About A.D. 1500 there was a 'belt of civilizations girdling the
Old World from the Japanese Isles on the north-east to the
British Isles on the north-west: Japan, China, Indo-China, Indo-
nesia, India, Dar-al-Islam, the Orthodox Christendom of Rum,
and another Christendom in the West.' They were in touch with
each other, but not so close as to feel members of the same
society. The main line of communication was provided by a chain
of steppes and deserts that cut across that belt from the Sahara to
Mongolia. 'The Steppe was an inland sea . . . of higher con-
ductivity for human intercourse than the saltwater sea ever was
before the close of the fifteenth century of the Christian era. This
waterless sea had its dry-shod ships and its quayless ports. The
steppe-galleons were camels, the steppe-galleys horses, and the
steppe-ports "caravan cities"— . . . Petra and Palmyra, Damascus
and Ur, Tamerlane's Samarkand and the Chinese emporia at the
gates of the Great Wall.'

In seeking a vantage-ground for his survey, Toynbee asked
himself 'who was the most centrally placed and most intelligent
observer . . . among notable non-Westerners' then alive, and
found his man in the Emperor Babur, the author of a brilliant
autobiography written in Turkish. Babur was a descendant of
Tamerlane, the Transoxanian conqueror who made the last
attempt to unify the world by land operations; and himself in
1519 invaded India. At that time Babur's capital, Farghana, was
'the central point, and the Turks were . . . the central family of
nations'; and there was some justification for 'a Turco-centric
history' seeing that from the fourth century of the Christian era,
when the Turks 'pushed the last of their Indo-European-speaking
predecessors off the steppe,' down to the seventeenth century,
which witnessed the collapse of Turkish power in Europe, Iran, and
India, 'the Turkish-speaking peoples really were the keystone of
the Asiatic arch from which the pre-da Gaman belt of civilizations
hung suspended'; and their conquests extended from Manchuria
to Algeria, and from the Ukraine to Deccan.

Yet, Toynbee points out, the Emperor Babur in his memoirs

never once mentions Western Christendom, though he must have been aware of the existence of the 'Franks'; nor even Vasco da Gama's landing in India, twenty-one years before his own invasion of that sub-continent. It may have escaped his attention, or else he may have felt that 'the wanderings of these water-gypsies were unworthy of a historian's notice.' He did not realize that 'these ocean-faring Franks had turned the flank of Islam and taken her in the rear.' And with 'the substitution of the Ocean for the Steppe as the principal medium of world-communication . . . the centre of the world made a sudden jump . . . from the steppe-ports of Central Asia to the ocean-ports of the Atlantic.' After hovering round Seville and Lisbon, it settled for a time in London; to remove in our own lifetime to New York.

About 1500, the social structure of the half-dozen civilizations was remarkably uniform: primitive peasantries ruled by a minority enjoying a monopoly of power, leisure, and skill. And there was a similar uniformity in their historical outlook: each had its own version of the 'Chosen People' myth. China was 'All that is under Heaven'; Japan 'the land of the Gods'; to the Brahmans all outside the Aryan Holy Land were untouchables; Moscow was 'the Third Rome'; and the 'Franks' were 'solemnly asserting A.D. 1500' that they, and not Orthodox Eastern Christendom, were the true heirs of Israel, Greece, and Rome. But while the others, shaken by the impact of Western civilization, have since given up their pretensions, 'the Franks are still singing the same old song: singing it solo now . . .' Their technology has unified the world; but they themselves still require an 'educative toss.' And it is by no means certain where the world centre of gravity will be in an age when neither the steppe, nor the ocean, but the air will be the medium of human intercourse.

NATIONALITY AND LIBERTY

LIBERTY WAS claimed in 1848 for the individual and liberty for nations, and a natural, wellnigh intrinsic connexion was assumed between the two; to be consummated—so the theory ran—in a peaceful fellowship of free nations. But there was a deeper antinomy between constitutional development in most of the States concerned, and the postulates of the new national movements. Individual and civic liberty requires a stable, uncontested political framework: internal freedom is best secured where the communal consciousness coincides with the territory of the State, that is, where nationality is territorial in character and the existing frontiers do not give rise to claims by, or against, neighbours. But the politically minded cannot feel truly free except in a State which they acknowledge as their own, and in which they are acknowledged as indigenous: that is, in their own national State; and the nationalisms which in 1848 entered the political arena, and held it during the next one hundred years, were primarily linguistic. 'The sole idea now fruitful and powerful in Europe is the idea of national liberty; the worship of principle has begun,' wrote Mazzini in 1832.[1] And further: 'The nation is the universality of the citizens speaking the same tongue.'[2] Territorial nationality is essentially conservative, for it is the product of a long historical development; nationalisms which place the emphasis on language almost invariably seek change, since no existing satiated community singles out one principle for its basis—the demand that the State should be coextensive with linguistic nationality was an internationally revolutionary postulate which, seeing that nations are seldom linguistically segregated, proved destructive both of constitutional growth

[1] *Life and Writings* (1864), vol. i, p. 147.   [2] Ibid, vol. i, p. 167.

and of international peace. National feeling was hailed in 1848 as a great and noble force which was to have regenerated Europe, and is denounced today as an obsession which has brought ruin upon her: but from the outset it was the expression of social and political maladjustment, and has since been at least as much the vehicle as the source of destructive passions.

I

The British and Swiss concepts of nationality are primarily territorial: it is the State which has created the nationality, and not *vice versa*. A historical process, operating within a geographically determined framework, has produced a British island nationality which comprises the English, Scots, and Welsh, and to which Ulster adheres; and neither within the island, nor in the English-speaking world outside, could language be the criterion of nationality, or else Scotland and Wales would each be split internally, while, for instance, Irishmen and Americans would have to count as 'English.' Liberty and self-government have moulded the territorial nation of Britain, and given content to its communal nationality. The political life of the British island community centres in its Parliament at Westminster, which represents men rooted in British soil. This is a territorial, and not a tribal, assembly; it was for centuries the representation of freeholders and householders, of men with a share in their native land; and 'every blade of grass in Great Britain' was said to be represented in it. Bound to the soil of Britain, it is limited to it: by now the British Parliament does not claim authority over communities even of British origin and English speech once they are rooted in other soil. And so close is the nexus between territory and nationality in English law that a child of whatever parentage if born under the British flag can claim British nationality. Indeed, the English language lacks a word to describe a 'nationality' distinct from, or contrasted with, the citizenship derived from territory and State; and the meaningless term of 'race' is often used for what in Continental languages is covered by 'nationality.'

The island character of Britain and the 'genius' of its people are acclaimed as factors which have produced that rare entity, a real, and not merely nominal, territorial nationality. But the argument must not be pressed too far: for in the adjoining island a similar mixture of Celt, Anglo-Saxon, and Norman has failed to evolve an Irish territorial nationality. Even unity of language has failed to bring its inhabitants together; and now the political dissonance has resulted in a deliberate and laborious attempt to revive linguistic separateness. The geographical factor is obvious also in the rise and development of the Swiss nationality, yet the frontiers of Switzerland are by no means preordained, nor amenable to a strict rational explanation. Undisputed territory has rendered possible the growth of orderly self-government and of civil liberty, which in turn has heightened the national consciousness and coherence of the community: so that any desire for territorial expansion, still more for merging into another State, is completely absent. In and even before 1848, the most far-sighted among the German nationalists desiring a union of all Germans, feared the growth of civic liberty and self-government in the separate German States as liable to consolidate and crystallize them, and thereby to hinder unification. Fichte wrote:[1] 'One might say: gradually a German nation will come to be. But how can the conception of one nation arise at all? (Nor was Greece ever united. What prevented it? Answer: the single State prematurely grown solid).'[2] Men cannot fit themselves into a new nation 'once a communal existence [das Volkseyn] has entered their natural existence and consciousness.' All men desire civil liberty, and mutual understanding and trust between representatives and represented is the basis of national life: 'Therefore a people can no longer be re-formed, or added to another, once it has started steadily to progress towards a free constitution.'

2

The Germans, more than any other European nation, had emptied the territorial State of communal contents and converted it into sheer dynastic property; and they brought forth dynasties without roots or substance, ready to rule over any country or people. The denationalized State with an unpolitical population was the product of German political incapacity and deadness, and of German administrative efficiency. The Habsburg Monarchy, an almost unique phenomenon in history, rooted in the German

[1] 'Politische Fragmente aus den Jahren 1807 und 1813,' Werke, vol. vii, p. 549.
[2] der schon zu feste Einzelstaat.

hereditary provinces, the *Erbländer*, yet seemingly unrelated to any land or people, unrestricted in its acquisitive ambitions and singularly successful, variegated and ever changeable, was private dynastic domain, and so were the innumerable German pygmy States, too small to rank as political entities. Even Prussia, a military and administrative organization turned State, was ready to absorb territory and population of any language or race. In such dynastic proprietary or organizational creations, German and non-German provinces were frequently yoked together, while the German dynasties and bureaucracies of Vienna, Berlin, and St. Petersburg encouraged fresh German settlements in non-German lands, adding considerably to the residue left by earlier, medieval, migrations. Lastly, Habsburg non-national territorialism extended the contradiction between nationality and State to other parts of Europe, especially to Italy; and when in 1848 the demand arose for national liberty and self-determination, it was against the Habsburgs that it was primarily directed.

The highest forms of communal life became the basis of West European nationalisms, the myth of the barbaric horde that of German nationalism.

> Nationalism in the West was based upon a nationality which was the product of social and political factors [writes Professor Hans Kohn[1]]; nationalism in Germany did not find its justification in a rational societal conception, it found it in the 'natural' fact of a community, held together . . . by traditional ties of kinship and status. German nationalism substituted for the legal and rational concept of 'citizenship' the infinitely vaguer concept of 'folk,' which, first discovered by the German humanists, was fully developed by Herder and the German romanticists.

> With roots which 'seemed to reach into the dark soil of primitive times,' that concept 'lent itself more easily to the embroideries of imagination and the excitations of emotion.' Moreover, the Germans transferred 'to the field of society and nationalism' Rousseau's ethical and cultural antithesis between the primitive and artificial.

> They established a distinction between State and nation: they regarded the State as a mechanical and juridical construction, the artificial product of historical accidents, while they believed the

[1] *The Idea of Nationalism* (1946), p. 331.

nation to be the work of nature, and therefore something sacred, eternal, organic, carrying a deeper justification than works of men.[1]

Here it was not the State which moulded nationality, but a pre-existent nationality which postulated a State. The German concept of nationality is linguistic and 'racial,' rather than political and territorial, and it finds its final expression in the doctrine of the *Volksdeutsche* which claims that anyone of German 'race' and language owes allegiance, first and foremost, to his German Fatherland, of whatever other State such an *Ausland-Deutsche* may claim to be a citizen. Nor is that idea a mere Nazi invention: for instance, in the Frankfurt Parliament of 1848 the suggestion was made that Germans resident in Paris should be represented in it; this patently absurd and impossible proposal received no support, yet it is symptomatic of certain trends in German thought that it should have been made at all. And though no other European nation has gone the same length as the Germans, the German concept of nationality, largely through the influence which German political formations and deformities had on Central and Eastern Europe, has become dominant on the Continent.

3

The French Monarchy was based on territory with a common literary language and a national culture and consciousness; the elements of a rich nationality were present, but the welding force of active civic development was wanting; and no synthesis was reached between the power of the State, the growing influence of Paris, and the vigorous life of the provinces. The final unification of France was achieved not through an organic growth preserving the historical individuality of the component parts but in the cataclysm of the Great Revolution: by abstract thought setting out to build on a non-historical basis. A new principle of unity was found in the community of men declared free and equal; the liberty of the individual and his rights were placed in the fore-front, yet he was completely integrated into the sovereign nation. The emphasis in the concept of nationality was shifted from the land to the people; the component countries and populations were merged into the Republic, one and indivisible: *la patrie* became a dogma and a principle. To the French people, coincident

[1] *The Idea of Nationalism* (1946), p. 249.

with the territory of its State, was ascribed a non-territorial and a-historical existence: it was as if the French nation had shaken off the bonds of locality and time, and taken wing. 'In the words of Siéyès,' writes Lord Acton,[1] 'it was no longer France, but some unknown country to which the nation was transported. . . . The idea of the sovereignty of the people, uncontrolled by the past, gave birth to the idea of nationality independent of the political influence of history. . . . Every effaceable trace and relic of national history was carefully wiped away—the system of administration, the physical divisions of the country, the classes of society, the corporations, the weights and measures, the calendar.' Here was a break in historical continuity which has left deep rifts in the nation; and the French, passionately attached both to nationality and liberty, have to this day failed to evolve political forms that would provide the consensus and stability which these two require. But so dazzling in its spiritual magnificence was the opening of the new era, so convincing intellectually the argument, so powerful the surge of the movement, and so generous and universal was the message of the Revolution, that men were slow in perceiving the losses which were suffered even in the realm of ideas. From the French Revolution dates the active rise of modern nationalism with some of its most dangerous features: of a mass movement centralizing and levelling, dynamic and ruthless, akin in nature to the horde.

It was the agrarian movement that rendered invincible the French Revolution of 1789 and the Russian of 1917, but it was the cities which supplied these two revolutions with their ideology and their striking force; and a metropolitan population is the common denominator of the nation detached from its lands. Michelet, himself a Parisian, extolled Paris as 'the great and complete symbol' of France formed into one city.

The genius of Paris is a most complex and at the same time the highest form of France. It might seem that something which resulted from the destruction of all local spirit, of all regionalism, must be something that is purely negative. It is not so: of all the negations of material, local, particular ideas results a living generality, a positive thing, a life force.[2]

[1] In his essay on 'Nationality,' published in the *Home and Foreign Review*, July 1862; reprinted in *The History of Freedom and other Essays* (1909), pp. 277–8.

[2] Quoted after Hans Kohn, *Prophets and Peoples* (1946), p. 53.

Indeed, Michelet rejoiced at the rapid effacement of the 'French provincial distinctions' (*nos provincialités françaises*).

> That sacrifice of the diverse interior nationalities to the great nationality which comprises them, undoubtedly strengthens the latter. . . . It was at the moment when France suppressed within herself the diverging French countries that she proclaimed her high and original revelation.[1]

And he reached the significant conclusion that 'nations will endure . . . if they do not take thought to suppress the towns, in which the nationalities have condensed their self-expression' (*ont résumé leur génie*).[2] Rousseau, on the contrary, 'hated the great metropolitan capitals which seemed to him to destroy the individuality of nations.'[3] 'It is in the distant provinces,' he wrote, '. . . where the inhabitants move about less, and experience fewer changes of fortune and status, that the genius and customs (*le génie et les mœurs*) of a nation have to be studied.' Yet the contradiction between Rousseau and Michelet is more apparent than real, for they were speaking about different things: Michelet had in mind the modern nationalist movements, now so curiously alike all the world over, while Rousseau thought of the distinct contents of each nationality.

4

For men rooted in the soil there is, as a rule, a hierarchy of allegiances: to their village community or estate, to their district, to their 'country'[4]—for them the nation is of a naturally federal structure. Traditional beliefs and hereditary ties persist; class and the way of living determine alignments; things are individual and concrete in the village or the small, old-fashioned town. But in the great modern cities men grow anonymous, become ciphers, and are regimented; thinking becomes more abstract and is forced into generalizations; inherited beliefs are shaken and old ties are broken; there is a void, uncertainty, and hidden fear which man tries to master by rational thought. He starts by proudly asserting the rights of the abstract average individual freed from the

---

[1] Michelet, *Le Peuple* (1946), p. 286.   [2] Op. cit., p. 288.
[3] Kohn, *The Idea of Nationalism*, p. 254.
[4] In France *pays* is used to this day for various provinces; in eighteenth-century England, 'country' was still frequently used for 'county.'

bondage of tradition, and then integrates him into the crowd, a collective personality, which unloads itself in mass movements. The mass is the refuge of the uprooted individual; and disintegration of spiritual values is as potent a process as the splitting of the atom: it releases demonic forces which burst all dams. The program may be social revolution, or national revolution, or both; the aim may be to right wrongs or to sweep away stultifying encumbrances; the result can be liberation, but it can hardly be liberty which is founded on restraint and not on force, even if genuine idealism guides it. 'Whenever a single definite object is made the supreme end of the State,' wrote Lord Acton,[1] 'be it the advantage of a class, the safety or the power of the country, or the support of any speculative idea, the State becomes for the time absolute. Liberty alone demands for its realization the limitation of the public authority. . . .' Liberty is the fruit of slow growth in a stable society; is based on respect for the rights of the individual, deeply embedded in the life and habits of the community; is in its origin an aristocratic idea: of the self-conscious individual, certain of himself and his position, and therefore perfectly at ease. It spreads when every man's house becomes 'his castle': yet he must have a house and be safely rooted.

In 1848 the political insufficiency of the existing States of Central and East-Central Europe was rendered even more glaring by a peak period in intellectual development. Cultural entities were forming which transcended meaningless frontiers or disrupted territorial agglomerations. British political practice and French revolutionary doctrine provided the runways for the new movements, and the work of the Napoleonic period, uncompleted or reversed, their starting-points; while the Metternich régime, negative and uncreative, had hollowed out still further the forms which it endeavoured to maintain, for it had impeded within them the growth of an active political life such as is apt to evolve nationality even within accidental territorial frameworks. The conception of dynastic property in States was of feudal origin and derived from property in land: it fitted into the ideology of a community whose relations and connexions were bound up with the soil. But it no longer made sense in urban communities: and it was these, with their strong educated class and their new proletariat, which were now coming to the fore. The uprooted individual becomes conscious of his personal rights,

[1] Op. cit., p. 288.

C

rational rather than traditional; and so does the crowd detached from the soil. There is a profound difference between a King of France and an Emperor or King of the French—but what if the territorial term does not even correspond to a human aggregate?

The first logical inference of individual liberty and popular sovereignty is the claim to national self-determination: 'One hardly knows what any division of the human race should be free to do, if not to determine with which of the various collective bodies of human beings they choose to associate themselves,' wrote J. S. Mill in 1861.[1] And he rightly concluded that 'it is in general a necessary condition of free institutions, that the bound-aries of governments should coincide in the main with those of nationalities.'[2] Liberty and nationality, especially when opposed to the concept of dynastic property in States, seemed therefore to be concordant ideas. The national movements demanded the union of nations disrupted between dynastic domains, and the indepen-dence of other nations engulfed in dynastic empires. It was taken for granted that representative and responsible government would be practised by the sovereign nations, with full guarantees of the rights of the individual; and it was hopefully assumed that no free people would ever attack another people. The problem of the territorial squaring of intersecting national circles did not as yet vex the minds of the theoretical exponents of the creed of nationality.

5

A foremost position among the prophets of nationality is due to Mazzini, a man outstanding for spiritual integrity and single-minded devotion to the cause he preached. A sincere lover of liberty, he believed in the rights and dignity of man, in the 'law of progress,' and the joint destiny of humanity; and he adhered passionately to the tenets and postulates of a truly humanitarian liberalism. 'Liberty is sacred, as the individual is sacred.' 'Without liberty there is no true morality.' And on what principle can an association of free men be founded except on 'that of the rights of the individual'? Yet he never wearied of contrasting the age which had placed rights in the forefront with the new age centred on duty—the doctrine of individualism with that of nationality. 'The epoch of *individuality* is concluded'; it has been 'replaced by the epoch of the peoples'; 'the question of nationalities is

---

[1] *Considerations on Representative Government*, p. 289.   [2] Ibid., pp. 291–2.

destined to give its name to the century.' 'Individuality' was 'a doctrine useful perhaps . . . in securing the exercise of some personal rights, but impotent to found nationality or association . . .'; and 'it is the duty of reformers to initiate the epoch of association. Collective man is omnipotent upon the earth he treads.' Mazzini yearned for a collective life which would reveal itself 'in regular and progressive development, similar to the gradual evolution of vegetation in the new world, wherein the separate trees continue to mingle their branches, until they form the gigantic unity of the forest.' Even art, 'vital art,' must be a collective performance, inspired by the collective purpose and serving it. He was prepared to subordinate the entire life of the community to a political aim—thus Young Italy was 'to comprehend all the various manifestations of national life in one sole conception, and direct . . . them all . . . towards one sole aim, the emancipation of our country and its brotherhood with free nations.' He saw Europe being transformed 'into vast and united masses.'

Mazzini himself said that his heart was stronger than his head; and the moral fervour, purity of purpose, and religious sincerity which pervade his writings—words of faith and action rather than of thought—were apt to conceal from contemporaries how deficient his teachings were in substance correlated to everyday reality, and what dangerous germs they contained. National self-glorification and claims to moral superiority were of their core: which entails a measure of depreciation of other peoples, and is not conducive to international comity. Nor are self-conscious apostles of an exalted creed easy to work with at home. Liberty calls for sanity, a modicum of scepticism, and tolerance: a man must be prepared to believe that he may be mistaken, if he is to treat others as equals. Mazzini was not; he had faith and was intolerant of 'opinions'; his aim was action which ill accords with doubt. He retained his contempt of the 'moderates' even after the goal of a united Italy had been achieved by them; and he never showed real understanding for the nature of Parliamentary government, which rests on a good many seeming absurdities but so far has proved the most efficient system for safeguarding civic liberty.

Mazzini claimed for Italy a position of primacy in the world, and assigned to her a unique mission. There was 'a void, a want in Europe'; 'no power of initiative' existed in any of its peoples; a 'regenerate Italy' could alone initiate a new and superior life and unity among them. Twice before has the world been united by Rome, Imperial and Papal; and the tradition of those two epochs bears witness to a further mission.

> Why should not a new Rome, the Rome of the Italian people . . . arise to create a third and still vaster unity; to link together and harmonize earth and heaven, right and duty; and utter, not to individuals but to peoples, the great word Association—to make known to free men and equals their mission here below?

But first, Italy had to be reconstituted 'as one independent sovereign nation of free men and equals'; and the basis was to be republican and unitarian, not monarchical and federal.

> Because without unity, there is no true nation.
> Because without unity, there is no real strength; and Italy surrounded as she is by powerful, united, and jealous nations, has need of strength before all things.
> Because federalism, by reducing her to the political impotence of Switzerland, would necessarily place her under the influence of one of the neighbouring nations.

Mazzini insisted that the first thing was 'to put an end to our servile subjection to French influence,' intellectual as much as political; and he seems hardly aware of how much his 'unitarian' programme was a response, both defensive and imitative, to the national France of the Great Revolution. 'I could wish,' he wrote in 1861, 'that all the artificial territorial divisions now existing were transformed into simple sections and circumscriptions. . . .'

'Young Italy,' when he started organizing it in 1831, was to be the instrument of Italy's regeneration: it was to be 'neither a sect nor a party but a faith and an apostolate'; and the emphasis was not on numbers but on the homogeneous character of the movement. 'I still believe,' he wrote on another occasion, 'that next to the capacity of rightly leading, the greatest merit consists in knowing how and when to follow.' During the period which might elapse before the movement achieved 'the complete liberation of Italian soil,' it would have to be directed 'by a provisional dictatorial power, concentrated in the hands of a small number of men.'

The banner of Young Italy was to bear 'on the one side the words—*Liberty, Equality, Humanity*; and on the other—*Unity, Independence*.' 'What is it we want?' wrote Mazzini in 1832.

We demand to exist. We demand a name. We desire to make our country powerful and respected, free and happy . . .

In other words, we demand independence, unity, and liberty, for ourselves and for our fellow-countrymen.

. . . All are agreed in the cry of *Out with the foreigner*.

The same process of unification Mazzini desired for other nations. He saw the future 'arousing extinct peoples, uniting divided races, proceeding by masses, and making individuals the mere stepping-stones to their ascent.' 'To reconstruct the map of Europe . . . in accordance with the special mission assigned to each people by geographical, ethnographical, and historical conditions, was the first step necessary for all.' 'Lasting liberty can only be achieved and maintained in Europe by strong and compact nations, equally balanced in power. . . .'

Here was real vision of the future though not of its dangers, and high idealism not devoid of elements which have since become dominant in nationalist movements. He wanted to see his country 'powerful and respected,' not merely free and secure: 'the political impotence of Switzerland' would not have been acceptable to his feelings. His conscious thought turned towards humanity and embraced the whole; but when stigmatizing an answer given in 1831 by the Provisional Government of Bologna, he says that they spoke 'like foreign barbarians.' He disliked Italy's two neighbours, France and Austria; his demand of an equal balance in Europe was directed against the French 'instinct of domination,' and his program of redrawing the map of Europe against Austria's survival. He spoke of 'the special mission assigned to each people,' but would hardly have endorsed those claimed by the nations themselves: they might not have left the 'mission Italy is destined to accomplish towards humanity' quite as great as Mazzini conceived it.

For in the romantic era the prophets of each nation found that it was destined to play the noblest part. 'La patrie, ma patrie peut seule sauver le monde,' wrote Michelet in 1846. The history of all the nations was 'mutilated,' that of France alone was 'complete': 'avec elle, vous savez le monde.' But France, after some experience in the redeeming of nations, knew that such attempts do not necessarily earn the love of those to be 'saved.' 'Children, children,' wrote Michelet, 'I say to you: ascend a mountain, provided it is sufficiently high; look to the four winds, and you will see nothing but enemies.'[1] Poland 'the Christ among the Nations' was at the time the doctrine of Polish Messianism propounded by her greatest poet, Mickiewicz; all the other nations were described as worshipping false gods who were no gods, while the Poles alone were 'from first to last faithful to the God of their fathers.'[2] Russia as 'the God-bearing nation' was the creed of her most inspired writers from Khomiakov to Dostoyevsky, coupled with contempt for the 'decaying West' (which did not impair their admiration for its achievements). Fichte, one of the discoverers of *Germanentum*, found that the Germans alone were a real nation, *ein Urvolk*, speaking a living language—the other languages were 'dead in their roots,' mere echoes. He thus apostrophized the Germans in 1808: 'Of all the modern nations it is you who carry most clearly the germ of human perfection, and it is your mission to develop it. Should this perish in you, all hope of humanity for salvation from the depths of its evils will perish with you.'[3] And the much applauded poetaster Geibel, wrote in 1861 on 'Germany's Calling':

> Und es mag am deutschen Wesen
> Einmal noch die Welt genesen!

Thus every nation was exalted above the rest: compensatory dreams of grandeur dreamt by suffering or afflicted nations and uprooted individuals—immature, comparable to the day-dreams of adolescents. Nations unified, regenerated, or resurrected, have since proved to be in no way better than other nations—there is a limit to miracles even in Wonderland, as Alice discovered when she ate the cake. And what remains after the idealistic gilt of nationalism has worn off is the claim to superiority, hence to dominion.

6

The impact of France on Europe during the Revolutionary and Napoleonic periods was the chief political factor in the arousing of its nationalisms. In France, united even before 1789, the process of revolutionary transformation had released forces which deluged Europe: a nation welded into an ideological entity, and freed from the bonds of territory and tradition,

[1] *Le Peuple*, p. 35.   [2] *Ksiegi narodu polskiego i pielgrzymstwa polskiego* (1832).
[3] *Reden an die deutsche Nation* (1808).

offered a spectacle of power of which the nature, cost, and consequences men did not as yet probe, but which evoked the wonder, envy, and fear of its neighbours. The Germans, superior in number to the French, and the Italians, not very much inferior, realized to what disadvantage they were put through the political fragmentation of their countries. Napoleon himself started the work of territorial 'rationalization' in both; and the fall of many governments and the frequent redistribution of territory 'deprived the political settlement of the dignity of permanence'—'tradition and prescription,' writes Lord Acton, 'ceased to be guardians of authority.' In Italy most of the previous States were re-established in 1815, but the foreign origin of so many of the rulers and the foreign support on which they relied, the foreign occupation of Lombardy and Venetia, and the oppressive character of most of the Governments rendered the territorial divisions even more galling. Genoa was merged into Piedmont; and one wonders how much this may have contributed to Mazzini's 'unitarianism' —if his native city had still been the glorious ancient republic, would he have wished to wipe out its identity? But after it had been placed under a dynasty strange to it, was it not more reasonable to go the whole length in national unification? In his 'General Instructions for Members of Young Italy' he used against a monarchical constitution for a united Italy the argument that 'while the populations of the various Italian States would cheerfully unite in the name of a principle which would give no umbrage to local ambition, they would not willingly submit to be governed by a man—the offspring of one of those States. . . .'

In Germany the territorial resettlement of the Napoleonic period was much more extensive and more permanent. More than two hundred small principalities, ecclesiastical States, and Free Cities were incorporated in the big and middle-sized States whose character was thereby changed very considerably. After the Rhineland and Westphalia had in 1815 been included in Prussia, the Roman Catholics came to form more than one-third of her population; the inclusion of Franconia and the Palatinate in Bavaria raised the proportion of her Protestants to over one-fourth of the whole; in Baden, originally a Protestant country, the Roman Catholics now formed two-thirds of the population, and in Württemberg one-third. The West-German Roman Catholics felt no affection for the Hohenzollerns, nor the Protestants, say, of Nuremberg for the Wittelsbachs, etc. And both in 1814-15 and in 1848, the small mediatized princes or Knights of the Empire were among the foremost champions of a united Germany: Stein, the Gagerns, Leiningen, and Chlodwig zu Hohenlohe-Schillingsfürst are outstanding examples. Men whose old territorial rights had been extinguished, or whose allegiance had been changed, wished to see all territorial rights merged in a Great Germany: in 1848 *Stock-Preussen* or *Alt-Bayern* showed a high degree of *Partikularismus* (local territorial consciousness), especially in the rural districts, but the newly acquired provinces clamoured for German national unity, the Roman Catholics hoping for a Habsburg Empire, and the Protestants for one under the Hohenzollerns. The territorial shufflings and re-shufflings in the Napoleonic period and at the Congress of Vienna facilitated the rise of a movement for a united Germany.

'The German people wanted a strong and free State: this is the content of the German revolution of 1848-9,' writes its historian, Veit Valentin, in the first volume of his work;[1] but by the time he reached the second, 'free' dropped out: 'The strong national Reich was the foremost aim of the German revolution.'[2] And while Mazzini's counterpart to the watchwords of the French Revolution was *Independence, Unity, Liberty*, that of the German revolution of 1848 was *Einheit, Freiheit, und Macht* ('Unity, Freedom, and Power'); which was soon abbreviated to *Einheit und Macht*. Bassermann, one of the foremost leaders of the South-Western Liberals and Chairman of the Constitutional Committee, said in the National Assembly on 16 February 1849: 'If I knew the unity and future greatness of Germany were to be attained through a temporary renunciation of all the freedoms (*sämmtlicher Freiheitsrechte*), I should be the first to submit to such a dictatorship.' And Stremayr, an Austrian member of the Left, said on 27 October 1848: 'Were Slavia to offer me freedom, and Germania to put me in chains, I would still follow Germany, for I am convinced that a united Germany will lead me to freedom.' Thus the emphasis was on nationality rather than on liberty, and even where liberty was placed in the forefront, it was not always for its own sake but rather as the means for realizing the over-riding purpose of national unification. As dynastic interests and rivalries were the main obstacle, and it was not possible to square them by negotiation or compromise, national unity could have

[1] *Geschichte der deutschen Revolution von 1848-49*, vol. i, p. 246
[2] Ibid., vol. ii, p. 31.

been easiest achieved in a German Republic, one and indivisible; and even to the moderates the doctrine of a joint German national sovereignty, superior to the claims of dynasties and constituent States, supplied the basis for their endeavours to achieve unity. But everywhere 'the German revolution stopped at the steps to the thrones'; and not one dynasty was overthrown. Indeed, again for the sake of unity some republicans considered it necessary to renounce their programme: 'I desire German unity,' wrote Heinrich Simon, a leader of the Left, in April 1848, 'but it would be impossible if in a few places the republic was now proclaimed.'

Aggrieved national feelings were perhaps the greatest and most universal force behind the revolution of 1848. Here are two passages from the oath to be taken by members of Young Italy:[1]

> By the blush that rises to my brow when I stand before citizens of other lands, to know that I have no rights of citizenship, no country, and no national flag . . .
> By the memory of our former greatness, and the sense of our present degradation . . .

And Prince Chlodwig zu Hohenlohe-Schillingsfürst wrote in December 1847:[2]

> *One* reason for dissatisfaction is universal in Germany, and every thinking German feels it deeply and painfully. It is the nullity [*Nullität*] of Germany vis-à-vis of other States. . . . It is sad and humiliating not to be able to say proudly abroad: 'I am a German,' not to see the German flag flying on ships, nor find a consul, but to have to say: 'I am a Kurhesse, Darmstädter, Bückeburger, my Fatherland was once a great, powerful country, but is now split into 38 fragments.'

And a Memorandum presented on 19 October 1848 by the Radical minority on the Constitutional Committee (including H. Simon and Robert Blum) declared that the German Revolution had been provoked as much by the princes suppressing popular freedom as by their 'failing to unite with a view to establishing Germany's power.' Germany's *Macht* was a concern of the Left no less than of the Centre and Right.

---

[1] Mazzini, *Life and Writings*, vol. i, p. 111.
[2] *Denkwürdigkeiten des Fürsten Chlodwig zu Hohenlohe-Schillingsfürst*, edited by F. Curtius (1906), vol. i, p. 38.

The longing for German unity was strongest where the State could not endue its educated and semi-educated classes with a 'consciousness of power' (*Machtbewusstsein*), which is the German substitute for freedom, as the organized violence of war is the German version of revolution: a commutation of particular importance in a study of liberty and nationality, many other nationalisms having since developed along similar lines. South-western, Western, and Central Germany were most solidly behind the endeavours of the Frankfurt Assembly: these were regions of small or middle-sized States and of disaffected provinces, where the most extensive territorial reshuffles and transfers of allegiance had occurred, and where the impact of France—the influence of French ideas, and the fear of a new French invasion—was felt most acutely. Austria and Prussia, or even Bavaria and Hanover, had developed a 'State consciousness' (*Staatsbewusstsein*), the territorial nationality of 'subjects'; but their 'nationality' being of dynastic or organizational origin, and not based on a free communal life, was as acquisitive as the dynasty or organization which had created the State.[1] Yet, their territorial ambitions being more realistic (they had existing States for basis), were moderate when compared with the formless, unmeasured, visionary Pan-Germanism of more or less Stateless Germans: most of the extra-vagant German claims of the two World Wars were raised and applauded by the 'freedom-loving' *idéologues* of the Frankfurt Parliament of 1848.

'What is the German's Fatherland?' The Frankfurt Assembly, being the parliament not of an existing State but of one to be created, had to decide the question. And a double, contradictory answer was given: *Was deutsch spricht, soll deutsch werden* ('What-ever speaks German, shall become German'), and *Was deutsch ist, soll deutsch bleiben* ('Whatever is German, shall remain German'). Thus linguistic claims were combined with another set based on history and the *status possidendi*, and each in detail was further garnished and extended—strategy, geography, the presumed wish or interest of some 'inferior' race, or the 'needs' of German expansion supplying the arguments. Even the linguistic test,

---

[1] The German language has no word to describe the 'nationality' of the separate States, and in 1848 the term employed for those territorial nationalities was *Stämme*, which means 'tribes' and was originally employed for the Franks, Swabians, Saxons, etc. To attach it to territorial formations, some of as recent origin as 1815, is rather comic.

wie weit die deutsche Zunge klingt (as far as the German language resounds) was indefinite, for it was left open how many Germans had to speak at the top of their voices for the claim to be established. Poland, martyred, partitioned Poland, the victim of Tsarism, enjoyed quite exceptional popularity with the exponents of liberty and nationality in 1848; and the Frankfurt Pre-Parliament started off with a resolution declaring the dismemberment of Poland a 'shameful wrong,' and her restoration 'a sacred duty of the German nation': but at no time did it occur to anyone that the Polish-speaking districts of West Prussia and Upper Silesia were due to the Poles, while in Posnania, recognized as Polish, a demarcation line was drawn between German and Polish districts which, after several consecutive corrections each favouring the Germans, gave the Poles less than one-fourth of a province in which they formed two-thirds of the population.

Even less liberal was the attitude of the Frankfurt Parliament concerning Trieste and the Trentino. Schuselka, a leader of the Left, thus defended the *Territorialpolitik* of the National Assembly in July 1848: 'Such must be our basis, for a great nation requires space (*Raum*) to fulfil its world destiny (*Weltberuf*), and I would rather die a thousand times than, for instance, renounce Trieste because they speak Italian.' Don Giovanni a Prato, a leading figure in the Trentino, had, against the opinion of the Trentino *émigrés* who had left with the Lombard *insorti*, persuaded the population to take part in the elections to the Frankfurt Parliament in the hope of having the national claims of the Trentino endorsed by it:[1] he left Frankfurt in December 1848 a deeply disappointed man. (Giovanni de Pretis, Count Festi,[2] and G. Vettorazzi had done so before him.)

When the Czechs, under Palacký's leadership, refused to send representatives to the German National Assembly, their refusal produced a storm of indignation among the Frankfurt 'Liberals': it was described as 'a direct challenge to the territorial integrity of Germany,' and their absence as in no way affecting the right of the Assembly to legislate for the Czech provinces. There was unanimity in condemning any possible claim of so-called 'a-historic' nations to an independent national existence. Heinrich von Gagern, an outstanding personality who dominated as no one else the Frankfurt Parliament, thus defined on 26 October

[1] See M. Manfroni, *Don Giovanni a Prato* (1920), pp. 50–1.
[2] See Livio Marchetti, *Il Trentino nel Risorgimento* (1913).

1848 Germany's 'task in the East': 'to include as satellites nations on the Danube which have neither a call nor a claim to independence.' And Wilhelm Jordan, one of the first on the Left to translate his political radicalism into ultra-nationalist terms, spoke on 20 June 1848 of 'the attempts of puny nationalities [*Nationalitätchen*] to found their own lives in our midst, and like parasites to destroy ours. . . .' Even Marx and Engels admitted the right only of 'the great European nations' to 'a separate and independent national existence,' but not of 'those numerous small relics of peoples' which have been (or should have been) absorbed by the 'more powerful nations.' But as they did not deny that right to the Magyars, who were hardly equal in number to the Czechs, and much inferior to the Yugoslavs and Rumans, one must presume that, unconsciously, these German middle-class prophets of class-war assigned the privilege of nationhood to peoples with a well-developed upper and middle class, and denied it to such as consisted almost entirely of 'a-historical' peasants and workmen.

7

The linguistic nationalism of the Germans, through its lore and example as well as through its impact, in turn stimulated the growth of linguistic nationalisms among their eastern neighbours, especially in the Habsburg Monarchy. But as Austria's *Staatsidee* was territorial, the Czech or Slovene cultural revival, so long as it remained a-political, received lenient, or even friendly, treatment from the dynasty and the feudal aristocracy, whose territorial concepts it did not as yet contravene. 'There is no such thing as an Austrian patriotism,' declared a speaker in the Hungarian Parliament in 1848. 'It is as unthinkable as a specific patriotism on the various estates of Prince Esterhazy.' Wherein he was wrong: every territorial unit is capable of developing a specific patriotism[1] in those truly rooted in it; which non-territorial mass-formations may, however, in time cut across, overshadow, or even destroy. 'Patriotism' need not be one of

[1] An amusing example of 'estate patriotism,' amazing in its inhumanity, occurs in Bismarck's early correspondence. On 9 April 1845, at a time of great floods, he wrote to his sister: 'I am proud to be able to report that my rivulet [*Nebenfluss*], the Zampel, has drowned a carrier and his horse' (see Horst Kohl, *Bismarckbriefe* (7th edition, 1898), pp. 24–5). As Klaczko put it, how proud was Bismarck to be one day, after Europe had become his domain, to see disappear in floods of blood *currum Galliae et aurigam ejus.*

'storm and stress'; there can be also a patriotism interested in what exists, and desirous of preserving it: such conservative sentiment, of varying intensity, gathers round every existing territorial formation.

The nationalities of the Habsburg Monarchy, barring the Italians and Serbs, all had, at one time or another, some interest of their own in its survival, developing accordingly their specific type of 'Austrian patriotism.' This was strongest and most permanent among the Austrian Germans: German was the official language of the Monarchy, they held the central position within it, supplied the largest proportion of administrative officials and army officers, and felt as if they were partners of the dynasty— even a democracy is apt to assume the role or inheritance of its late rulers.[1] But the fact that the Habsburg Monarchy tended to show tolerance to nationalities which did not threaten its territorial integrity, even in 1848 very much sharpened the hostility to it of the extremer German nationalists, especially in the Czech provinces, and enhanced their desire to break up the Monarchy and engulf its western provinces in a united Germany, which would enable them to crush completely the Czech national movement: a program openly avowed in the Frankfurt Parliament. Naturally the danger of such inclusion made the Czechs wish for Austria's survival: they developed the idea of 'Austro-Slavism' of the Habsburg Monarchy reconstructed on a Slav basis. This program enjoyed the support of a great many aristocrats who were of very mixed national origin and talked at home German or French, but developed a Bohemian territorial nationality, favoured the Czech national movement (as dynasties, whatever their origin, assume the nationality of the country over which they rule), and demanded within the framework of the Habsburg Monarchy, autonomy for the Czech provinces, expecting to maintain their own primacy in the provincial self-government. When the Czech national movement assumed during the next fifty years a markedly democratic character, the Bohemian territorial nationalism of the magnates steeply declined.

The Magyars were at all times opposed to a federalist reconstruction of the Habsburg Monarchy which would have conceded territorial or linguistic rights to any of the 'subject' races, since freedom

[1] When in 1536 the citizens of Geneva drove out the Bishop and the Vidomne, they cried with joy, 'Nous sommes princes,' and proceeded to rule in an autocratic manner thirty surrounding villages.

for the Czechs (the nearest kinsmen of the Slovaks), the Yugoslavs, Little Russians, or Rumans in Austria, would have encouraged parallel movements in Hungary; and the Magyars, who insisted on Hungary's right to an independent State existence, within that State insisted on their own absolute dominion over Slavs and Rumans. They were bitterly hostile to the concept of a *Gesammt-monarchie* (a monarchy embracing all Habsburg dominions) upheld by the Vienna centralists, for which these tried to enlist the support of Hungary's subject races. Yet while all Magyars were united in the defence of Hungary's constitutional rights and territorial integrity, the views on how best to secure them ranged from those of nationalists even more *enragé* than Kossuth, to those of the Old-Hungarian magnates who on a conservative basis wished to arrive at a compromise with the dynasty and the Vienna Court; and the less radical a group was politically the more tolerant it was as a rule toward the non-Magyar nationalities of Hungary: an early example of conflict between nationality and liberty, and, in the case of Kossuth, of a spurious reputation for liberalism.

In 1848 most of the Poles were hostile to the Habsburgs and the Vienna Government. They still expected an early restoration of a free and united Poland; in 1846 they had experienced the catastrophe of the West Galician *jacquerie* in which Polish peasants, incited by Austrian officials, turned on the Polish gentry as these were about to start an insurrection of a national and, in fact, democratic, character; and in East Galicia they were faced by an alliance of the Vienna Government with the Little Russian peasants on a socially and nationally anti-Polish basis. But even then there was a group of Polish aristocrats and Conservatives who aimed at a co-operation with the Habsburgs such as was established afterwards. And while the Poles continued to suffer persecution under Russia and Prussia, in Austria they attained a privileged position, enjoying after 1867 self-government and dominion over the Little Russians. Consequently during the fifty years preceding the First World War, they developed a remarkable Austrian patriotism.

The Slovenes, Croats, Rumans, Slovaks, and 'Ruthenes' or Ukrainians in various periods developed varying degrees of pro-Austrian feeling; but in time all these Austrian 'patriotisms' were disappointed, barring that of the 'partners' of the dynasty. No civic territorial nationality could unite the different nationalities of Austria-Hungary, for such community is possible only between linguistic groups acknowledging each other as equals, whereas the Germans, Magyars, and Poles claimed cultural, social, and political superiority over those on whom they looked down as 'a-historic' subject races, not entitled to an independent national existence. The Compromise of 1867 resulted in a division of the Habsburg dominions into three distinct domains: Western Austria of the Germans—approximately the territory which in 1848 these had wanted to see included in the Frankfurt Parliament; Hungary of the Magyars; and Galicia, which in 1919–20 the Poles managed to carry over entire into the restored Poland against the armed opposition of the Ruthenes.

8

In 1789 two nations on the European continent, Poland and Hungary, could look back to an unbroken tradition of Parliamentary Government, with a concomitant territorial nationality and a high degree of personal liberty for their citizens; these, however, in contrast to England, were of a single Estate or caste: the gentry, a very numerous body comprising about one-tenth of the population, yet an exclusive, privileged class. Towards the end of the Middle Ages, under the impact of German aggression or infiltration, the Poles had developed an early form of conscious linguistic nationality. But in their own subsequent expansion to the east they changed their concept of nationality: Poland and Lithuania, constitutionally united, became a gentry-Republic (under elected kings), based not on a common language or religion but on caste: the gentry-nation spoke Polish, White and Little Russian, and Lithuanian; in some western and northern districts also German and Swedish; and it comprised even Moslem Tartars, Armenians, and baptized Jews. Citizenship depended on being of the gentry, or being received into it. In Poland, in the sixteenth century, the official language was Latin, in Lithuania it was White Russian; and the Greek Orthodox and Protestants together may at one time have equalled in number the Roman Catholics. But gradually, across Reformation and Counter-Reformation and the Uniat Church, the overwhelming majority of the gentry joined Rome, and with Polish superseding Latin as the literary language, became Polonized. Similarly in Hungary the gentry-class was of very mixed national extraction, and its nationality was originally territorial rather than linguistic; the language of State and Parliament was Latin, and so remained till the nineteenth century, when a growing Magyar linguistic nationalism transformed the nature of the Hungarian State.

Had the landed gentry of the non-Polish or non-Magyar provinces remained united to the peasants in language and religion, the territorial nationality of the two realms might possibly have been capable of modern development and re-adjustments, and might consequently have survived. But when the deep cleavage of the agrarian problem became exacerbated by differences in language and religion, a joint territorial national-ity became utterly impossible: Poland and Hungary could claim their historic frontiers only so long as the peasant masses did not count politically. Consequently the modern Polish and Magyar nationalisms, which were no longer those of 'single-class' com-munities but which none the less aspired to taking over the territorial inheritance of the gentry-nations, were driven into hopeless contradictions and manœuvres. In 1848 these two nations were looked upon as foremost champions of liberty and national-ity: they had had within their historic frontiers a fuller and freer political life than most Continental nations, and therefore a stronger civic consciousness and patriotism; and now they were fighting the despots of the Holy Alliance to re-establish those free and independent communities; that these had in the meantime become social anachronisms and could not be rebuilt on modern foundations, was realized by very few among the men of 1848 in Western and Central Europe, and was never acknowledged.

9

The revolution of 1848 was urban in its character and ideology. It started in the capitals, spread to other towns, and was directed or turned to account by the urban middle-class intelligentsia. The countryside remained indifferent or hostile, or, if revolution-ary, pursued aims extraneous and alien to the distinctive purposes of that year. In France it was Paris which made the February Revolution without encountering any active opposition from the provinces; but the June Days and the Presidential election of December 1848 disclosed the social conservatism of the peasantry. In Italy the peasants gave no support to the liberal and national revolution which remained entirely urban, while in Sicily and

Naples the rural movement bore a purely agrarian character. In northern Germany the countryside was almost entirely conservative, far more so than appeared in the April elections, and Prussian Junkers, like Bismarck, chafed to lead their peasants against Berlin. F. Th. Vischer, a Württemberger who in the Frankfurt Parliament belonged to the Left, wrote to a friend on 28 May 1848: 'Here are Pomeranians and East Prussians, some of them hefty fellows with the best will who say that if we proceed too sharply, we shall provoke a reaction not from the Government but from the provinces. . . . A German Vendée.'[1] And there was more than one potential Vendée in Germany; while revolutionary agragrian movements—in Silesia, Baden, Württemberg, or Hesse—threatened to result in *jacqueries*, but were completely indifferent to national or constitutional ideas. In the Habsburg Monarchy there was a strong peasant movement but again of a purely agrarian character: the leaders in the Austrian Parliament clearly realized that once the peasant was freed from the remainders of servitude and from feudal rights and dues, and was given his land, he would turn reactionary. On the whole Governments and Oppositions alike avoided appealing to the peasants, a dark, incalculable force which, if roused, could not easily be directed or mastered. Thus neither the landed classes nor the peasants had a share in determining the character of the revolution of 1848 which used to be described as 'the awakening of the Peoples.'

10

The year 1848 marks, for good or evil, the opening of the era of linguistic nationalisms shaping mass personalities and producing their inevitable conflicts: a nation which bases its unity on language cannot easily renounce groups of co-nationals intermingled with those of the neighbouring nation; and an alien minority within the State, or an intensely coveted *terra irredenta*, are both likely to distort the life of the nation, and impair the growth of its civic liberty. The alien community within the disputed borderland, hostile to the State and possibly plotting against it, provokes repressions which are apt to abase the standards of government; while fellow-countrymen across the border awaiting liberation keep up international tensions, which again are destructive of a

[1] 'Achtzehn Briefe aus der Paulskirche,' edited by Engelhaaf, *Deutsche Revue* (1909).

D

free civic life. Moreover, the strongly knitted mass formations of the neo-horde are based on positive feelings which keep the nation together; but the negative feelings, which have to be suppressed within the group, turn with increased virulence against 'the stranger in our midst,' or against the neighbour. Freedom is safest in the self-contained community with a territorial nationality; and where this has not by some miracle or the grace of God grown up spontaneously, it might perhaps best be secured by a transfer of populations. But it serves no purpose to expostulate with history: *on ne fait pas le procès aux révolutions,* nor to any other historical phenomena.

1848: SEED-PLOT OF HISTORY

THE MEN of 1848, victorious in Paris, Vienna, and Berlin, stood amazed at their own success and moderation. A revolution had swept over Europe, wider than any before it, but eminently humane in its principles and practice. It had its dead but no victims; it made refugees but no political prisoners. Louis-Philippe crossed the Channel—not the first French ruler nor the last to take to that route. The other sovereigns remained, shaken but not overthrown. Metternich, Guizot, and the Prince of Prussia (the later William I) one by one arrived in London: exponents of three systems, disparate in nature and aims, but seemingly obliterated by the same storm. The strongholds of reaction had fallen, rubble had to be carted away, new structures were to arise; there was a great void, filled by sun and air; and over it brooded a singularly enlightened *Zeitgeist*. Men dreamed dreams and saw visions, and anything the spirit could conceive seemed attainable in that year of unlimited possibilities. Next year the light and airy visions had faded, and it was as if they had never been.

A gale blows down whatever it encounters, and does not distinguish. Revolutions are anonymous, undenominational, and inarticulate. If there is an inherent program, as in agrarian revolutions, it is of a most primitive character. The elemental forces of a mass movement can be made to do the work of men whose quest is alien to them. Most revolutions are filched or deflected: groups or parties with elaborate programs—panaceas or nostrums—try to stamp them with their own ideology and, if successful, claim to be their spokesmen or even their makers. But revolutions are not made; they occur. Discontent with government there always is; still, even when grievous and

45

well founded, it seldom engenders revolution till the moral bases of government have rotted away: which are the feeling of community between the masses and their rulers, and in the rulers a consciousness of their right and capacity to rule. Revolutions are usually preceded by periods of high intellectual achievement and travail, of critical analysis and doubt, of unrest among the educated classes, and of guilt-consciousness in the rulers: so it was in France in 1789, in Europe in 1848, and in Russia in 1917. If such corrosion of the moral and mental bases of government coincides with a period of social upheaval, and the conviction spreads, even to the rulers themselves, that the ramshackle building cannot last, government disintegrates and revolution ensues. Revolutions, as distinct from mere revolts, usually start at the centre of government, in the capital; but the nature of the actual outbreak and its purpose almost invariably escape analysis. What aim did the labouring poor of Paris pursue in the Great Revolution, and what did they attain? What was it that made them fight in July 1830, or in February 1848? And what would they have done had they been successful in the June Days or in the Paris Commune? Agrarian movements are far more articulate in form and aim, and therefore, if extensive and determined, are usually successful. The village is a living organism and its communal consciousness transcends other loyalties; and the peasants' demand to be relieved of dues, or to be given the land of the nobles and the Church, can be met or enforced overnight. The weakness of agrarian movements usually is in that they break out sporadically, and therefore can be suppressed. But if linked with a rising in the urban centres and with self-doubt in the upper classes, if fanned by generalizing factors, such as *la grande peur* in 1789 or the effect of war in 1917, they become overpowering; and then urban groups or parties graft on to them their own programs.

The revolution of 1848 followed on a period of intellectual efflorescence such as Europe has never known before or since; it supervened at a time when the Governments themselves came to feel unequal to the new circumstances and problems; in a period of financial crisis and economic distress, but of disjointed, or even contradictory, social movements. A numerous urban proletariat gathered in the rapidly growing capitals; the independent artisans were fighting a long-drawn losing battle against modern industry; the factory workers started their struggle for a human existence; while the incidence of the agrarian problem was uneven and varied. In France it had been solved by the Great Revolution; in Germany it was confined to several large areas; in the Habsburg Monarchy it was general and acute: there the peasants were determined to sweep away the surviving feudal burdens and jurisdictions. Before the first gusts of the revolutionary storm the Governments collapsed without offering serious resistance; there was a paralysis of will and a consciousness of defeat almost before the fight was joined. But there was no uniform or unified social-revolutionary force to continue the struggle; and the educated middle classes, the successors or new partners of the princes, from an exaggerated fear of the Reds quickly turned counter-revolutionary, though they still counted on preserving the conquests of the initial victory which they had appropriated. The peasants were bought off by timely and extensive concessions; the proletariat was defeated in Paris in the June Days, in Vienna in October, while in Berlin (as in 1933) it succumbed without fighting. In France, where 1789 had done most of the work which still awaited accomplishment elsewhere, 1848 followed a path apart; in the rest of Europe the conflict was between the principle of dynastic property in countries and that of national sovereignty: from which devolved the problems of self-government and self-determination, of constitutional rights and of national union and independence.

The year 1830 brought a reaction against ingenious solutions which the Congress of Vienna had devised for France, Belgium, and Poland; outside France, 1848 was largely an endeavour to find solutions where the Congress had not seriously attempted any. The movement of 1848 was European, yet consciously French in origin. In 1847 Karl Mathy, a Baden bookseller and publisher, had planned a pamphlet putting forward the demands of the German people, to be distributed broadcast on the death of Louis-Philippe: for this was expected to set the European revolution going. 'Our revolutions, like our fashions, we were wont to receive from Paris,' wrote in 1849 his partner, F. D. Bassermann, a leader of the moderate liberals in the Frankfurt Parliament. The European revolution, when it came, operated within the area of Napoleon's work and influence; for he had sapped inherited forms and loyalties, regrouped territories, established modern administrations, and familiarized tens of millions of men with change in political and social conditions—and new ideas are not nearly as potent as broken habits. When Napoleon was overthrown there had to be restoration. Even had the monarchs and ministers assembled in Vienna wished to reconstruct Europe on a rational basis, how could they by agreement have squared Austrian and Prussian aims and claims in Germany, solved the problem of the Papal State in Italy, or resettled the Habsburg Monarchy on any but dynastic foundations? The failures of 1848 go far to justify 1815. Incapable of devising, men are forced back to the *status quo ante*; and with the pristine facts return ideas in which men no longer wholly believe: in every restoration there is an element of make-believe. The Vienna Congress reaffirmed the idea of indefeasible monarchical rights—and over wide areas failed to restore the previous rulers. And while, for instance, in *Alt-Preussen* and *Alt-Bayern* the countryside was in 1848 *stockpreussisch* and *bayuvarisch*, and therefore hardly affected by revolution, the Roman Catholic Rhineland felt little allegiance to the Hohenzollern, or Protestant Franconia to the Wittelsbach. Nor were the proprietary and quasi-contractual rights attributed to dynasties or Estates compatible with the new social and economic conditions: for those ideas were connected with the land; they were alien to the intelligentsia (including the bureaucracy which supplied a remarkable percentage of members to the Parliaments of 1848) and to the modern cities. With them conceptions of the neo-horde replace those of rooted populations. In 1848 a considerable advance was made towards the State untrammelled by contract and custom; and a non-territorial, linguistic nationality asserted its sway. The privileged orders entered into partnership with the educated middle classes, accepting their intellectual lead. As early as 12 December 1847 the Prince Consort advised the King of Prussia to meet the coming onslaught by attaching 'the well-to-do and intelligent sections of the population—that is, the real people (*das eigentliche Volk*)' to the Government by a share in the administration of the country.

Guizot and Metternich had voluntarily left their countries. Prince William had to be persuaded, nay, made to leave in order to put an end to rumours that he was about to march on Berlin. They quitted, and he did not—and all three proved right; their systems were dead, his was to be the foremost beneficiary of 1848. There was philosophic elevation and spiritual pride in the fallen Ministers, while the Prince was single-minded and *borné*. 'Je ne connais guère l'embarras et je ne crains pas la responsabilité,' was Guizot's dictum. 'L'erreur ne s'est jamais approché de mon

esprit,' said Metternich with a faint smile when in March 1848 he
met Guizot on the steps of the British Museum. But Metternich,
on the night of his fall, had replied to his wife: 'Oui, ma chère,
nous sommes morts'—and never again did he try to force his
way among the living. Nor did Guizot: in France, he wrote, in
great crises the vanquished *deviennent des morts*. Neither was quite
of the country he had governed. Metternich, a Rhinelander, had
first come to Vienna at the age of twenty-one: the exponent of a
non-national ideal, he tried to uphold the Habsburg Monarchy,
that dynastic creation *par excellence*, by tying all Europe to the
principle which alone could secure Austria's survival. Internal
reform he never seriously contemplated: he apprehended its
hopelessness—'je passe ma vie à étayer un édifice vermoulu.'
When asked by Guizot to explain how it was that revolution had
spread to Austria governed by him, he replied: 'J'ai quelquefois
gouverné l'Europe, l'Autriche jamais.' Guizot, on the other hand,
was a Protestant attracted by British institutions and ideas, and
self-nurtured on them, who tried to establish constitutional
monarchy in France. Under Louis-Philippe France had enjoyed
what the rest of the Continent aspired to in 1848: a Parliamentary
régime, equality before the law, civic freedoms. And what
Guizot's *toryisme bourgeois* tried to cultivate in France were the
civic virtues of Victorian England; 'l'esprit de famille, le goût du
travail régulier, le respect des supériorités, des lois et des traditions,
les sollicitudes prévoyantes, les habitudes religieuses. . . .' For him
French history neither stopped nor started in 1789; he wanted to
secure the achievements of the Revolution and lay its ghosts. He
thought of 'ces millions d'existences qui ne font point de bruit
mais qui sont la France.' But beyond these were men he combated
and feared:

The French Revolution and the Emperor Napoleon I have thrown
a certain number of minds, including some of the most distinguished,
into a feverish excitement which becomes a moral and, I would
almost say, a mental disease. They yearn for events, immense, sudden,
and strange; they busy themselves with making and unmaking
governments, nations, religions, society, Europe, the world. . . .
They are intoxicated with the greatness of their design, and blind
to the chances of success. To hear them talk, one might think that
they had the elements and ages at their command . . . and that these
were the first days of creation or the last days of the world.

And Louis-Philippe would say to Guizot:

> You are a thousand times right; it is in the depth of men's minds that the revolutionary spirit must be fought, for it is there that it reigns; *mais pour chasser les démons, il faudrait un prophète.*

Le juste milieu was uninspiring, and no compromise, for neither wing accepted it: to the Legitimists the July Monarchy was a 'profanation of monarchy,' to the Republicans a perversion and usurpation of national sovereignty. Sainte-Beuve wrote in 1861:

> The Orleans dynasty were neither a principle, nor a national glory; they were a utility, an expedient; and they were taken for what they were.

And this was his account of the period:

> I appreciated the joys of that reign of eighteen years, the facilities it afforded to the mind and for study, for all pacific pursuits, its humanity, the pleasures offered, even to those not possessed of a vote, by the wonderful display of Parliamentary talent and of eloquence from the tribune. . . . Yet it was impossible to view that régime, in its spirit and ensemble, as in any way grand . . . as something of which one could be proud to have been a contemporary. . . .

Guizot himself writes:

> It makes the greatness of our nation . . . that purely material and immediate success does not suffice, and that the mind has to be satisfied as much as the interests.

When the revolution started in the streets of Paris even those who valued the July Monarchy as a 'utility' would not die for it. As de Tocqueville puts it 'the government was not overthrown, it was allowed to fall.' It flopped.

The February Revolution had been universally expected, and after it had occurred no one could account for it. Its course was meaningless, or at least unproductive of immediate results. Memories were relived, and the circle of repetition was completed by the Second Republic, the Presidency of Louis-Napoleon, and the Second Empire. Only in the June Days a new reality pierced through the counterfeit displays; the people of Paris, with a tradition and consciousness of power, but without clear aim, took action. In 1848 the French monarchy was consigned to the grave, and with it an element essential to the proper working of the Parliamentary system was lost. Since then France has faced an uneasy choice between a Parliamentary Republic in which President and Prime Minister to some extent duplicate each other, and a system based on an independent Executive which is a cross between the American Presidency and the Napoleonic dictatorship. The principles of equality and national sovereignty, bequeathed by the Great Revolution, found in 1848 their logical fulfilment in universal suffrage and the Republic, two principles not contravened even by a plebiscitarian Empire. While British radicals adhered to the tenets of classical economy and free trade, French thought in 1848 moved toward new social concepts: the organization and protection of labour, 'the right to work' (with its concomitant: relief for the unemployed), universal education as a citizen right, a graduated income-tax— most of which were realized in Britain before they were in France. To begin with, the February Revolution was not anti-clerical, still less anti-religious: the revolutionaries were romantics rather than free-thinkers, while the clergy were largely Legitimists. Lammenais and Lacordaire were forerunners of a socially radical Catholicism. It was only after the June Days that the cleavage between the Church and the radicals reopened, while the big bourgeois drew closer to the Church in a political clericalism. The problem of Church and State was now sharply put, and the battle joined which was to reach its climax fifty years later.

When Metternich fell, aged seventy-five, he was replaced by Kolowrat, aged seventy, and at the Foreign Office by Ficquelmont, aged seventy-one; in May, Pillersdorf, an official aged only sixty-two, became Prime Minister; but on 8 July he was succeeded by Wessenberg, aged seventy-five, who continued the septuagenarian set-up of Austria's 'rejuvenation' till after the October rising in Vienna. And when Bach (aged thirty-five), a politician of revolutionary origin, attained office, within a few weeks he turned into a heavy-handed reactionary. The Vienna revolution was indeed a peculiar affair. But any radical handling of the situation was bound to endanger Austria, immediately or ultimately. Joseph II, Schwarzenberg and Bach, and the men of 1906–14, were exponents of sharp, centralizing authoritarian systems; Maria Theresa, Metternich, and Francis Joseph in his later years temporized; *immer fortwurschteln* ('always muddle along') was the precept of the Emperor's most accordant Premier, Count Taaffe. Where historic survival is both *raison d'être* and

aim, logical conceptions are a deadly poison. And Austria survived
because of the inherent impossibilities and contradictions of the
situation. Metternich knew it, but preferred to bedeck the dismal
truth with philosophical dissertations.

The pattern of Austria's existence becomes patent in 1848,
though it takes time before it is discerned and the consequences
are drawn. There were four dominant nationalities within the
Habsburg Monarchy whose upper and middle classes covered
also the territories of the subject races: Germans, Italians, Magyars, and Poles, versus Czechs, Slovaks, Yugoslavs, Ruthenes,
and Rumans. The four master races demanded a united Germany,
a united Italy, an independent Hungary, and a reunited Poland,
including between them all the territories of the subject races
inhabiting the Monarchy. Their programs carried to their logical
conclusion implied the complete disruption of the Austrian
Empire, and were therefore opposed by the dynasty, and by those
among the Austrian Germans who were more Austrian than
German. The subject races, too, desired national unity and independence, but they preferred the rule of the non-national
Habsburgs to that of the master races. Some of their leaders,
especially among the Czechs, went the length of developing a
program of 'Austro-Slavism'—of an Austria reconstructed on
a Slav basis. But this was a phantasm: for it offered no possible
basis for the existence and survival of the Habsburg Monarchy.
In the long run the dynasty had to take for partners nationalities
which shared their proprietary interests in their territories, as did
the Germans, Magyars, and Poles, and which, therefore, were
prepared to defend every square mile. But the Germans, inside
and outside Austria, would only accept her continued existence
in lieu of complete national unity if the German predominance
within Austria was maintained and reinforced by a German
alliance, which in turn the Habsburgs themselves required to safe-
guard their dominions; and the Magyars and Poles would only
accept it provided it did not touch, and indeed safeguarded, their
dominion over Hungary and Galicia. Socially also the German-
Magyar-Polish basis best suited the Habsburgs: an ancient dynasty
cannot permanently ally itself to peasants against their masters. In
1848–9 the peasant nations supported the dynasty; in 1867 they
were abandoned by it to the dominant races. In 1866–7 the
German, Italian, and Magyar programs of 1848 were realized
in modified forms, and the Polish, in so far as this was possible

within the framework of the Habsburg Monarchy alone. In 1918–19 came the time for the subject races of the German and Magyar spheres, and for the Poles; in 1939–45, for the Yugoslavs and Ruthenes in the Italian and Polish spheres. Every idea put forward by the nationalities of the Habsburg Monarchy in 1848 was realized at some juncture, in one form or another. And perhaps even Austro-Slavism will ultimately find its realization in a Danubian Union under Slav ægis.

With 1848 starts the German bid for power, for European predominance, for world dominion: the national movement was the common denominator of the German revolution in 1848, and a mighty Germany, fit to give the law to other nations, its foremost aim. *Einheit, Freiheit, und Macht* ('Unity, Freedom, and Power') was the slogan, with the emphasis on the first and third concepts. 'Through power to freedom, this is Germany's predestined path,' wrote in April 1848 the outstanding intellectual leader of the Frankfurt assemblies, Professor Dahlmann. Even some of the Republicans were Republicans primarily because they were Nationalists: the existence of thirty-odd dynasties and the rival claims of Habsburgs and Hohenzollern were the foremost obstacles to German unity, easiest removed by proclaiming a German Republic, one and indivisible. The movement for German unity originated in 1848 in the west, south-west, and in the centre of Germany, in the small States which gave no scope to the German *Wille zur Macht*, and in the newly acquired, disaffected provinces of Prussia and Bavaria. But although the aim of the Frankfurt Parliament was a real Pan-Germany, not a Greater Prussia or Great Austria, one of the two German Great Powers had to be the core of the new German Federal State. And here started the difficulties: Austria was the greatest State within the Federation and its traditional 'head,' but of its 36 million inhabitants less than six were German; while of 16 million in Prussia, 14 were German. Austria obviously could not merge into a German national State, whereas Prussia could—theoretically. It became clear in 1848–9 that a united Greater Germany (*Gross-Deutschland*), comprising the German provinces of Austria, implied the disruption of Austria; otherwise it had to be a Lesser Germany (*Klein-Deutschland*). With an undivided Austria within Germany, the German Confederation could not change into a Federal State; but a Federation of States offered no prospect of real national unity or of power. The Frankfurt Parliament therefore finished by accepting *Klein-Deutschland*, and offered its Crown to the King of Prussia; who refused from respect for Austria and because he could only have accepted the Crown if offered to him by his fellow-sovereigns. Nor would the new Empire as planned at Frankfurt have proved acceptable to the true Prussians: Frankfurt, not Berlin, was to have been its capital, and Prussia was 'to merge into Germany' (there was intense jealousy at Frankfurt against the Berlin Parliament, and as a safe-guard against Prussian predominance in a *Klein-Deutschland* it was planned to break up Prussia into her eight provinces, each about the size of a German middle-sized State). When in March 1848 Frederick William IV sported the German tricolour and made his troops assume it, the Second Regiment of the Guards replied by a song about 'the cry which pierced the faithful hearts: you shall be Prussians no longer, you shall be Germans.' When Bismarck showed its text to the Prince of Prussia, tears ran down William's cheeks. But it was his system based on Prussia, her army and administration, which was to be established by the man who showed him the song.

The year 1848 proved in Germany that union could not be achieved through discussion and by agreement; that it could be achieved only by force; that there were not sufficient revolutionary forces in Germany to impose it from below; and that therefore, if it was to be, it had to be imposed by the Prussian army. Again the future was mapped out. There were four programmes in 1848-9. That of *Gross-Oesterreich*, a centralized Germanic Austria, retaining her traditional preponderance in Germany, was realized by Schwarzenberg in 1850, after Olmütz. That of a Greater Prussia was realized in the North German Confederation of 1866, and was extended in 1870-1 to cover the entire territory of the Frankfurt *Klein-Deutschland*. That programme itself, with the capital removed from Berlin, was haltingly attempted under the Weimar Republic; while the other Frankfurt programme of *Gross-Deutschland*, including the German and Czech provinces of Austria, was achieved by Hitler in 1938-9.

In 1800, after some forty years in politics, Lord Shelburne wrote in his memoirs:

It requires experience in government to know the immense distance between planning and executing. All the difficulty is with the last. It requires no small labour to open the eyes of either the public or of individuals, but when that is accomplished, you are not got a third of the way. The real difficulty remains in getting people to apply the principles which they have admitted, and of which they are now so fully convinced. Then springs the mine of private interests and personal animosity. . . . If the Emperor Joseph had been content to sow and not to plant, he would have done more good, and saved a great deal of ill.

Most of the men of 1848 lacked political experience, and before a year was out the 'trees of liberty' planted by them had withered away. None the less, 1848 remains a seed-plot of history. It crystallized ideas and projected the pattern of things to come; it determined the course of the century which followed. It planned, and its schemes have been realized: but—*non vi si pensa quanto sangue costa.*

TWO AUSTRIAN EMPERORS

I

FRANCIS I

THE PROGRESSIVE decay of the Habsburg Monarchy and of the Ottoman Empire accounts for most of the territorial changes in Europe between the Congress of Vienna and the end of the First World War. Austria had arisen in the struggle against the Turks and lost her primary *raison d'être* when they ceased to be a danger. Henceforth an affinity grew up between the two conservative Empires, threatened by nationalist movements from within and by national States from without. Maria Theresa talked about *mes chers Turcs* and Metternich described them as a neighbour safer even than the sea; Andrassy wished to maintain their power, and his successors understood that in a division of the Turkish inheritance Austria would take the place of 'the sick man of Europe.' In spite of differences in cultural level and international position, there was a resemblance between the policies of the two Empires and the uninspired meanderings of their rulers who had to fight against time and shear it of events.

The reigns of Francis I (1792–1835) and Francis Joseph I (1848–1916), with the intervening nominal reign of the feeble-minded Ferdinand, cover one hundred and twenty-four years of Austrian history. Time seemed to spare even the persons of the Habsburg Emperors, and so did historical literature: their servants, though frequently made into scapegoats, preserved silence, some from loyalty, others from mental insignificance, most because of the overwhelming tedium of their political existence. As events proved, the growth of normal political life within the Habsburg Monarchy was bound to destroy its framework, and conservatism of the mollusc type could alone prolong its existence. Given international stability, it was possible for Francis I—tenacious, inert, unimaginative, and impervious to ideas—to maintain his dominion. But to have made the entire European continent adopt a policy primarily devised in the Habsburg interest was the work of Metternich—a great political and diplomatic achievement.

Fresh research confirms the traditional picture of the Emperor Francis I.[1] 'By nature he is rather slow, insincere, and indifferent,' wrote Joseph II about his nephew. Everything about him is 'mechanical, mere repetition; he has no original ideas and no style in writing or talking.' Any apparent desire to improve is merely meant 'to shut the mouths of his teachers . . . and then he remains the same as before'; the only argument which works with him being 'fear and the apprehension of getting into trouble.' As Emperor he distrusted able men, even his own brothers, the Archdukes Charles and John. Metternich was the only one he could put up with.

> Nothing good comes from so-called men of genius or learning; they think they know everything better, obstruct business, and find no pleasure in day-to-day work. The best thing is common sense and the ability to sit tight [*brav Sitzfleisch*]. I need no men of learning, but quiet citizens. . . . My servants must teach what I command. Whoever can't, or comes along with new ideas, had better go or I shall remove him.

Francis I was devoid of active ambition, lacked self-confidence, and even personal dignity. In 1799 his old tutor had to remind him that 'his pastimes should be appropriate to his years, position, and birth.' He accepted French preponderence, while it lasted, with cynical indifference. 'The French will soon attack us again,' he said about 1799; 'we shall probably be thrashed once more, and then we shall have to restart negotiations.'

When events and Metternich had secured for him peace and power, he effectively imposed his own listlessness on the Empire. He suffered from a mania of conspiracies, which he meant to crush by deterrent examples: trumped-up cases, resulting in miscarriage of justice. Police control was his panacea. The mother of

[1] Professor Dr. Viktor Bibl, *Der Zerfall Oesterreichs. Kaiser Franz und sein Erbe* (Vienna: Rikola Verlag).

Otmar Rauscher, the later Cardinal, wished her son to study law and complained to the Emperor of her son's religious zeal—'My dear woman,' answered the Emperor, 'if you like, I shall have the matter examined by the police.' The unrelievedly wretched condition of public finance left him unmoved. 'What of it? State bankruptcy is a tax like any other. One has merely to arrange it in such a manner that everyone should lose in proportion, just as happens when an honest merchant goes broke.' Morally, too, his system was bankrupt. But most dangerous of all to the Habsburg Monarchy were rulers such as Joseph II, the men of 1849–66, and of 1906–14, who tried to base Austria's existence on quasi-intellectual principles. Nonentities playing for time against fate were better custodians.

2

FRANCIS JOSEPH I

Francis Joseph I was born in August 1830. As a small child he played at the feet of the Emperor Francis, the enemy, father-in-law, and finally quasi-conqueror of Napoleon; and his plan of studies at seventeen included one hour a week with Prince Metternich. At the close of 1848, when the disruption of the Habsburg Monarchy—not to come off until seventy years later—had seemed at hand, Francis Joseph entered upon the contested dynastic heritage of his house, soon to be fully re-established in a truly proprietary spirit.

The youth of Francis Joseph passed under peculiar conditions; heir to an ultra-conservative tradition, he had no man to look up to in the generation which immediately preceded him. His uncle, the Emperor Ferdinand, retained the throne only till Francis Joseph could be declared of age; when he died in 1875 Francis Joseph agreed with his friend King Albert of Saxony that 'in this case there could be no question of true mourning.' His own father, in mind and character but slightly superior to Ferdinand, let himself be passed over in favour of Francis Joseph; and when his long and insignificant life reached its close in 1878, this, too, seems hardly to have been an occasion for 'true mourning' to his son. Anyhow, he at eighteen was considered fit to displace his

uncle and father. To his mother alone, who was largely instrumental in removing the two from the throne, Francis Joseph was
attached; but in awe. In childhood, to judge by his letters,[1] he
sincerely cared for his brother Maximilian, by two years his
junior. But in later years the Emperor seems to have distrusted
and disliked anyone who might have thought of succeeding him.

The marriage of Francis Joseph was not happy, and his gifted,
rather eccentric wife never pierced the ice which covered the
poor, frozen life of this, after all, rather mediocre man. Their
correspondence shows Francis Joseph behaving to her with perfect
courtesy, which she reciprocated; of lively feelings there is, however, no trace. He appears cold in the wearisome, stereotype
cordiality which he displays in family relations, and numbed by
grief on tragic occasions. Perhaps indeed this was the deepest
tragedy of the Emperor's life that he passed through it emotionally
inarticulate; pain is worst when repressed in dull silence. In public
and in private relations alike Francis Joseph was the same almost
throughout his life—poor in ideas and poor in feelings, bare of
deeper understanding and of live passion, stiff, unimaginative, un-
impressionable, and unimpressive. He was buffeted by events and
movements which he did not understand and was therefore
utterly unable to control. His ideas, when he was young, were as
primitive as his vocabulary. There were 'bad men' (*die Schlechten*)
who had to be supervised by the police; subjects were sometimes
'naughty' (*ungezogen*) and had to be punished; but his soldiers
were invariably 'good boys' (*brav*) and went to war singing and
cheering if ever a brother monarch proved 'iniquitous.' There is
something pathetically underdeveloped in the Francis Joseph of
those younger years.

Nor did his horizon widen much with age, merely his sphere of
action was narrowed down by the achievements of stronger,
wiser men, and perhaps also by a recognition of his own in-
feriority. The lifeless, conscientious manner with which he fitted
himself into new situations imposed on him by events was un-
canny, almost inhuman. In time he became merely the first
bureaucrat of his Empire (which his grandfather too had been
during the later part of his reign). '*Vive la bagatelle!*' might have
been his motto—except that he did not know, or refused to
realize, that he spent his life on trifles. He was endowed with a

[1] *Franz Joseph I in seinen Briefen*, edited by Dr. Otto Ernst (Vienna: Rikola
Verlag).

E

narrow, unemotional conscience which found employment and
relief in the discharge of 'duty,' though its positive contents and
meaning were probably never clear to him. He clung to it, a self-
condemned galley-slave; and it imparted the semblance of
impressive steadiness to his life. Invariably at work, he always
remained the Emperor. Unable to make history, by way of
compensation he interfered in thousands of administrative details.
But in the midst of dreary platitudes, here and there one suddenly
comes across a piece of sound common sense or even of shrewd
discrimination. For within a very limited sphere Francis Joseph
had clear vision; his mind was not weak, but narrow and unproductive. He belonged to a type which is by no means rare, is
hardly ever interesting, appears very respectable in common life,
but is highly oppressive to itself and to those whom ill-chance
happens closely to chain to anyone of that type.

UNE AMITIÉ AMOUREUSE

FRANCIS JOSEPH AND FRAU SCHRATT

PRINCE BÜLOW wrote in his *Memoirs, 1897–1903*:

Francis Joseph was human only in his relationship with Frau Katharina Schratt. I will add at once that the relationship was purely one of friendship. Frau Schratt was not merely a talented actress; she was also an amiable and agreeable woman, sprightly, gracious, and above all natural as Viennese women are. She kept aloof from politics completely, a fact which did not keep the industrious envoys of the smaller Powers from paying zealous court to her and with grave importance reporting her harmless chatter to Dresden and Munich. Frau Schratt stood in completely good relations with the Empress Elizabeth who was genuinely glad that her exalted spouse found, in conversation with Katharina, the relaxation and compensation for the checks to his policy and the terrible ordeals which he had to undergo in his private family life. In his letters to her, Francis Joseph always addressed Frau Schratt ceremoniously. In her drawing-room hung a large picture of the Empress Elizabeth who had sent it to this friend of the Emperor's.

But Bülow's account, which deals even with the style of the Emperor's letters to Frau Schratt, seems to suggest that 'the industrious envoys of the smaller [German] Powers' were not alone in cultivating her acquaintance. And indeed, Francis Joseph wrote to her from Cap Martin, on 5 March 1896:[1]

My dear, good Friend,

. . . I received your dear letter just as I was starting with the Empress for Mentone, to lunch at the Perimont Rumpelmeier, and

[1] *Briefe Kaiser Franz Josephs au Frau Katharina Schratt*, edited by Jean de Bourgoing (Vienna: Ullstein Verlag).

so could not read the second half till in the pastry-shop, and when I communicated its contents to the Empress, who sends you her most cordial greetings, she immediately remarked that Count Eulenburg [German Ambassador in Vienna] will prove dangerous to me. As you know, I have long feared it, for the Ambassador is very amiable, and much cleverer and more amusing than I, and will soon have ousted me from your heart. Thus I am constantly beset by grievous thoughts, and it is indeed high time for you to reassure me by giving me a chance to look into your dear clear eyes. . . .

And four days later: 'That Count Eulenburg should have seen you three times is too much for my taste.' Count (subsequently Prince) Eulenburg himself admits in his diary that at times he

communicated with the Emperor through Frau Kathi in short questions and answers: whether this or that would be pleasing, or displeasing, to him.

The Emperor's letter of 5 March to Frau Schratt contains this further remark:

Your views on the line to take about the Vienna [communal] elections pleased me very much as fresh evidence of your clear and sound political judgment.

Thus even at that time politics were not absent from their talks and correspondence; and with the passing years they fill more and more space in the Emperor's letters.

Fragments of a Political Diary of Joseph M. Baernreither, a Minister in Count Thun's Cabinet, 1898–9, is one of the few published memoirs of Austrian statesmen or politicians; he writes on 5 February 1913:

Marchet [another ex-Minister] telephoned me to-day that he had told Frau Schratt about the warlike plans of the military party and she had said to him that she would speak to the Emperor about it at 5 o'clock to-day.

And on 8 November 1913, while the Emperor was in search of a new Prime Minister, Baernreither wrote:

Frau Schratt proposed to the Emperor Baron Beck and myself. About the former, the Emperor's tone was not at all sympathetic. Of me, he remarked that I was a very intelligent man, and had many friends, but also many enemies.

'Frau Kathi' was not so completely a-political after all.

The first meeting between her and the Emperor occurred apparently on 20 May 1886, in the studio of the painter von Angeli and in the presence of the Empress Elizabeth, who had commissioned him to paint for the Emperor a portait of Frau Schratt—a singular opening to a strange relationship. He was fifty-five, and she thirty-two; and their friendship continued for thirty years, till his death. The published correspondence consists of some 560 letters from him, which cover about 400 pages, though only very few are printed in full. But none from her appears in the book, except one, of February 1895, found in draft among her papers; yet they are essential to a full appreciation even of his part in the correspondence and friendship. Have they perished? The Emperor kept and treasured, numbered and counted them. By 15 January 1888 he had forty, and hoped that they would 'grow into a voluminous library of letters.' 'I employ my leisure in rereading your entire correspondence from the beginning,' he wrote on 28 January. By November 1888 he had one hundred, and still addressed her as *Meine liebe gnädige Frau*; but at last she changes into *Meine liebe Freundin* (and a few years later small crosses begin to appear at the end of his letters). On 10 June 1890 he announces receipt of her 200th letter. 'Your letters are my greatest joy,' he wrote on 9 May 1888. 'I await them always with longing and impatience, and always read them several times. . . .' His own are worth reading for their cumulative effect, though, except one or two, none deserves being reread. 'You might ask why I write again, and I could really give no sufficient answer . . .' (19 May 1887). 'I close this letter as I have nothing sensible (*nichts Gescheidtes*) left to say, and in fact what I have written is not very sensible either' (5 July 1888). He praises her letters for being 'so pretty and delightful,' and apologizes for the 'deficient form' of his own (5 October 1888)—'I have no time to correct them,' he explains on one occasion, and on another puts *pardon* against a blot. 'And now my paper has come to an end, and also my anyhow not very profound thoughts. . . .' (10 October 1889). 'I am constantly amazed at my ability to produce such long and empty letters, and apologize for their lack of contents. . . .' (10 November 1889). A correct appreciation— but what unfeigned modesty in one who had been Emperor for more than forty years.

Lonely, never sure of himself, and very seldom satisfied with his own performance, he worked exceedingly hard from a compelling sense of duty, but without deriving real satisfaction from his work. Shy, sensitive, and vulnerable, and apprehensive that he might cut a poor or ridiculous figure, he took refuge in a still and lifeless formalism, which made him appear wooden, and in a spiritual isolation, which made him seem unfeeling or even callous. Never in all these letters is there the least trace of pride in the part he had to fill, and hardly ever any sign of pleasure in it, except when he thought he met with genuine attachment from his people: human warmth and sympathy touched him deeply, and he seemed in need of them. But human contacts were difficult for him; and he disliked social gatherings and shunned 'clever conversation.' He could not, and would not, 'improvise': everything had to be fixed beforehand, and no freedom was given to thought or to impulses. This was not the rigid 'Spanish etiquette,' as which it is sometimes described, but the self-imposed slavery of one painfully aware of his own insufficiency: and the heavy burden of the task, to which he felt unequal, he had to carry for sixty-eight years. But the things eliminated from his own life attracted him: frivolous gaiety, carefree enjoyment, sensuality, volatile moods, especially if rendered innocent by a basic decency. He found an unwonted release in his relationship with Kathi Schratt: and his deeper self—tender, immature, frustrated, and impoverished by lifelong imprisonment—appears in these letters.

How he loathed the publicity which attached to his every word and movement! At parliamentary dinners or public receptions he had to be amiable and talk 'with sparkling intelligence' (*und geistreich sprechen soll man auch mit den Leuten*), for 'all the twaddle I talk appears in the Press.' His one wish on such occasions was to escape—*aussi möcht i*, is his stereotyped phrase in Vienna dialect. Even more trying were the visits of brother-sovereigns. In October 1888 he had to entertain the speechifying William II: 'My toast at yesterday's dinner, which I dreaded terribly, I managed to deliver without getting stuck, and yet without a prompter. . . .' Similarly, when 'ordered' to give the toast at a family wedding—'I did it very briefly and, thank God, without coming a cropper' (5 July 1892). However pleasant his 'exalted guests' may have been, he felt ill at ease—*gemütlich ist die Sache doch nicht*. But the visit of the King of Serbia, in October 1894, was excruciating—'he continually asks questions and repeats the same thing ten times over.' (For once Francis Joseph did not realize that he was portraying himself—though on innumerable occasions he avows that asking tiresome questions was his own 'bad habit,' for which he was 'constantly pulled up by the Empress.' 'Again a question,' he wrote on 5 March 1893. 'The Empress says that it may be an honour to be my lady-friend, but that it is *assommant. . . .*)' Most of all he disliked the visits of women with a claim to intellectual distinction. 'I shall have to pull myself together; and appear highly intelligent and educated.' The wife of Charles I of Rumania was an authoress writing under the name of 'Carmen Silva,' and she managed to inflict one of her plays on the Vienna Court Theatre: what Francis Joseph dreaded most was that she might come to its production. Her high-falutin exhibition-ism grated upon him; he writes a few years later from Budapest (1 October 1897):

> The Rumanian visit passed off well and according to program, but was very exhausting. Carmen Silva, who was most amiable and very friendly, got on my nerves with her ecstatic delight at the truly excellent reception with which they met here. I naturally grew colder and colder, and almost uncivil. . . .

He squirmed at any display of feelings—what would he not have endured had he known that the story of the *amitié amoureuse* of his old age would one day be exhibited in print?

Frau Schratt, an actress of the Court Theatre subsidized from the Emperor's Civil List, tried even early in their acquaintance to gain his support in an argument with its director. The Emperor wrote to her in January 1886:

> I had meant . . . to speak about your business, but did not dare, since so far I have never meddled with the repertory or the casting of parts, as I consider that the theatre is for the public and not for me, and besides I do not trust my judgment in these matters. Moreover, I feared that my interference might place you in a false position, and do harm rather than good. But to please you I shall state your wishes at the next opportunity. . . .

A few weeks later Frau Schratt fainted in church in the Emperor's presence, and the next day he wrote to apologize for not having stayed after she had regained consciousness: 'I wanted to avoid a sensation.' In the same letter he reproached himself with not having had the courage to speak to her at a ball but he was watched from all sides 'through, or without, opera glasses, and the Press hyenas were about who get hold of every word I say. Well, I did not dare.' And on 21 April 1887:

Forgive my having troubled you with my views about our friendship and the chatter of our dear fellow-men. I felt a real need to speak frankly to you about it. . . . Your honour and reputation are sacred to me above all, and I wanted to tell you how I endeavour to make our friendship, in which I see nothing wrong, appear in a proper light before the world, and wanted to hear what you think of my failure to do so. What you said the other day, and wrote yesterday, reassures me, and is new proof of your goodness and indulgence toward me.

30 May 1887: 'the three weeks since I saw you, seem to me an eternity.' 29 November: 'I would be happy to see you again, but of course only if it pleases you, if you feel well, and can spare the time.' 6 January 1888: he saw her cross the square in front of the Imperial Palace without her seeing him, 'but to my joy you looked up several times, to my window.' 20 January: 'I could shout with joy at the idea that to-morrow I shall probably meet you again.' And next came a clarifying talk, followed by two letters. 14 February 1888:

This morning I was overjoyed to receive your dear, good, long letter of the 12th. . . . The enclosed 'Letter of Meditations' made me immeasurably happy, and if I did not know that you always tell me the truth, I could hardly believe it, especially when I see in the mirror my wrinkled old face. . . .

That I adore you, you must know or at least guess, and in me that feeling grows steadily. . . .

So now it is out, and it may be as well, for out it had to come.

But that's enough, and our relation must remain the same as till now, if it is to last, and last it should, for it makes me so happy. You say that you will hold yourself in hand, and I shall do the same on my part, even if it is not easy, for I don't want to do anything that is wrong, I love my wife, and do not want to abuse her confidence and her friendship for you. . . .

And on 18 February:

. . . you again have scruples and a *panicky* fear that I shall think you a seductress and be angry with you. The latter is impossible, and as for the first, you are indeed so beautiful and lovable and good that you could be dangerous to me, but I shall remain firm, and since I have your 'Letter of Meditations' I am happy and reassured. Clarity is best, and even if it is perhaps not altogether proper, still it is better so, and it saves me now from my stupid jealousy, which often plagued me.

. . . It has been snowing all day, and the mood is melancholy; but how jolly all this snow would be if we were walking in Schön-brunn, and if the slope above the Tyrolese Garden is again slippery, I might perhaps be allowed to take your arm!

A most satisfactory existence à *trois* ensued: the Empress publicly avowed friendship for Frau Schratt, while the Emperor revelled in the calf-love of a mid-nineteenth-century adolescent. 20 May 1888: 'Tuesday afternoon I had luck. Thinking that this was about the time for you to drive to the theatre, I kept careful watch'—and he saw her pass in her carriage: 'I then laughed with joy over your friendly greeting.' 24 May: 'The last two days were lucky for me, because . . . at last I saw you again from a distance, and I am most grateful to you for having rendered this possible by clever manœuvring. . . .' The moment he caught sight of her grey hat or her red umbrella in the square in front of the palace he would try quickly to get rid of whoever was with him and rush to the window to greet her. 'I remain in longing (*Sehnsucht*), attachment, and most devoted love, yours. . . .'

Then, in January 1889, the Mayerling tragedy broke upon them: the suicide of his only son, the Archduke Rudolph, together with Baronesse Mary Vetsera. Frau Schratt drew even nearer to the Imperial couple. 12 February 1889:

I often think of you with deep love and gratitude, and we often talk of you. The Empress was glad to hear that you propose to come in the spring to Hietzing, because, she says, you will be nearer to us.

I again thank you with all my heart for your intention to go to Lourdes. Pray there above all for our poor, dear Rudolph, the best of sons, and pray to the Mother of God, our Lady of Dolours, for the poor mother whom Heaven has visited with the greatest imaginable pain.

16 February 1889: 'Outwardly the Empress is quiet and only con-cerned for my health and distraction, but I can see she is filled with deep, silent pain. A great, rare woman!' 28 February: 'The sad mood continues. . . . I begin to worry about the Empress. She

daily grows more sad and silent. . . .' The Empress had been
ordered to go to Wiesbaden for a cure, but, wrote the Emperor
on 12 March, 'stubbornly refuses to leave me before you are back
in Vienna.' On the 16th, having transmitted theatre news to Frau
Schratt (a frequent subject in their correspondence), he remarks:
'You see that I again take some interest in gossip. . . .' Next he
went to Budapest for 'the manufacturing of new Ministers';
and in April to Ischl, to recuperate and 'shoot capercailzie.'

So I drift back into my old habits and resume the old life, though
things can never be the same.

She had her difficulties in the theatre, and he with his Ministers
and Parliaments. The Hungarian crises loom large in his correspondence: a genuinely Parliamentary system rendered them more difficult to settle than in Austria, where Parliament, paralysed by inter-
racial divisions, left the Emperor free to make his own choice;
moreover, while in Budapest he had to communicate with her by
letter. 'It would of course be splendid,' he wrote on 13 February
1890, 'if you could come here, but how to find a plausible excuse,
and our dear fellow-men would say that you have followed me,
and probably invent some additional stories.' And another time
about Press reporters: 'These reptiles are even worse here than in
Vienna.' Frau Schratt did not share the Emperor's dislike of
publicity and occasionally caused him worry by indiscretions.
Thus she went up in a balloon with Alexander Baltazzi, a relation
of Baronesse Mary Vetsera. The Emperor wrote on 7 June 1890:

I cannot get over your flight. It is the first time . . . I could be angry
with you, but as this cannot be, I am merely aggrieved (not offended).
That flying is very rash, I told you before, and even the Empress,
who fears nothing, thought it dangerous and wrong. Moreover, I
immediately apprehended that the newspapers would not keep
silent.

Here followed a selection from the Press.

I know you too well to doubt that for you this was merely an
amusement to satisfy your curiosity, but the papers . . . make it look
like self-advertising and a bid for renown in an alien field, which fits
neither your style nor your natural simplicity, for which I have the
greatest regard. . . . I have never objected to your social relations
with Alexander Baltazzi . . . on the contrary, I was grateful, for it

enabled me in a difficult period to learn through you things which were of importance to me. That you should have undertaken the flight under his auspices is truly indifferent to me, but in the eyes of a wicked world this fact, picked out by the Press, will harm you. . . . If you should ever again think of such a silly prank, please let me know beforehand.

He was much relieved at her mild reception of what he later described as his 'wicked letter and bold remarks.'

Even ordinary forms of active sport worried the timid Emperor. The yacht of the Empress, he wrote on 5 September 1890, 'is already at Bordeaux, and so restarts the sea-voyaging, but for me constant anxiety and worry. . . .' When she reached Oporto he was relieved. When she left Algiers in a rough sea: 'I shall have no peace till I learn that she has arrived safely.' And hearing of some boating accident: 'It is terrible, and further proof of how careful one should be on the water.'

Frau Schratt's mountaineering, however mild, filled him with similar dread. 'No more glacier expeditions,' he begged. And next bicycles were invented: Frau Schratt and one of his daughters started cycling. 'A real epidemic!' he groaned. 'Naturally I worry constantly because of your cycling and other dangerous pursuits.' A few years later spiritualism and hypnotism became the fashion. 'This can only harm you and affect your nerves still more.' By 1907 there were motor-cars. 'I am less pleased with your having hired a car,' wrote the Emperor on 18 March 'this causes me constant anxiety.' 7 April: 'That you should have met with a motor accident is disturbing, but was to be expected. . . .'

There was another side to mountaineering and cycling: slimming had become the craze among women. 'Don't forget to report whether cycling has de-fattened our friend (*die Freundin*),' wrote the Empress. Baths, waters, gymnastics, massage, patent medicines, glandular extracts, milk and fruit cures, diets, fasting —everything was tried by the two women: and detailed informa- tion was exchanged through the Emperor. There was daily weighing: 'I consider the weighing-machine nonsense and a mis- fortune.' Or again: 'I reported to the Empress that your weight has remained the same, whereupon she immediately inquired whether you were taking certain dangerous medicines, which un- fortunately I had to confirm. . . .' Another time he begged Frau

Schratt not to talk too much to the Empress about health, 'and above all not to recommend any new cure or remedies.'

On the other hand, a wellnigh comic importance was attached to eating. Thus with an invitation to tea: 'The Empress . . . asks you not to have too much for lunch, so that you should have a good appetite at 5. Like all *Hausfrauen*, she has a passion for stuffing her guests as much as possible.' (On another occasion Frau Schratt is told beforehand that the afternoon tea will consist of cold meat and chocolate ice!) And when the Imperial couple went to Territet (his letters sound as if he had never been abroad, at least not outside courts), there were continuous reports on the quality of food and the dishes consumed. 12 March 1894, from Cap Martin:

> We are well, although we try all kinds of restaurants, and really eat far too much and too varied a fare. . . . The main purpose of life here is after all only in eating. With this sparkling remark I conclude my letter.

Altogether his accounts are of an engaging naivety. This from Cap Martin, in March 1896, *æt.* 65, in the forty-seventh year of his reign:

> The interview with President Faure passed off very well. . . . When I visited him in the morning at Mentone, rows of Chasseurs des Alpes stood from the Cap to the Hotel de Ville at Mentone, and cuirassiers paraded in front of it. . . . When he came to return my visit, he was escorted by a squadron of the cuirassiers who paraded in front of the hotel. The trumpeters blew their trumpets. It was magnificent. . . . At 7 I went with my three companions to the Hotel de Paris, where we had an excellent dinner, as per enclosed menu, much better than at Noel's or Patard's.

On 10 September 1898 the Empress Elizabeth was murdered by an anarchist at Geneva. 11 September: '. . . with whom can I talk better about the noble dead (*die Verklärte*) than with you.' 16 October: 'I feel best in your company, for I can talk so well with you about the unforgettable one, whom we both loved so much, and because I love you.' He needed Frau Schratt more than ever. But soon shadows fell on their friendship. On the fiftieth anniversary of the Emperor's accession, 2 December 1898, an 'Elizabeth Order' was to be founded, and the Empress had promised it to Frau Schratt, who failed to understand that the

Emperor could not now fulfil that promise without causing a painful sensation. Archduchess Valerie, because of a promise given to her mother, invited Frau Schratt to her country house, but the Emperor, who knew the real feelings of his daughter and her husband, advised Frau Schratt to decline the invitation—which she resented. Lastly, over some differences with the director of the Court Theatre, she sent in her resignation; and the Emperor allowed it to be accepted. She would now absent herself from Vienna, in bad health and worse humour, and make the Emperor pay for having displeased her. Undoubtedly he must often have been very trying—even *assommant*. He was an old dear but a bore. He was exacting in a naive way—he would, for instance, rise at 4 a.m. to get through his work, and then think nothing of asking Frau Schratt to receive him between 7 and 7.30 a.m. In Austria, on all levels, matters were settled by *Protektion*—but the Emperor, even if appealed to by Frau Schratt, would strive to decide them in accordance with justice. When the director of his own Court Theatre was allowed to flout her wishes, how much prestige could attach to being the Emperor's friend? Besides, their relationship, notwithstanding its innocence, appeared equivocal; and the Emperor was visibly embarrassed by what people might think of it: indeed, but for the encouragement and sanction given to their friendship by the Empress, he would never have dared to enter upon or to proceed with it. His attitude must have irritated Frau Schratt, free and easy in outlook and manner. And yet it is difficult to justify the callous and whimsical ill-humour with which she treated the poor old man when he needed her most.

He wrote on 17 January 1899:

I have just received your note which distresses me all the more as I fear that it is I who have caused your nervous depression, and yet my intentions toward you are so good, and I love you more than I can say. But I hope that you will soon regain equanimity and I shall be permitted to see you, for the hour which I spend with you is the only relief and comfort I get in my sadness and worries. With a heartfelt prayer to love me still a little bit and not to be so very angry with me,

I remain, in faithful devotion,

Yours,

FRANCIS JOSEPH

But her bad mood continued, and throughout 1899 meetings seem to have been comparatively rare. 14 November 1899: 'Your nerves must be in a truly bad condition if it took you so long to make up your mind to open my last letter. Did you expect something so awful in it?' On 27 December he asks her, if she feels 'a little more friendly and kindly' toward him, to send round her servant with a message about her health. Early in March 1900 his refusal to intervene in her conflict with the director of the Court Theatre seems to have produced a painful scene between them— Frau Schratt 'passionately and obstinately' rejected the Emperor's arguments and suggestions, and left him in an 'abrupt and deeply hurting manner.' He appealed to her once more:

> Think of the long years of our unclouded friendship, of the joys and pain which we shared—unfortunately more pain, which you helped me to bear—think of the beloved, unforgettable one whom we both loved and who is like a guardian angel above us, and then I hope you will incline toward reconciliation. . . . May God protect you, and turn your heart to mercy and reconciliation. . . .

Another year went by: highly strung, she travelled about Europe, planning more distant journeys—perhaps unconsciously imitating the late Empress. She had even 'the awful intention of going to Egypt,' but first meant to come to Vienna. Overjoyed, the Emperor wrote on 9 December 1900:

> . . . if only it was possible to keep you here and put an end to your nomadic life, if only a way could be found to meet your—unfortunately undeclared—wishes, and to quieten you. . . . Your journey to Egypt you must drop in any case, and think a little of me, of my sorrows and anxiety, were you to go so far and was I to be without news from you.

After a separation of five months, he merely hoped that he would not irritate and annoy her again. But apparently they did not meet, and when in March she was once more in Vienna, he wondered whether he would be permitted to see her or even to write to her in future. And when in a letter of 5 April she asked 'why had it all to happen in that way,' he replied that it was rather for him to ask that question, 'for you yourself had wanted things to happen as they did.' At last, in June 1901, he saw her 'dear, though not friendly face'; and once more he appealed to the love which they had both borne to 'our dear dead one'—'the last tie between us.'

There was some improvement that summer; but she continued her travels, going even to the Canaries. He wrote before her return, on 12 May 1902: 'I am sad and tired, and you will find me much aged and enfeebled in mind.' He was not quite seventy-two, and had still fourteen years to live and rule. Yet he was old and weary. Their relations now resumed a more steady character. But the once frequent and chatty letters seem to have become fewer and shorter. Perhaps what had once been a passionate longing was now a settled habit.

THE STORY OF A
GERMAN DIPLOMATIST

HERR VON KÜHLMANN, well known in London society during the years preceding the First World War, stepped for a while, in its last phase, into the very forefront of international politics, achieving considerable though ephemeral prominence. His *Memoirs*, published in 1949,[1] even in this country gained a measure of recognition apt to endow them with undeserved credence. In the *Spectator* of 24 June 1949, Mr. Harold Nicolson attributed 'great historical importance' to 'this calm, serious, saddened, and in some ways honourable book'; while the reviewer in *The Times Literary Supplement* of 30 September called it a 'revealing book which historians of the period 1905–18 cannot well leave unread'—'it shows how near its author came to the attainment of aims that would have left Great Britain friendless and discredited in a Europe and a world made safe for Germany.' Revealing this autobiography certainly is as a self-exposure, and as such deserves being read; but it cannot be admitted in evidence. Trifling and self-important, suffused with the malignancy of a frustrated intriguer, these *Memoirs* if accepted would be more damaging to the men Kühlmann commends than to those whom he tries to disparage. But his inaccuracy in matters big and small —the result of a failing memory, of slovenly workmanship, and of an innate disregard of truth—eliminates him as a witness: on closer examination many of the transactions remembered by him in great and lively detail, change into mere comic potpourris, which must not be allowed to gain currency even in the lighter type of historical literature. It is stated by the publisher that Kühlmann

[1] Richard von Kühlmann, *Erinnerungen* (Lambert Schneider, Heidelberg).

died before he could revise his proofs, and that only obvious errors were corrected ('and not nearly all of these,' adds the reviewer in *The Times Literary Supplement*); but had all been removed, the remnants of the book might no longer have been fit for publication.

There is a deceptive façade to these *Memoirs*, as there was to their author. Contemporaries knew him for an 'entirely unscrupulous intriguer'[1]—a judgment confirmed by his autobiography; but they credited him with a first-rate brain—'of his ability as a diplomatist there can be no doubt,' writes Lloyd George in his *War Memoirs*.[2] Yet his contemporary dispatches, published in the *Grosse Politik*, are nowise remarkable, while even his earlier books lack poise, depth, and judgment, and sometimes descend to puerility. As an author he falls into one class with the Kaiser and Bülow: a representative of the *Wilhelminische Aera*.

Richard von Kühlmann, the son of a German director of the Anatolian Railways, was born in Constantinople, in 1873; entered the German diplomatic service in 1899;[3] was Secretary at the Tangier Legation, 1903–05; Counsellor at the London Embassy, 1909–14; State Secretary from August 1917 till 9 July 1918, and chief German delegate to the peace conferences of Brest-Litovsk and Bucharest. At these historical junctures in his career, his chiefs happened to be absent or weak, or at least not equal to their forceful assistant. At the age of thirty-one, as Chargé d'Affaires at Tangier, he played a busy part in the first Morocco crisis, and at forty-four virtually directed Germany's foreign policy, Kaiser and Army Command permitting. But dismissed in 1918, he lived another thirty years without re-entering politics: not for the lack of trying. One such attempt attained publicity. In 1929, while the Young Plan for German reparations was being settled in Paris, Kühlmann approached the British Ambassador, Lord Tyrrell, with his pet idea of colonies for Germany.

[1] See the note 'An Ephemeral Career,' in *The Times* of 11 July 1918. On the role he played at the London Embassy see Asquith, *The Genesis of the War*, p. 105. Even Mr. Nicolson, though lenient to him, describes him as 'not too scrupulous'—'a remarkable man' possessed of 'intelligence unaccompanied by strength of character.'

[2] Vol. iv, p. 2082.

[3] Hardly any dates are given in Kühlmann's *Memoirs*, and his entry in *Wer ist's?* (the German *Who's Who*) supplies a list of his decorations, but no proper service record. The above date, computed on the basis of his narrative, may be merely approximately correct.

F

But he overreached himself when he followed up the talks with a letter; this, duly transmitted to London, produced an angry communication from Austen Chamberlain to Stresemann, who replied by completely disavowing Kühlmann's unauthorized activities and unwarranted intrusion.[1] It was perhaps the hope of a come-back, joined to easy financial circumstances, which made him keep silent in the 1920's when others rushed into print with their memoirs: the Kaiser, Bülow, Bethmann Hollweg, Hertling,[2] and Lichnowsky, Hindenburg, Ludendorff, Tirpitz, and Hoffman, Erzberger and Scheidemann, Czernin, Burian, Conrad von Hötzendorf, and Auffenberg, or even secondary figures such as Schoen, Eckardstein, Musulin, J. Andrassy, jun., General Arz, etc. All that Kühlmann published in the interwar period was several excursions into history and politics, superficial even when plausible,[3] flimsy,[4] or primitive to a staggering degree.[5] He prided himself on his historical erudition: 'I could never resist the temptation to get to understand the present in the light of the past.'

In 1943, at the age of seventy, he started writing his autobiography, finishing it in September 1944. By the time Hitler was tottering, Kühlmann obviously felt it opportune to relate how he had tried to stave off the First World War, and next to bring it to a timely close; how he had endeavoured to secure a glorious future for Germany in Central Africa; how he very nearly saved both her and the world from the disasters which have befallen them since; and how he was frustrated. It were a pity had he not gone on record: for at certain crucial moments he did get hold of the right end of the stick, and without knowledge of the man it might seem strange that after having risen so high he achieved so little, and that he went down never to emerge again.

So-called humour has its stereotypes. Some fifty years ago, Central European comic papers of the genteel, bourgeois variety went in for stories about the ageing spinster and the absent-minded professor, while inferior productions would sport, for instance, the vulgar figure of a semi-Balkanic commercial traveller. Herr von Kühlmann, on his own level, somehow

---

[1] See *Gustav Stresemann, His Diaries, Letters, and Papers*, vol. iii (1940), pp. 424–9.

[2] The book, *Ein Jahr in der Reichskanzelei*, is actually by Hertling's son.

[3] *Thoughts on Germany* (German editions 1931 and 1933; English edition 1932).

[4] *Die Diplomaten* (1939), with a chapter on decorations.

[5] *The Heritage of Yesterday* (German edition 1936; English edition 1938).

manages to recall that unattractive type and his enjoyments. Not that there is anything improper in his book—it is his personality, polished yet crude and gross, that offends. He unconsciously depicts himself in writing of a friend: 'When he spoke of truffles in red wine, his eye of a poet would shine just as when he described the beauty of a divine woman.' Food, women, and the splendour of rich houses and luxury hotels is what Herr von Kühlmann seems to remember best, seeing himself as a refined *bon viveur*, a sportsman and traveller, a man of the great world, and an art connoisseur and collector. In short, here are 581 pages of 'high life,' decked with the appropriate adjectives and clichés. Every woman is beautiful and accomplished—*schön, reizend, charmant, elegant*, (though of one he says that she was 'really very beautiful'); the meals which his memory treasures are rich, succulent, delectable; while the houses he visited are described in the language of a classy house-agent or auctioneer. Nor is the reader ever allowed to forget Kühlmann's interest in art, 'which invariably absorbed a substantial part of my working powers.'

The least part of Kühlmann's laudations goes to his chiefs. His first post was St. Petersburg, where Prince Radolin, a friend of his father's, treated him with wellnigh 'parental kindness.' A *grand seigneur*, 'kind and soft, and without any sharpness or hard precision,' Radolin, according to Kühlmann, owed 'his, after all unusually brilliant, career,' to the sinister Holstein, whose confidential letters he would read out to Kühlmann 'under seal of secrecy.' Similarly, at a later date in Paris, Radolin is shown having regular confabulations with Kühlmann, kept secret especially from the Counsellor of the Embassy. With Kühlmann there is usually someone to be short-circuited or circumvented.

His next chief, Count Rex at Teheran, is merely seen worrying lest that 'exile' might be his last diplomatic post. In 1903 followed a short assignment to London, and Count Metternich, under whom Kühlmann was to serve again 1909-12, comes in for a first dose of disparagement. His week-ends lasted four or five days; he would take long holidays to shoot in Scotland or recuperate on the South Coast; but packets of blank sheets, signed in various places, were left to be filled in with non-committal stuff by his officials. On his return he would dictate brilliant dispatches. 'Were it sufficient in a diplomatist to write courageous and accurate reports, Count Paul Metternich would have to be placed among the remarkable diplomatists of his time'; but 'the essential part of an Ambassador's task consists in inducing correct decisions at home,' while, by gaining influence with the leading men where accredited, he should 'carry on an active, constructive, go-ahead policy.' 'In that matter an appraisal of Metternich's activities in England would yield less favourable results.'

Kühlmann's next post was Tangier. The Minister, Freiherr von Mentzingen, was 'an experienced, painstaking diplomat, probably too painstaking'—he lacked 'wider horizons' or any desire 'to assume responsibilities.' Instead of intriguing against France he tried to see justice done to German subjects by the Shereefian Government.

> All my endeavours to convince him how inopportune his policy was just at that time, and all attempts, partly made through his charming wife and his clever mother-in-law, to deflect him from that course, proved unavailing.

But Mentzingen soon went on leave, not to return. 'I never had . . . any conflicts with him'; but may not Kühlmann have had a hand in this timely disappearance?

1906: Washington. Freiherr Speck von Sternburg, a cavalry officer, had in 1898, as German Military Attaché, helped Theodore Roosevelt with his Rough Riders. To please him when President, Speck was appointed Ambassador. 'I was never able to detect a great politician in him.' 1907–09: at The Hague, where the Minister, Herr von Schlözer, was 'an amiable man, devoid of political passions'; and was rescued by Kühlmann from comic embarrassments caused to him by the Kaiser's visit to Holland.

And then back to London, to the lonely bachelor and morose hypochondriac Metternich, who, when things grew critical, would do nothing but 'sit passive with folded arms.' Hence a cleavage arose between them—but never 'any controversy or even argument'; Kühlmann would merely do things behind the Ambassador's back, or try to short-circuit him. Here is a typical tale. Kühlmann was attending a fashionable wedding in Berlin at a date unnamed, but ascertainable through the Gotha Almanac as 12 March 1912. During the 'excellent wedding dinner,' he was summoned to the State Secretary, Herr von Kiderlen-Wächter, who made him report on the situation in London; and agreeing with his conclusions, took him, in spite of the late hour, to the Chancellor Bethmann Hollweg. It was decided that Kühlmann should the next day return to London and seek an interview with Haldane (this was a month after Haldane's 'mission' to Berlin). 'The Chancellor added quite casually: "Please also inform the Ambassador of what was settled to-day."' But on hearing Kühlmann's report Metternich's face darkened visibly, and

> he said somewhat abruptly: 'Obviously they told you that I myself should discuss the matter with Haldane.' I replied that nothing of the kind had been said. . . . Still, if he desired to make the communication, I would comply with his wish.

And next Kühlmann was reprimanded from Berlin for his claim to deal with Haldane himself—'which did not impress me with Bethmann Hollweg's strength of character.' The new draft for a German-British agreement, brought by him from Berlin, is printed in the *Grosse Politik*,[1] which also shows that on 14 March —possibly before his return—Metternich saw Grey in the presence of Haldane, and was given a draft approved by the British Cabinet:[2] it is difficult to see how he could have let Kühlmann handle the German counter-proposals.

Metternich was informed at the end of April 1912 that he would be recalled from London, and left early in June. His successor, Freiherr Marschall von Bieberstein, arrived at the end of the month, and in August went home for a holiday: he died in September. 'I am convinced even now,' writes Kühlmann, 'that he would have been able to prevent the outbreak of the World War'—'he had the advantage of working in London on ground which was well prepared' (obviously not by Metternich). But then came Prince Lichnowsky, who had made his career 'under the wing of Princess Marie von Bülow'—

> a *grand seigneur* whose forte was magnificent entertainments and an amiable personality. . . . Brilliant dinners, and a number of footmen and butlers, surprising even for English conditions, dressed in splendid, absolutely correct, liveries, masses of silver and flowers, soon became the talk of the town among the upper classes.

But what were his qualifications as Ambassador? Sir Edward Grey, writes Kühlmann, once asked permission

> to put to me a somewhat delicate question, fully relying on my discretion. . . . He was in the habit of dictating minutes of conversations while these were fresh in his memory. . . . So he did also

[1] Vol. xxxi, pp. 167-9. [2] Ibid., p. 178.

after visits from Prince Lichnowsky. But he thought he had noticed that the Prince was 'most inaccurate' about particulars, and therefore asked permission to submit to me his minutes of conversations with the Prince: I should tell him whether he had correctly understood the Ambassador. . . . I agreed to this being done. But in the few months which separated us from the outbreak of war, it never so happened that Grey asked me to examine his notes.

The concluding statement would seem the most credible part of the story.

In August 1914 Kühlmann was sent to Stockholm, where the burden of work and responsibility seemed too great for the German Minister, Herr von Reichenau: while in Brazil he had suffered a severe sunstroke.

I received a secret instruction to take as much as possible off his shoulders and to keep a watchful eye on him. Should I find that his nerves were no longer equal to the task . . . he would be sent on sick-leave and I would carry on as Chargé d'Affaires.

Two months later Kühlmann was transferred to Constantinople, only to find that his new mission resembled his previous one.

Baron Wangenheim was apparently thought to be highly strung, and a robust assistant was deemed necessary. Much importance was attached in Berlin to bringing Turkey into the war, and it was felt that the Ambassador was remiss in pressing the matter. Still, to my great relief, I was not expected, as in Sweden, to take over if I thought it necessary, but to try, with the utmost consideration for Wangenheim, to overcome his inhibitions.

And so Turkey was brought into the war; 'the Ambassador was inwardly pleased when it was accomplished without his having had to take the crucial decision'; and Kühlmann's relations with him remained 'perfectly harmonious.' Wangenheim was Kühlmann's tenth and last diplomatic chief, and looking back at the series one can merely wonder at the dictum in his *Thoughts on Germany* (p. 68): 'Our pre-war diplomacy was at least equal to the average of the diplomats of other countries. . . .'

Kühlmann's next post was that of Minister to The Hague, from April 1915 till September 1916, when he returned as Ambassador to Constantinople: but this period seems blacked-out or confused in his memory—he mumbles something about The Hague, and then passes straight on to the final phase of his career. Bethmann

Hollweg and his Secretary of State having resigned in July 1917, the new Chancellor, Michaelis, 'persuaded' Kühlmann to accept the Foreign Office. 'After we had reached basic agreement on the broad principles ... Michaelis, I can truly say, left me completely independent in the conduct of foreign policy.' Even so he does not escape censure for 'political disloyalty,' which 'unfavourably affected' Kühlmann's judgment of his character. By October, Michaelis got into difficulties with the Reichstag, and asked Kühlmann, on the point of going with the Emperor to Constantinople, to intervene in a stormy debate. Kühlmann took the opportunity to deliver

> a serious and sharp speech about Alsace-Lorraine, which concluded with a most heartfelt 'never.' . . . The Reichstag was deeply impressed and seemingly reunited . . . by this appeal to its patriotic feelings. . . . As I descended the great staircase . . . I was surrounded by crowds of members . . . who excitedly . . . argued that the political position of the Chancellor . . . was too seriously affected by that most unfortunate debate, for him to remain in office . . . and begged me to report to the Emperor accordingly.

At that time 'the idea seems to have arisen in certain Parliamentary circles, probably in connexion with my speech on Alsace-Lorraine, that I should be his successor. No such thoughts entered my head. . . .' And so, wholly disinterested, Kühlmann took the first opportunity to report against his chief, and to tell the Emperor

> that the leaders of the most important majority parties had asked me, before I left, to submit to him that in their opinion there was no chance of further fruitful co-operation with Chancellor Michaelis. . . .

His successor, Count von Hertling, like Kühlmann a Bavarian,

> from the first moment left me, I can truly say, in completely sovereign direction of foreign affairs, and never during the whole period of our collaboration was there the least, even momentary, clouding of relations between us.

These were 'absolutely harmonious'; 'the aged Chancellor,' who complained that at such time he, 'a worn-out Professor of Philosophy,' should be burdened with that office, in private conversation frequently spoke of Kühlmann as his successor. But at the end of June the 'demi-gods' of the Army Command,

Hindenburg and Ludendorff, demanded Kühlmann's dismissal. He, when told by the Emperor that their 'paths must part,' pleaded the need of being allowed to bring to some conclusion secret peace talks which he claimed to have started with London. Finding that the decision was final, he felt that this would cost the Emperor his Crown.

Thus in a diplomatic career of almost twenty years, Kühlmann had but two chiefs he fully approved of: one who died soon, and the other who was 'dead above ground.'

In Kühlmann's subjective story it is his attitude and emotions that matter rather than his facts. But from the way he remembers things which are of common knowledge and can easily be checked, conclusions must be drawn for events of which he is sole witness.

Here are a few examples. In 1900, in St. Petersburg, Kühlmann was presented to 'the beautiful, melancholic-looking Empress' who 'was unhappy because her eldest son . . . was a so-called "bleeder." ' Her only son was born in August 1904.

At the end of September 1914, Kühlmann learnt that he would be moved from Stockholm; 'some time later' he was transferred to Constantinople; he arrived in Berlin for instructions just when the Polish State was proclaimed by the Central Powers (which happened two years later, on 5 November 1916); in Vienna he discussed that proclamation with the Austrian Premier, Dr. von Koerber (appointed in October 1916); and having visited Sofia, spent a few days in Bucharest, where the German Minister told him that the anti-German elements would not prevail in the life-time of King Carol (who died on 10 October 1914). Kühlmann has mixed up his first journey to Constantinople with the (forgotten) second journey.

Similarly confused is his account of his London negotiations. In September 1911 he went to stay with friends in the Isle of Mull, in order

to recover somewhat after the exciting and exhausting days of the [Agadir] crisis. Sir William Tyrrell had been in attendance at Balmoral[1] during the visit of the Russian Foreign Minister, Isvolsky, and now likewise arrived at the house. . . .

[1] Grey might have been 'in attendance' at Balmoral, but not his Private Secretary.

As Kühlmann was leaving, Tyrrell offered to accompany him to the landing place; and having reviewed the events of the preceding few weeks, asked:

'Are you satisfied with the state of our relations?' I expressed my deep dissatisfaction, and he declared himself in complete agreement. He argued that radical measures were required to place the relations of the two great countries on a satisfactory basis. We reached agreement that proper positive negotiations were needed to achieve a *rapprochement*, and that the old Anglo-German treaty concerning the Portuguese colonies offered a suitable basis. Tyrrell asked me whether I was prepared and determined to throw in my weight in favour of a *rapprochement*, and I, in clear terms, promised my co-operation. He, for his part, assured me that he would not fail us.

Pondering over the talk, Kühlmann concluded that Isvolsky must have spoken at Balmoral about the Balkan League which was being formed under Russian patronage, and that Isvolsky's 'personal policy,' actuated by a desire of revenge for his discomfiture in the Bosnian crisis, must have moved Tyrrell to abandon his reserve and offer Germany a closer understanding. 'The great historical value of the conversation was that Tyrrell, who was nearly all-powerful in British foreign policy, favoured Anglo-German co-operation'; 'the true director of British foreign policy for the first time unreservedly showed me his hand.' Kühlmann's suppositions were soon confirmed by a talk with Grey, to which he was invited in Metternich's absence. Grey spoke of the need of Anglo-German co-operation to prevent the Great Powers from being drawn into the imminent Turco-Bulgar War.

Such is Kühlmann's story. But Isvolsky left the Russian Foreign Office for the Paris Embassy in 1910; he did not visit Balmoral in 1911; the Balkan League was started in the spring of 1912; and the Balkan War broke out in October 1912. Sazonov (not Isvolsky) was at Balmoral 23–29 September 1912; and Kühlmann's talk with Grey can be identified as that of 7 October 1912,[1] with another of 14 October added to it.[2] But then where does Kühlmann's historical conversation with Tyrrell come in?

[1] See Kühlmann's cipher-wire of 7 October 1912, *Grosse Politik*, vol. xxxiii, No. 12240, pp. 175–6.
[2] See No. 12276, pp. 221–2, and No. 12284, pp. 228–32.

If it occurred in September 1911[1] it loses its connexion with
Russia's Balkan policy and Kühlmann's talk with Grey. On the
other hand, there is no room for such a walk and talk in September 1912: on the 24th, when the news of Marschall's death
reached Kühlmann, he was shooting clay-pigeons in London,[2]
and not deer in Scotland; and his wires and dispatches in the
Grosse Politik place him in London throughout the period (unless
signed blanks were used in his absence). Moreover, dating it
September 1912 would make nonsense of a number of other
statements in Kühlmann's account.[3]

'The foundation of my political creed' and 'the lodestar of
all my diplomatic work,' writes Kühlmann, was to gain for
Germany a Colonial Empire in Africa 'commensurate with the
power and the greatness of the mother country.'[4] Even Angola
and Mozambique would have made that Empire 'sufficiently
great and rich to give scope to German energy for generations to
come, and to lay solid foundations for Germany's economic well-
being.'[5] This gives the measure of Kühlmann's judgment:
Germany's pre-1914 Colonial Empire accounted for half a per
cent of her foreign trade, and between 1887 and 1914 cost the
German tax-payer about £100,000,000; doubling its size would
probably have increased these figures proportionately.

Morocco supplied Kühlmann with his first chance: he quickly
'realized' the importance of Germany's economic interests,
boosted them in Berlin, and tried to convince the French that
Germany would uphold them; he claims to have instigated the
Kaiser's visit to Tangier,[6] which ostentatiously acknowledged
Morocco's independence, to Kühlmann an object of bargain to
be used in a 'sharp and quick action.'[7] But Bülow and Holstein

[1] Grey was at Balmoral 11–14 September 1911, and Tyrrell may have
accompanied him.

[2] See *Erinnerungen*, p. 373.

[3] For instance, that Tyrrell and he were by no means pleased with the Haldane
Mission (of February 1912), because it was liable to break the 'fine silk threads'
of their conversations; or that Tyrrell advised Kühlmann to have a talk with the
Colonial Secretary, Lewis Harcourt, when, in fact, many talks between Harcourt
and Metternich, Marschall, and Kühlmann himself about the Portuguese
colonies and the Congo are recorded in March-July 1912.

[4] *Erinnerungen*, pp. 245–6.   [5] Ibid., p. 343.

[6] In his *Thoughts on Germany*, p. 183, Kühlmann includes that visit among
Germany's untoward 'threatening gestures.'

[7] *Erinnerungen*, pp. 203–45, and *Thoughts on Germany*, pp. 225–6.

were out to humiliate France instead of blackmailing her; and even Kühlmann's last overtures which, he thinks, 'might well have led to a profitable understanding for the future,' were frustrated by 'unfortunate influences in Berlin' when the work 'was nearly completed.'[1]

Here is the story as told in his *Memoirs*.[2] On leave in Paris he met by chance the Tangier correspondent of the *Agence Havas*, with whom he claims to have had a curiously close association,[3] and who now suggested a private talk between him and some representative Frenchman. Kühlmann picked for it Count de Chérisey, French Chargé d'Affaires at Tangier. They met, and over lunch roughed out the basis for an agreement with which, completed but unavowed, France and Germany were to go to the Algeciras Conference: Germany was to offer no serious opposition to a French mandate for policing Morocco, and in exchange was to receive the entire French Congo and the French right to pre-emption over the Belgian Congo, besides certain economic rights in Morocco. With this splendid bargain Kühl-mann rushed off to Berlin, merely to see it turned down by the nefarious Holstein. And next Kühlmann's report vanished from the German archives. All that appears in the *Grosse Politik* is a memorandum, whose 'very unclear tenor (*sehr unklare Fassung*) suggests that Holstein had but imperfectly informed his colleagues of the matter.' (In stating the terms the memorandum speaks of 'compensation in the French Congo,' and not of 'the French Congo as compensation,' and while ascribing the initiative to the French, adds that 'it is not clear from whom on the French side it came.') Next Kühlmann, having kept no copy of the text settled with Chérisey, asked him to obtain it from the Quai d'Orsay, only to learn that there, too, it had mysteriously vanished: 'the docu-ment obviously inconvenienced so many people that on both sides unscrupulous politicians decided to suppress it.'

A very different story was told by Chérisey to the French Commission on the Origins of the War.[4] He had made merely a verbal report to the Premier (who was also Foreign Minister),

[1] *Thoughts on Germany*, p. 226.
[2] *Erinnerungen*, pp. 246–50.
[3] See *Erinnerungen*, p. 206: 'Hardly ever was a more important message sent to the semi-official French telegraphic agency without my having previously been given an opportunity to talk over its contents.'
[4] See *Documents Diplomatiques Français*, 2nd series, vol. viii, p. 90, note 2.

and himself had preserved nothing in writing. But he well remembered the transaction: the initiative was Kühlmann's, and what Germany was to receive was a share in Moroccan public works and frontier rectifications in the French Congo; but when Chérisey tried to discover whether Kühlmann was authorized to make such proposals, he was merely told 'that they had the approval of influential men.' Here, in short, is a Kühlmann intrigue, too clever to succeed, but now furbished up into a historical transaction.

Kühlmann magnifies the colonial negotiations which he carried on in London into 'a great, constructive policy,' fraught with far-reaching possibilities, and misinterprets (ill-advised) British attempts at meeting the Germans in a friendly manner. Could anyone have seriously expected a contingent agreement about Central Africa to extinguish Germany's naval ambitions or Britain's interest in the balance of power on the Continent? Elsewhere Kühlmann admits that war may have been rendered 'scarcely avoidable' by the problem of Austria-Hungary's future,[1] and that Britain was bound to join in immediately, lest she be 'confronted in a few weeks by a victorious Germany in occupation of the entire Channel coast.'[2] No wonder then if in July–August 1914 Kühlmann's spurious achievements proved piffle before the wind.

Kühlmann, in his account of the London negotiations, tries to make out that, while Arthur Nicolson and Crowe adhered to the Entente, Grey and Tyrrell were veering toward Germany and working with him behind the backs of the other two. But there is evidence of the distrust which Grey felt of Kühlmann,[3] and Kühlmann's story of his close understanding and collaboration with Tyrrell seems about as accurate as of its inception in the Isle of Mull. Of Tyrrell I can speak from personal knowledge, having served under him in the Political Intelligence Department of the Foreign Office from April 1918 till May 1920; and I agree with the reviewer in *The Times Literary Supplement* that Kühlmann 'seems never to have understood either the limitations of Tyrrell's influence or

[1] *Thoughts on Germany*, p. 78.   [2] Ibid., p. 257.

[3] Mr. Alwyn Parker, who in 1912 on behalf of the Foreign Office negotiated with Kühlmann about the Baghdad Railway, wrote in the *Times Literary Supplement* of 7 October 1949: 'Nobody in the Foreign Office had any illusions about Kühlmann. Sir Edward Grey warned me to be careful, adding that he had rather a full measure of self-esteem and was very *débrouillard*, and not over-careful to bring his actions to the touchstone of the moral sense.'

the mental reservations that may well have lain behind Tyrrell's politeness': Tyrrell was neither 'the true director of British foreign policy,' nor the man 'unreservedly to show his hand' to Kühlmann. Complex, versatile, talkative, but exceedingly secretive, he was amiable, and even yielding on the surface, but a stubborn fighter underneath. He avoided, if he could, personal collisions, and professed a preference for 'long-range artillery'; yet he disliked writing—active and restless, he shunned the drudgery of office drafts, and, cultivating the laziness which Talleyrand enjoined on diplomats, was selective even in his reading of office files.[1] He was a contrast to that austere, somewhat rigid, tireless worker Eyre Crowe, one of the greatest Civil Servants this country ever had; but they were on the closest terms and never would Crowe have shown so much friendship to a pro-German within the Foreign Office. Tyrrell's curious, occasionally even impish, ways gave rise to doubts among some people; in reality he was a loyal friend, who fought the battles of his chiefs, colleagues, and subordinates, often with complete disregard for his own person. Because even after the Foreign Office files have been opened, it may be found difficult to ascertain Tyrrell's views or actions, it is now incumbent on those who worked with him to defend him from Kühlmann's encomiums.

As for the negotiations about the Portuguese colonies, these were not conducted by Tyrrell, then Principal Private Secretary to Grey (and as such not in charge of negotiations with foreign Governments independently of the relevant departments of the Foreign Office), but first by Harcourt and the Colonial Office, and next by Crowe for the Foreign Office. Further, after the agreement had been initialled on 20 October 1913, it remained unsigned because the British Government insisted on publishing it together with the Anglo-Portuguese Treaty of 1899, while Berlin objected, discerning a contradiction between the two. 'If that apparent perfidy of England against her old ally Portugal could trouble anyone,' writes Kühlmann, 'it was the English, but it was hardly a concern of Germany.' Does Kühlmann fail, or does he refuse, to understand that publicity was to deprive the

[1] An administrative question concerning our department was once submitted to Tyrrell in a long minute on the jacket of its file. Tyrrell, uninterested in the subject, initialled the minute unread. It was returned to him with the remark: 'This matter requires your decision.' Reply: 'I agree, W. T.' The decision was then obtained orally, and the jacket of the file was changed.

Anglo-German agreement of the very character which he meant to give it?

While Kühlmann boasts of having managed in the East (on the basis of 'self-determination') 'to carve out of the body politic of Russia' whatever territories were coveted by Germany, in the West he claims to have aimed at a peace 'without annexations,' negotiated and not dictated; this, he says, he meant to attain through secret negotiations with London. The story of his official approaches is told, at some length, in Lloyd George's *War Memoirs*.[1] His good faith was always in doubt, but the approach being made (in Balfour's words) 'through the orthodox channel of a neutral Foreign Office' (Spain), H.M. Government were prepared to deal with the matter in a proper understanding with their major Allies. But Kühlmann's 'No, never!' with regard to Alsace-Lorraine in his Reichstag speech of 9 October 1917 put an end to it.

Now Kühlmann in his memoirs has a story about peace approaches in which Tyrrell is made to appear as his opposite number.

> Certain signs seemed to me to warrant the assumption that Sir William Tyrrell thought a moderate peace settlement in the British interest, presumably because he foresaw that a fight to the finish would produce an unsound French preponderance on the Continent.

And next:

> Through a neutral personality I had entered into communication with my old political friend Sir William Tyrrell, and informed him that I could discuss peace only on the basis of territorial integrity for Germany and Austria-Hungary. . . . Tyrrell replied he was ready to start from that basis.

Indeed, it requires a Kühlmann to imagine, and to try to make others believe, that anyone in the Foreign Office could have, off his own bat, engaged in peace talks—and Tyrrell, the friend of Grey and Asquith, had no personal connexion with Lloyd George.

> My immediate aim [Kühlmann goes on to say] was to meet an English statesman for an informal talk at some Dutch castle in order to ascertain what possibilities there were of peace. German and

[1] Vol. iv, pp. 2081-107.

British delegates were about to meet at The Hague to discuss an exchange of prisoners-of-war. This seemed to me a good opportunity to establish at least a first contact.

With this in view, Kühlmann included in the German delegation Prince Hatzfeldt, son of a late German Ambassador to London, educated and subsequently resident in England. To this hint, claims Kühlmann,

> the British duly responded . . . and Lord Newton led their delegation—Tyrrell must have taken special care in selecting it. At the end of the very first session, Hermann Hatzfeldt and Lord Newton remained behind. . . . Newton immediately started talking about a general peace, and Hatzfeldt, in accordance with his instructions, promptly entered into the subject.

And once more Kühlmann's story can be proved to be rubbish from beginning to end. Since February 1916 Newton had been in charge of the Prisoners-of-War Department of the Foreign Office, and as such had been chief British delegate to the Anglo-German conference on prisoners-of-war at The Hague in June 1917, and to the Anglo-Turkish conference at Berne in December 1917: there would have been no need to 'select' him for it, and anyhow this would not have been within Tyrrell's competence. But in view of a bitter Press campaign which had preceded the Conference of June 1918, Newton, for once, did not lead the British delegation. He writes in his diary under date of 31 May:[1]

> Sent for by Bonar Law, who told me that it had been decided to send Cave,[2] myself and Belfield[3] as delegates to The Hague. The agitation had been so great that the Government had determined to send a Cabinet Minister and, according to Bonar Law, Cave had proposed himself.

That Hatzfeldt would be on the German delegation the British only learnt at The Hague. Newton writes on 7 June:

> Vredenburch[4] says that the Germans are much exercised over Cave's appointment, and in order to be represented by a man of

[1] See Lord Newton, *Retrospection* (1941), p. 256.
[3] Lord Cave, at that time Home Secretary.
[2] Major-General Belfield, Director of Prisoners-of-War Department, War Office.
[4] Jonkheer van Vredenburch, a Dutch diplomatist, was chairman of the conference.

equal official rank have sent Prince Hermann Hatzfeldt, son of the former German Ambassador in London.

And here is the story of the peace talks as they appear in Newton's diary:

. . . although the work of our delegation had been to some extent disappointing, I had during our stay made a discovery that was at once important and unexpected, for we had not been there long when it came to my knowledge that the Germans were acutely, almost passionately, anxious to enter upon peace negotiations. We had been directed to confine ourselves to our own immediate business, but if two parties are in constant close communication for about six weeks it is a practical certainty that each side will learn something about the plans and intentions of the other. The information came to me as a complete surprise, for there was no indication of a German collapse. . . . The important fact was that the Germans obviously realized that they were going to lose the war, otherwise they would never have made any such approach. I determined to keep my information secret until I could convey it personally to the Prime Minister.

He did so on 25 July more than a fortnight after Kühlmann's dismissal. Tyrrell is never mentioned.

Nor is there any ground to suppose that Tyrrell favoured lenient peace terms for the Central Powers. At the Paris Peace Conference, Crowe and he were in agreement with the French about Poland's western frontier. It was Lloyd George, supported by Philip Kerr and Headlam-Morley, who reduced Poland's acquisitions in Posnania, set up the Free City of Danzig, and conceded a plebiscite in Upper Silesia: while Tyrrell, in protest against such modifications, withdrew from the post of British representative on the Polish Committee. Of these matters I can again speak from personal knowledge; and so I can of an earlier significant transaction, on the very eve of the Hague Conference. In May 1918 the Czechs asked the Western Powers to acknowledge the National Committee under Masaryk as a quasi-governmental representation. This was during the Ludendorff offensive, and even some, not averse to Czechoslovak independence, doubted whether it was the time to assume new and far-reaching commitments. I myself was of those who thought that if a new Austerlitz was imminent, we had better unroll our future map of Europe, a sign of hope to nations engulfed by the German flood.

Tyrrell knew this, and on 17 May, late in the afternoon, came to my room, carrying a pack of files; said that Beneš was to see Balfour next morning; that there was disagreement concerning the line to be taken about the Czech request; and asked me to prepare from those files a short minute of our previous dealings with the Czechs, and a memorandum on further action. I do not know what use was made of my paper which urged recognition of the Czechoslovak National Committee; but this was officially extended to them on June 11, and the mere fact that Tyrrell had the matter put into my hands—it was not usual for our Department to deal with current executive work—illustrates his own attitude towards the 'territorial integrity' of the Central Powers. In April 1918, Clemenceau said about Kühlmann's Austrian colleague: 'Count Czernin has lied.' The same can now be said of Herr von Kühlmann.

GERMAN UNITY AND THE
GERMAN WARS

IT WOULD be better if World War I and World War II were called the First and Second German Wars: which would define their origin and character, and their place in history. Other nations, before the Germans, had fought wars of aggression and aimed at world dominion; even so it is the ethos of a nation which determines the nature of its wars and dominion: hence again the importance of the German character of the two wars of our generation. The rise of a united Germany completely changed the political physiognomy of Europe and, which may seem singular, the mental and moral physiognomy of the German people. From excessive, and often nonsensical, political fragmentation, Germany passed over to a disciplined, centralized unity, and from unmeasured subjectivism the German gradually passed over to totalitarian *Gleichschaltung*. But pygmy principalities and the Leviathan State, spiritual anarchy and spiritual regimentation, are opposite expressions of the same political incapacity to build up a sound human community. The political creations of the German are inorganic and grotesque; the work of the typical introvert,

> of men with poor human contacts, isolated and tense: who require rigid rules and regulations in their intercourse with fellow-men, and if forced into gregarious life, fit themselves into it to the point of self-annihilation, but cannot attain the culture of the *agora*.
> .. Introversion and divorce from reality produce a colossal, doctrinaire totalitarianism even in the realm of ideas: still, so long as the Germans remained *das Volk der Denker*, such peculiarities, at their worst, merely made them comic. But when these introverts were

92

swept into action, when their inner tensions were translated into a supreme power-drive . . . the world catastrophe was at hand. And when defeated and demented they developed a mass-movement, it assumed inhuman forms; from introverse isolation they plunged into the heat and intoxication of undifferentiated, uncritical mass-hysteria.[1]

To the State the German surrendered his individualism and individuality, and argued that freedom consists in the deliberate acceptance of self-imposed constraint. 'The will to power' (*der Wille zur Macht*) was the urge behind Germany's unification; and in national dominion over others the German came to seek compensation for what he as an individual had renounced.

When the French in the revolutionary period and under Napoleon overran Europe, they carried a message to the world; and the glory they sought was not one of military victories only. Wherever they went it is possible to this day to discern their great constructive, civilizing work. But there was not one redeeming feature to the German invasions and occupation in the two German Wars to compensate for the immense destruction and untold sufferings which they deliberately inflicted on the conquered nations. A century after Napoleon's death, Heine's song about 'The Two Grenadiers', returning from Russian captivity and mourning when they heard of Napoleon's downfall, was still one of the most popular songs both in Germany and in Russia. But in all the ages to come never will a non-German write or sing a song about two Gestapo or S.S. men mourning Hitler's end. Pro-Germans would be well advised to refrain from comparing the bids for dominion of the French and the Germans, for nothing could better drive home the difference in spiritual values than a juxtaposition of the great humanizing influence of post-revolutionary France with the inhuman and de-humanizing régime of Nazi Germany.

But to what extent is the average German responsible for the misdeeds of his rulers? Attempts to absolve the German people of responsibility even for the Second Reich, the creation of the Hohenzollern kings and the Junkers, are unconvincing in view of the wide and genuine popularity it enjoyed and the devotion it commanded. And as for Hitler and his Third Reich, these arose from the people, indeed from the lower depths of the people,

[1] See my book, *Facing East*, pp. 38–9.

and the unmeasured adulation of which the Führer became the object was as spontaneous as the man was self-made. Friends of the Germans, most appreciative of them as individuals, must ask themselves why individual Germans in non-German surroundings become useful, decent citizens, but in groups, both at home and abroad, are apt to develop tendencies that make them a menace to their fellow-men? Which leads to the problem of group formation. Even with regard to inanimate matter, it is dangerous to argue from the particular to the aggregate: from the way in which a lump of coal burns it would not be safe to infer how a bed of that coal will burn; and the atom is the same in graphite and in diamonds—the difference is in crystallization. From the behaviour of individuals it is hardly possible to forecast the character of the national aggregate, and a nation can crystallize above or below the average moral level of the individuals who compose it.[1] The workings of the German group formations during the last hundred years should make their best friends ponder and hesitate before they commit themselves to the program of a Fourth Reich.

The idea of German unity enjoyed, in its formative period, a high degree of popularity in this country (inspired, to some extent, by belated anti-French feelings). Basic to it was a misconception of the character and motives of the German movement for unity. Thus Sir Robert Peel, in a letter to Baron von Bunsen on 10 October 1841,[2] having paid tribute to the Germans as 'a noble people, distinguished in every art of war and peace,' went on to say:

The union and patriotism of that people spread over the centre of Europe, will contribute the surest guarantee for the peace of the world, and the most powerful check upon the spread of all pernicious doctrines injurious to the cause of religion, and order, and that liberty which respects the rights of others.

My earnest hope is, that every member of this illustrious race, while he may cherish the particular country of his birth, as he does his home—will extend his devotion beyond its narrow limits, and exult in the name of a *German*, and recognize the claim of *Germany* to the love and affection and patriotic exertions of all her sons.

[1] See the essay on 'Germany. The National Character,' in my book *Conflicts*, pp. 78–82.
[2] Frances Baroness Bunsen, *A Memoir of Baron Bunsen* (1868), vol. i, pp. 622–3.

Bunsen himself saw more clearly the future development of a united Germany; not satisfied with the sympathy shown by this country, he taxed it, in a letter of 24 April 1848,[1] with

> fear of the power of a nation of forty-four millions with one customs system, one army, with coasts, ports, ships, and perhaps a protectionist policy in the offing.

And in another letter, of 1 July 1848, he, in spite of the friendship lavished on him in England, wrote to his English mother-in-law:[2]

> In this country, the cause which I have at heart has to encounter two great enemies: first, a commercial jealousy of one united Germany; and secondly, that apathy which is the offspring of egotism and the parent of ignorance. . . . The English press has done but too much to make the name of England an object of hatred. Fortunately, it must be the interest of both countries to stand well together; and we can dispense with English sympathies. As to myself . . . all delusions have been destroyed as to the politics of England. . . .

To the Germans themselves it was clear from the outset that the purpose of unification was not cultural, and not even primarily economic: it was political, and its aim was power, preponderance, and ultimately dominion. About 1770 there were far-sighted Germans, some of them now forgotten, others for ever in the front rank of German intellectual life, who foresaw and foretold the dangers of German unification. Thus a man called Pütter, writing in 1786 on the structure of Germany at that time,

> warned 'the peace-loving world against the pernicious hour of German unity' and ended his praise of the Holy Roman Empire with the fervent admonition: 'Woe to the liberty of the continent, when the hundreds of thousands of German bayonets should ever obey one ruler!'[3]

Similarly the poet Wieland praised the Imperial constitution because 'it prevented the development of a strong and coercive State in Germany,' and thereby secured for the Germans the highest degree 'of human and civic liberty.'[4] And Goethe in 1772

---

[1] *A Memoir of Baron Bunsen*, vol. ii, p. 185.   [2] Ibid., vol. ii, p. 185.
[3] Quoted after Hans Kohn, *The Idea of Nationalism*, p. 372.
[4] Hans Kohn, *The Idea of Nationalism*, p. 372.

protested against the ideas of a nascent German patriotism: 'Patriotism like the Roman! God protect us from it as from a giant's stature! We could not find any chair to sit on, any bed to lie on.'[1] But there were others who even then dreamt of German greatness: 'Already we are superior to all other nations in numbers, measure, and weight . . . united . . . we shall soon be the first nation of the world.'[2] Germany's greatest cultural development falls into the hundred years which preceded her unification, and closes with its attainment; in 1871, as Nietzsche rightly diagnosed at the time, the German mind was uprooted 'for the benefit of the German Empire.'

Heinrich von Gagern, the outstanding personality in the Frankfurt Parliament, thus analysed the origin of the German Revolution of 1848:

> The Revolution which has summoned the National Assembly to the Paulskirche, here to establish a constitution for Germany, had for its main cause the depressing consciousness that the place which is due to the German people among the nations is being withheld from it.

And he, and others, repeatedly explained their conception of the place due to the German nation—'I have conceived the vocation of the German people as great and dominating the world.' That unity and power, much rather than liberty, were the prime aim of the German Liberals of 1848 could even at that time be gathered from their speeches and actions,[3] and is proved beyond all doubt by their attitude toward Bismarck, when he achieved German unity in a way which might be thought diametrically opposed to theirs. Nor did 'the men of 1848' need to learn the militarist outlook from Bismarck or the Prussian army-leaders. Von Radowitz, the leader of the Roman Catholic group in the Frankfurt Parliament, wrote on 28 March 1848 about Europe having been 'ruined by thirty years of obtuse (stumpfsinnig) peace'; Heinrich von Gagern spoke of war as the most effective remedy 'for countering the dislike of a standing army which thirty years

---

[1] The Idea of Nationalism, p. 377.
[2] Ibid., pp. 386–7.
[3] I have dealt with that side of the German revolution of 1848 in my Raleigh Lecture to the British Academy, 1848: The Revolution of the Intellectuals (1947); and in my Waynflete Lectures given on The German Problem in 1848–9, at Magdalen College, Oxford, in 1947.

of peace had fostered in the nation'; and Professor Dahlmann declared:

> The wars which for a whole generation have been repressed in an unnatural manner, will come upon us with a vengeance; . . . we shall have to be more bellicose. . . . We have good grounds to prepare for war, and take care that its results should benefit the Reich.

Like Bismarck and Hitler, the German 'Liberals' gave advance notice of their program; but no one outside Germany seems to have taken it seriously. The merging of Germany into Prussia produced what German unification was from the outset intended to produce; and F. W. Foerster, one of the sincerest, most far-sighted, and most courageous among the German pacifists and humanitarians of our time, had to admit in 1941:

> From the democratic standpoint, Hitler is the most legitimate ruler Germany has ever had, a Kaiser who owes his crown to the most genuine popular vote. He is the spokesman of all the ideas held by the leading groups in Germany ever since 1850 . . . the logical expression of a century's illusion . . . which in National Socialism has donned the garb of primitive savagery and become the program of Germany's renewal. Were a plebiscite held to-day, ninety per cent of the voters would vote for Hitler.

What the majority of Germans now seem to deplore and resent is not Hitler's deeds but Hitler's failure. None the less, German unity, which is logically the fount and origin of the two German Wars, remains for a great many people in this country a moral axiom, something to strive for: to doubt its value is heresy. But is there any cultural or economic aim which the Germans could not attain without political unity and centralization? These are indispensable only for power and war, the gods whom the Second and Third Reich served with such disastrous consequences. Indeed, the importance which Germans now attach to that type of unity can serve as a touchstone for their future intentions.

Extraneous attempts to prevent, or to break up, German unity never served, and cannot serve, any useful purpose: even if their sole aim is security, they will be looked upon by the Germans as insidious power politics, to be countered by an even more intent pursuit of power politics of their own. None the less it matters what ideas non-Germans hold about German unity: whether they see in it something of moral and cultural value worth sacrifices, or whether they discern in it a danger to Europe, and even to the Germans themselves. Had this question been clearly envisaged at the end of the Second German War, a very different demarcation line would have been drawn across Germany. For the present line is based on the axiom of German unity, and effectively promotes reunion. Each of the four occupying Powers received its sector in Berlin. This was done on the assumption that Berlin shall remain the capital of a centralized, united Germany; which, in turn, reasserts the unity achieved by Bismarck. On the other hand, the Western Powers left districts to Russia which form an essential part of non-Prussian Germany: Saxony and Thuringia, with Leipzig and Dresden, Weimar and Jena. Had these been included in the Western zones, and Berlin left entirely to the Russians, the emphasis would have been on the line which separates *Ostelbien* (the lands east of the Elbe) from the old cultural Germany, and not on the unity basic to the Second and Third Reich. And then the German West and South might have been integrated into Western Europe (if there is truth in German declarations of their preference for the Western way of life) while a great deal of friction might have been avoided between Soviet Russia and the Western Powers.

A reunion of Germany and the recovery of the lost territories in the east are now the avowed aim of all non-Communist Germans. But they can be achieved only through a Third German War: the hostility between the Western Powers and the Soviet bloc is the basis of the new German power politics. The Germans may try to found their Fourth Reich by acting as 'vanguard of the West' or as 'the torch-bearers of Asian hordes' —as they offer or threaten; and once they have regained strength and freedom of manœuvre they may attempt either, or both in turn—they have never been squeamish about methods. But even if there were to be no Molotov-Ribbentrop agreement in reverse, if the Germans staunchly adhered to the West, and the Third German War ended in a complete victory over Soviet Russia and her satellites, the verdict of the First and Second Wars would be reversed. A reunited, victorious Germany would once more become by far the greatest Power in Europe, and a menace to the world: and it would not be long before Germany and Japan, re-allied, took Russia and China in tow, and on a new basis achieved their old dreams of domination.

THE GERMAN FINALE
TO AN EPOCH IN HISTORY

HITLER AND the Third Reich were the gruesome and incongruous consummation of an age which, as none other, believed in progress and felt assured that it was being achieved. The 150 years 1789–1939 were an era of confident hope and strenuous endeavour, of trust in the human mind and in the power of reason. The rights of man were to be secured in self-governing democracies, humanized by education and increasingly equalitarian; the rights of nations, in States recast on the principle of self-determination, national unity, and independence. On the European continent language rather than territorial tradition, the bond of the intellectuals rather than the heritage of rooted communities, became the basis of nationality; the age was formed by the intellectuals and the city populations, uprooted men in undiversified surroundings.

Nationalism became a disruptive force intertwining with social radicalism. When in Eastern and Central Europe the war of 1914–18 unleashed revolution, the moderate Socialists, heirs and exponents of the progressive creed, seemed to come into their own—only to succumb, mostly without resistance, to the modern dictators. Intellectuals, who had seen themselves as the rational leaders of mankind set free by their thought, were to find that the disintegration of spiritual values—their work to some extent—had released demoniac forces, beyond control by reason. There was even travesty of thought—*la trahison des clercs*. Hitler was the grotesque German finale to the epoch.

Territorially the Habsburg Monarchy and the Ottoman Empire were Europe's engrossing problems from 1815 to 1919. Once adversaries, next joined in destiny, they were forced back and finally disrupted by linguistic nationality. Bismarck thrust the Habsburgs from the Reich and propped them up on the Danube, to hold and manage for the Germans their doubtful assets—uncompleted conquests and jagged linguistic frontiers—in a monarchy in which the Germans were predominant, yet not masters. On the European continent the nineteenth century saw a rapid growth of German supremacy, intellectual, political, military, and economic. Yet linguistic nationality, the foundation of Germany's unity and power, was imperilling her Austrian 'heritage.' Could her will arrest a European process? This was the initial question in 1914.

Germany in command of Europe would have been a menace to the Anglo-Saxon countries. Their intervention decided the issue. The Habsburg Monarchy was broken up; Germany and Russia lost their alien fringes; territories on the Continent were redistributed on the linguistic principle (greed and the intermixture of races permitting). The settlement favoured the weak—but who in future was to defend them against Germany, Russia, and Italy? The United States had withdrawn from Europe, the British Empire wished it could do the same, while France grew increasingly averse to fighting. The League of Nations was but a paper phantom, invoked by France to prevent change, and by Britain to effect it by negotiation. Germany and Russia were recovering strength: together they might in a measurable time have dominated Europe.

Then the German scene was transformed by the entry of Hitler: never before had a man so malignant attained such power, nor a nation shown so little revulsion from evil. Crude and hysterical, full of virulent hatreds and envy, he powerfully appealed to the Germans, and set about doing their work in Europe. He knew the war-weariness of his generation, and with gangster-like audacity traded on it: first he took risks, and then he practised blackmail. Each time he raised his stakes, and each time he won. Every man, says Machiavelli, has but one method, and when it suits the circumstances we speak of good luck. Hitler had shrewd skill but no wisdom; with him there was no appealing to reason or even to rational interests—which fact men like Chamberlain were slow to grasp. Nor was there in him a conscious control of his own moves; hence he appeared incalculable and chaotic.

Yet a study of pre-1914 Vienna and of the Bohemian Pan-

Germans, by giving the background to Hitler's confused political thinking, might have supplied a clue to his actions. He remained an Austrian, and to the Austrian Germans, in contradistinction to the Prussians, Russia was the enemy and the Poles were acceptable partners. Vienna was not interested in the sea or in colonies. The Bohemian Pan-Germans despised the Habsburgs and Austria, adored Prussia, and revelled in the glories of 1870. That Hitler would attempt the *Anschluss* was obvious. But to the Great-Germans of 1848 and the Pan-Germans of 1898 'German Austria' included the Czech and Slovene provinces, and it was unthinkable that Hitler should permanently renounce Prague. He set out to reconstruct a Greater Germany, next a *Mittel-Europa*— and then? He had none of the realist restraint of the Prussian Junker, but a truly German *Masslosigkeit*—lack of measure and balance.

At no time did Hitler treat Munich as the close of his conquests. On the way to Munich he explained to Mussolini the need of reducing Czechoslovakia which otherwise, in a war against France, would immobilize forty German divisions. At Munich Ribbentrop talked to Ciano of a Triple Alliance with Japan. Hitler, on his return from Munich, ordered plans to be prepared for Czechoslovakia's final liquidation. He was not interested in the trappings and tinsel of Munich: a fortnight later, in his Saarbrücken speech, he attacked England. He expected France to keep out of Eastern and Central Europe. He offered to accept Poland as a satellite into his system, limiting his demands to Danzig and an extra-territorial line of communications across the Corridor. His immediate purpose was not necessarily joint action against Russia; on the Schlieffen principle he might have first turned against the West. Had he pressed his demand for Danzig before entering Prague, one may well wonder what would have been the reaction of the 'men of Munich'.

Prague was a blunder; Hitler's method ceased to suit circumstances, and he did not understand England. After Prague he pressed his 'offer' on Poland with greatly sharpened insistence, still hoping that she would agree. Poland's refusal, followed by her acceptance of a British guarantee, made Hitler order plans to be prepared for an attack on Poland: as she would not cover his flank in a war against the West, she had to be liquidated first. The final dispositions were made on 23 May 1939, the day after the signing of the 'Pact of Steel' with Italy.

His aim was now to isolate Poland. The Western Powers were negotiating with the Soviet Union. Between 23 and 26 May a dispatch was drafted in Berlin with a frank offer to Russia; it was not sent. But two months later Hitler reverted to the idea. He expected the Ribbentrop-Molotov agreement of 23 August to deter the Western Powers from supporting Poland. The attack was ordered for the 26th, but revoked when the news of the signing of the Anglo-Polish agreement of 25 August reached Hitler.

The attitude of the British Government was conciliatory but firm. Attempts to stage a second Munich failed. The declaration of war on 3 September 1939 is one of the great turning-points of history, and should be remembered in awe and gratitude. At the last moment Britain, though fully conscious of the mortal danger she was facing and of her own weakness, called a halt to a process which had gone much too far, and which, had Hitler pulled off his trick once more, would have subjected all Europe, and perhaps ultimately the world, to Nazi Germany.

In the end it was the entry into the war of the two great extra-European Powers, the Soviet Union, attacked by Germany, and the United States, attacked by Japan, which decided the issue. And when their armies met on 25 April 1945 at Torgau, in the heart of Germany and the centre of the European Continent, the victory was won and the century of German preponderance in Europe had reached its term. So, too, had the supremacy of Europe in the world. Within Europe the system of 1919 has been obliterated.

PART II

THE ELIZABETHAN PARLIAMENT

'IN THESE days of institutional *malaise*,' writes Professor Neale, 'a historical study of our English Parliament, though it be of far-off days in the sixteenth century, cannot be entirely remote from our interests.'[1] Indeed, history seems a corrective for the *malaise* which is largely due to an unhistorical approach: to insufficient understanding of institutions that have grown up organically, and to a wellnigh inevitable malformation in those constructed of set purpose. And although ingrained institutional conservatism tends in this country to protect their living organisms against the clever conceits of reforming logic, it seems appropriate to fortify instinctive defences with historical perception and conscious thought. At one time the Mother of Parliaments herself seemed in danger of being affected by the 'new look' of her reputed European progeny; the danger passed with their failure, which on the Continent brought parliamentary government into disrepute, and in this country discredited it as practised on the Continent. None the less, nations freed from the misery of dictatorship and under the impact of disaster now turn once more to the parliamentary 'system'; not with the naive enthusiasm of previous generations, nor even with a heightened critical understanding, but for want of anything better to put in its place. And practice without faith engenders *malaise*.

The failure of most Continental Parliaments springs from a basic misconception: the English Parliament was never an 'institution,' still less a contrivance; organically interwoven with the religious, social, and political life of the nation, Parliament has for centuries been its expression and guide. Had its nature been fully understood men would have hesitated to preach parliamentary

[1] J. E. Neale, *The Elizabethan House of Commons* (Cape).

103

government as a 'system,' or to attempt copying it. For it is the bane of the copyist that his creations must be rational and schematic: he picks out what appear to be the essential features of the prototype, and tries to reproduce them pure and perfect. But chemically pure water is unfit for human consumption, and 'impurities' are necessary ingredients of life. The basis of British parliamentary government is admittedly representation and majority rule, and these principles were adopted on the Continent, and improved upon—for instance, by the elaborate refinements of proportional representation. But the concept of arithmetical accuracy in representation is wholly alien to the origin and nature of the English Parliament, and by no means conducive to the way in which majority rule is practised in this country. Ever since the work of Parliament assumed a legislative character it has been the function of national representation in an indefinable manner to reproduce and balance the complex pattern of live forces and dominant interests, including that of the Crown or Executive. Votes are both counted and weighed; and our present parliamentary practice, basic to the constitution itself, demands that small turnovers in the constituencies should produce wholly disproportionate changes in the composition of the House. One of the consequences of this vastly enhanced weight of the marginal votes is to compel both sides to bid for the intervening, uncertain 'no party's land,' and therefore to steer their course toward the centre: which tends to transform majority rule into government by wider consent. But it is hardly possible for copyists to reproduce useful anomalies: or next they would find that this or that anomaly depended for its successful working on some other 'absurdity' which has been omitted.

Of what inestimable value were the rotten or pocket boroughs in the development of the British Parliament and the making of the nation! How dull the Commons would have been had the House consisted of none but typical country gentlemen and genuine representatives of prosperous boroughs! Moreover, representation would have preserved the local character which is its logical attribute, and which in France it has retained throughout—with deplorable results: for the greater the hold of the individual member over his constituency the more independent is he in Parliament (which in theory he should be), and the more difficult is it to form and maintain a stable, disciplined majority, which is the basis of parliamentary government. But while the 'political nation' had its proper representation in the knights of the shire and the burgesses of populous towns, the rotten boroughs formed a reserve of parliamentary seats at the disposal of the strong and of the interested: of the magnates while dominant in the country, of the Court or Crown or Executive, of economic and financial interests as they entered into the balance of forces. That peculiar interplay of influence and independence produced a House representative of the nation, though not of any rationally defined electorate.

Moreover, the rotten boroughs, by enabling men in search of parliamentary seats to roam up and down the country, helped to unify it politically; which process was furthered by the rule that every member, wherever and however elected, sat in the House as representative of the entire nation and not as delegate of his constituency—the latter concept would clearly have been inapplicable to an Old Sarum or Gatton. Lastly, the rotten boroughs opened the door to men of ability and application needed in the House but, because of lack of standing, wealth, or of such personal qualities as appeal to an electorate, ill-suited to the test of a free election. In short, those boroughs discharged essential functions now taken over by the party organizations; and they prepared the ground for the party system which, though again open to clever criticisms and objections, seems indispensable to the proper working of parliamentary government and of constitutional monarchy as understood in this country.

To trace the history of Parliament in correlation to the life of the community the student requires a thorough and detailed knowledge of the period and must free himself of ideas and conceptions derived from other ages, most of all from the present. Neale brings to his work the results and experience of many years of research into the period which he has made his own. The book is 'a study of the membership of Parliament' during the reign of Elizabeth, and besides 'aims at conveying a picture of the House of Commons at work; of its officials, its ceremonies, its procedure, its manners and conventions, even the style of speaking there.' The chronological story of the Elizabethan Parliaments is left to a subsequent volume; 'and there the constitutional theme will find its appropriate place.' Had we a series of studies such as Neale's, the history of Parliament could be seen in its proper perspective. So far the eighteenth century offers perhaps the best opportunities for comparisons.

Clientage, 'a vestige of feudalism adapted to new social purposes,' was a marked feature of Elizabethan society; both in counties and boroughs the tendency survived 'to move within the orbit of some magnate,' who could still openly describe his parliamentary candidate as his 'servant.' Focused in the Court, clientage supplied Privy Councillors and important Court officials with electoral influence and was apt to carry Court rivalries or factions into the counties, aligning with local faction and strengthening it.

> The grouping and interdependence of the gentry, with its accompanying and constant struggle for prestige and supremacy, permeated English life. It assumed the part played by politics in our modern society. . . .

County elections were a test of the social standing of individuals or of the relative strength of groups, and would at times attain the level of a struggle for hegemony. And such was the concern with precedence in the 'ordered aristocracy' of Elizabethan society that the question (forgotten by 1760), which of the two knights of the shire should rank first, offered occasion for bitter controversy, the second place being in these cases 'only less hard to bear than total defeat.'

In the eighteenth century the gentry of several counties were in the habit of complimenting the leading family (for instance, the Cavendishes in Derbyshire or the Stanleys in Lancashire) with one seat, while it accepted the choice of the gentlemen of the county for the other; but, barring Westmorland, no county was the domain of one family. In the reign of Elizabeth both types were frequent: counties whose representation was engrossed by one family and those 'virtually reduced to a one-seat constituency.' And when in 1593 the Earl of Essex asked Staffordshire to accept his candidates for both seats, he could write to them: 'I should think my credit little in my own country if it should not afford so small a matter as this. . . .' Still, in spite of changes in the social structure, the electoral pattern of certain counties is seen to persist for centuries. Huntingdonshire, writes Professor Neale, was in Elizabethan days 'without men of noble rank,' but the owners of three great houses or estates 'for long determined the county elections': the Tyrwhitts of Leighton Bromswold, the Wingfields of Kimbolton, and the Cromwells, *alias* Williamses, of Hinchingbrooke. In the seventeenth century Kimbolton and Hinchingbrooke were sold to younger sons of the Montagus of

Boughton, who became the founders of the Manchester and Sandwich branches; and these continued to dominate the county, not so much because of the size of their estates (even for a small county like Huntingdonshire the Sandwich estates were never extensive) or merely because of their rank, but probably also because of a tradition of houses in the literal sense, not unknown in the electoral pattern of England. 'In the western counties of Cornwall, Devon, and Dorset a sustained monopoly of [representation] was apparently out of the question,' writes Professor Neale. 'In Devon, Sir William Courtney alone managed to secure a county seat three times during Elizabeth's reign, while in Dorset no one exceeded twice.' Between 1707 and 1801 the independent spirit of the gentry in Cornwall, Devon, Somerset, Dorset, and Wiltshire showed itself in a refusal to return sons of peers for the county, except for one who had started representing Dorset before his father obtained a peerage.

At the opening of Elizabeth's reign the discovery was made 'that the Star Chamber could serve as a tribunal for election cases'; and as its proceedings, before the final hearing, were in writing, its dossiers, with their detailed examinations of witnesses, have supplied Neale with rich material about the conduct of elections. A surprising latitude of powers was possessed by the Sheriff, often an unabashed partisan whose repertoire of tricks started the moment the parliamentary writ was received. Obliged by statute to hold an election at the first county court after its receipt, he could, by concealing it, juggle with the date to suit his own side and hurt the other. Or again, he might try to mislead the opponents with regard to the place where the election was to be held, and go through with it in their absence. 'When there was no contest, the vote by voices terminated the election'; otherwise it was supposed 'to proceed either to "the view" or directly to the poll.' The view 'was taken by separating candidates' supporters into distinct companies, which the Sheriff or a party of gentlemen could survey, and guess at the relative size of each.' A poll, if demanded and conceded, offered the Sheriff new scope for tricks, ranging from the order in which the scrutiny was made to the time when the poll was closed.

The last word in an election was necessarily with the Sheriff. It was he who drew up the indenture, sealed by a selection of freeholders, and made the official return to Chancery. If prepared to

H

face the legal consequences, he could do exactly as he pleased. He could conclude the election after the initial acclamation, or refuse to proceed beyond 'the view,' or break off the poll, or falsify its manifest verdict.

There was a remarkable growth in the membership of the House of Commons from 296 at the beginning of the sixteenth century to 462 at its end; of these 166 new seats, 135 were in sixty-nine English boroughs (not counting Monmouth). But Neale exposes the 'essential fallacy' of the view once held 'that the motive for creating these additional seats was to pack Parliament.' The initiative in the enfranchisement was local, not central, and came 'from the boroughs themselves, or to speak more realistically, usually from their lords or patrons,' the monarch merely 'yielding to pressure for more seats.' But such

> lordly patrons of boroughs as Hunsdon, Huntingdon, Leicester, Mountjoy, Rutland, and Winchester, and 'eminent commoners like Sir Robert Cecil, did not want the seats for themselves. Their pressure on the Queen was simply a transmission of the pressure that was being put upon them. It was the country gentry from whom the demand came.

The infiltration of country gentlemen into the boroughs goes back a long way, but after the Reformation becomes a veritable invasion. In the Parliament of 1584-5, out of a total of 447 members whom it was possible to classify, the number of merchants or borough officials was fifty-three (a proportion approximately maintained till about the beginning of the nineteenth century, when the great rise in the wealth and ambitions of the urban middle classes led to an increase in their parliamentary representation, checked at first, and not promoted, by the Reform of 1832). Adding to these fifty-three the border-line cases of Recorders and gentlemen who held borough offices, we obtain a total of seventy-seven. 'The country gentlemen and his cousin, the lawyer, had captured the House of Commons.'

> If we ask why the Elizabethan gentry were so desirous of a seat in Parliament, we might answer, as we should answer for more recent times—ambition, dignity, curiosity, a desire to be at the centre of things, or even business reasons. . . . In any case, as the gentry swarmed into borough seats, mere emulation increased the demand; and the keener the competition, the more attractive and interesting an assembly the House of Commons became.

The legal term, Parliament, and 'good company' were bringing people to London for the 'season.'

'I am one that loves to see fashions, and desires to know wonders; therefore, if I be elected, I will not refuse it,' wrote Thomas Bulkeley, Recorder of Beaumaris, when the great John Wynn of Gwydir sought to persuade him to forgo the seat in favour of a friend.

There is a distinctly modern touch in all this. But Parliament was not yet a career, either in the eighteenth-century sense, or in that of the age of party. Parliaments were mostly summoned for one session only, measured in weeks: hardly a sufficient basis for profit-making. Hence also elections differed widely from those held under the Septennial Act, when a seat in Parliament had become akin to a long-term lease on a fairly secure tenure.

Bribery was practically unknown. There was no cash nexus either between patron and borough or patron and nominee. The bond was social.

Few will bribe when they can bully—the 'corruption' of the eighteenth century was a sign of growing freedom and independence.

The law prescribed that the representatives of boroughs should be resident citizens or burgesses, and placed the constituencies under obligation to pay them. Hence in earlier times representation was often deemed a burden. This frequently led in small and poor boroughs to the choice of strangers ready to forgo financial claims. In the Parliament of 1584-5, only about one-fourth of the borough members were 'resident,' and of these a good many had probably acquired residence for the purpose. Naturally the larger and richer boroughs, headed by London and Bristol, continued to elect citizens of their own; some, like York, Shrewsbury, Salisbury, or Cambridge, tried to maintain their independence, but did not always succeed; many divided their representation: thus 'Ipswich in 1584 adopted the principle of one Suffolk gentleman and one townsman.' But even a borough like Leicester was asked in 1584 by Thomas Heneage, Chancellor of the Duchy of Lancaster (whose influence extended far beyond that county) to leave 'the choice of both your burgesses to me as heretofore it hath been to my predecessors.' Leicester took refuge in the law, and elected two townsmen—but on other occasions they returned also 'strangers.' At the end of the scale 'were boroughs so petty that neither financially nor socially could they do otherwise than return outsiders.' Sometimes the indenture would be sent to the patron with one or both names blank, to fill in as he pleased. And lastly there were some purely nominal constituencies. Thus in 1547 the return for Gatton declared the members to have been elected by 'Sir Roger Copley, knight, burgess and only inhabitant of Gatton.' After his death, the Sheriff in 1554 addressed the writ to his widow, and

> the said Dame Elizabeth Copley, after proclamation there duly made hath chosen and elected William Wootton of Lincoln's Inn, gentleman, and Thomas Copley of the Inner Temple, gentleman, to be burgesses for the said borough of Gatton.

And here is another case of a woman choosing members:

> To all Christian people to whom this present writing shall come. I, Dame Dorothy Packington, widow, late wife of Sir Thomas Packington, knight, lord and owner of the town of Aylesbury, sendeth greeting. Know ye, me, the said Dame Dorothy Packington to have chosen, named, and appointed my trusty and well-beloved Thomas Lichfield and George Burden, esquires, to be my burgesses of my said town of Aylesbury. . . .

Or here is parliamentary representation treated as a freehold: in 1594, Thomas Langton sold

> the barony of Newton . . . and the nomination, election, and appointment of two burgesses of the parliament, which hath been used by the baron, lord, or owner of the said barony . . . with all other appurtenances belonging thereto.

On the other hand, cases are on record of even small boroughs standing up to powerful patrons; as instanced by the long struggle which the Cinque Ports waged against their Warden in the last quarter of the sixteenth century—Sandwich in 1584, and New Romney in 1588, refused him the nomination for one seat claimed by him as of right.

Boroughs often voluntarily accepted patrons: for there were few which had not, from time to time, interests to promote at Court. 'They hitched their fortunes to the leading favourite rather than the leading statesman.' Less clearly appears the motive for patrons in going to considerable trouble to acquire and accumulate borough interest. Thus Neale writes about the Duke of Norfolk:

So far as we can tell, none of these boroughs was completely and persistently subject to the Duke's dictatorship; and most interesting point of all, his nominees were not government men, but gentlemen-servants and dependants. They did not even constitute a political party. If we had the evidence, we should almost certainly discover that they themselves asked for seats, and that in satisfying their wishes the Duke was merely carrying out the social obligations of his class.

Was, then, a numerous retinue in the House of Commons merely a matter of prestige?

The patronage of the great nobles or the leading Court officials was wide and territorially varied, but it is difficult to form a conclusive judgment of the degree to which it was decisive, or of how it combined with other interests—even for the eighteenth century the extent of electoral influence wielded by single individuals was frequently exaggerated, as has appeared on a careful examination of the great mass of extant correspondence. Far less material is available for the Elizabethan Parliaments, and the lists given by Neale of boroughs controlled or influenced by various patrons are again very long. Still, all will be well if his successors will read and quote with the care and caution with which he writes. Thus, on the three pages (196-8) which deal with the borough interest of the Earl of Bedford, no fewer than eight times his statements are qualified by phrases such as 'there can be little doubt,' 'we can assume,' 'we may surmise,' etc. But the wear and tear of quotation only too often transforms the suppositions of the scholar into the assertions of the pseudo-scholar.

It would be rash to contradict so great an expert as Neale, but his own evidence makes one wonder whether his dictum that before Essex and Robert Cecil appeared the Elizabethan electoral system 'served social, not political purposes' is not too categorical in its formulation; for the political element present during the earlier part of the century, and again towards the end of Elizabeth's reign, can hardly have been wholly absent from the groups and factions of the intervening period, though the basic unity of the nation would have reduced the incentive to mould Parliament with a clearly political purpose.

The Tudors [writes Neale] did . . . influence elections. . . . Some degree of interference was inevitable . . . as the government took to framing a program of official legislation. . . . The planned society of the sixteenth century, with its great measures of religious, economic, and social regulation, could not have sprung spontaneously from a haphazard assembly of country gentlemen and townsmen. Preparation and organization were needed . . . it was essential that the House of Commons should contain . . . a group of King's Councillors and Household servants and their servants.

'All Privy Councillors who were commoners were expected to find seats in parliament'; and there were many 'ambitious officials,' or such as 'by the very nature of their life were unusually eager to enter Parliament.' As a result 'Elizabethan parliaments probably contained a larger Court element than any in earlier times.' An analysis of the Parliament of 1559 puts the number of such members at fifty-four, which Neale thinks 'probably too low an estimate'; in 1584

> the Court group was approximately seventy-five. In addition there were fourteen gentlemen-servants of noblemen and statesmen, who may be regarded as indirectly associated with the government. If we put the Court element in the last parliaments of the reign as not much short of one hundred, or between twenty and twenty-five per cent of the total membership, we shall be near the mark.

In the second half of the eighteenth century the 'Party of the Crown,' including all those who, in the words of an analysis of 1788, 'would probably support His Majesty's Government under any Minister not peculiarly unpopular,' was something like 150–190 in a House of 558: a somewhat higher proportion, but obtained on a rather different basis—an exact comparison is hardly possible in the greatly changed circumstances. But both in the eighteenth century and in Elizabeth's reign it required no 'packing' of the House to obtain the return of 'well-affected' members: a good many felt in conscience bound to support what was truly the Sovereign's Government as long as this was at all compatible with their conscience; and if such loyalty met with rewards, these did not necessarily bear the sinister character ascribed to them by the 'ill-affected.' Still, while admitting the administrative character both of the Elizabethan Court element and of the 'King's friends' under George III, is it possible to deny all political significance to such groups?

> That Henry VIII took a personal interest in the elections of 1529 seems quite clear. . . . But the first assured evidence of organized and systematic interference comes . . . with the rise to power of . . . Thomas Cromwell.

But Neale adds:

> Cromwell was not creating a pliant majority in the House of Commons. He was providing a group of 'King's friends' to lead the House.

Court influence assumed a different significance under Mary Tudor; in 1554 she had letters sent out "to admonish electors both in counties and boroughs to choose representatives" of the wise, grave, and catholic sort" '; and when in 1555 Philip discussed the elections with Privy Councillors, these 'were instructed to see that "none but Catholics and none who are suspect" were elected.' Under Elizabeth the policy of direct and systematic government interference was dropped. But whenever a group of politically active men earnestly pursues a program, a party arises, and elections assume a new character. Thus the Puritans are seen in the 1580's 'putting forth their maximum efforts in a political campaign,' markedly modern in character; 'they were at pains to secure the election to Parliament of a number of their supporters. . . .' And the 'sense of puritan brotherhood,' which was a feature of the Earl of Bedford's parliamentary patronage, came to be shared by other patrons. If our evidence was fuller, might not at least an embryonic political element be found also in some of the other groups? And might not political faction, in full blast with Essex and Robert Cecil, be found smouldering under the surface during the earlier period? Such things are seldom a sudden outcrop. Essex, 'a young man cursed with an urge towards monopoly that became a craze,' started a wide hunt for parliamentary seats. His supreme effort was made in 1597.

> Eight of his servants were elected. . . . About a dozen or more of his friends and relatives . . . as were eighteen of that peculiar clientele of Essex knights, not all of whom, however, belonged to his faction. . . . They constituted a substantial group; and our numbers are perhaps an underestimate. Twelve of these M.P.s took part in the Essex Rebellion.

'It may well be that in these elections of 1597, in addition to the ordinary motive of patronage, there was a conscious effort to secure what we may loosely call a party in the House of Commons.' If so, Essex and his followers deliberately imported a motive into Elizabethan elections which, according to Neale, 'was a striking departure from current practice. Patronage, a natural and more or less harmless feature of aristocratic society, was being turned into a political weapon.' Cecil took counter-measures, and the novel device to which he had recourse 'was the transfer of nominations from other borough patrons to himself.' He continued that policy even after Essex's death, and 'must have nominated quite an appreciable number of the burgesses' in the Parliament of 1601. But 'his policy of organizing and canalizing nominations . . . was the antithesis of high Elizabethan practice,' and marks a transition to that of the early Stuarts.

The concluding one hundred pages of Neale's book deal with the Officers of the House, and their 'rewards,' a device employed 'to supplement inadequate salaries' (as were often 'sinecures' in the eighteenth century, or certain offices in Oxford and Cambridge colleges—not always sinecures—in our own time); and further with the vast and difficult subject of parliamentary procedure. What a wealth there is of significant customs! Here is one example:

> There was an 'ancient order' that when a division resulted in the passing of a bill, the whole House, as well opponents as supporters, must go out with the bill and fetch it in again, presenting it to the Speaker, and saying they affirm it. The Clerk, for example, noted in his Journal in 1589: '. . . the bill was afterwards, according to the ancient orders of this House in such cases, carried out and brought in again by Mr. Vice-Chamberlain with the bill in his hand, followed and attended on by all the members of this House then present, as well those that had first before given their voices against the passing . . . as those . . . with the passing.' The practice clearly had its origin in the twin medieval ideas that law-making involved the consent of the whole community and that members were attorneys for their constituencies. Hooker in 1571 describes it as normal procedure. Probably at that date it was . . . but as the number of divisions increased and time became more pressing, this ritual tended to pass out of use. . . .

On many academic bodies in this country it is still the custom, especially in the case of elections, to try to convert majority votes into unanimous decisions; while the verdict of the English jury to this day must be unanimous, and the English are probably among the few nations capable of successfully working such a system of *liberum veto*. Here is matter for thought on the subject of 'majority rule.'

THE RUSSELLS IN BLOOMSBURY

MONOGRAPHS ABOUT country houses are a well-established form of English history writing. It is fully justified: as I put it in my book on *England in the Age of the American Revolution*, 'English history . . . is made by families rather than by individuals,' and 'the English political family is a compound of "blood," name, and estate, this last, as the dominions of monarchs' being the most important of the three. . . .' Miss Scott Thomson's book[1] covers much wider ground than most works in this class; at least five main strands can be distinguished in it. There are, first of all, the two integral elements of such a work, the history of the family, and the history of the mansion. But as Bedford House in Bloomsbury stood on the outskirts of the City, and a 'little town' soon grew up on the adjoining estate, its story tells also about the growth of London. Joined to the Russell property in Covent Garden and the Strand, Bloomsbury was, even in the eighteenth century, by no means unimportant among the estates of which the administration centred in Bedford House: the story of that administration, and of its gerents, forms a fourth aspect of the book. Lastly, the central theme, so brilliantly developed by Miss Scott Thomson in her first book on *Life in a Noble Household*, is continued through another century.

The story of *The Russells in Bloomsbury* starts in 1669 with the marriage of Lord William Russell to Rachel, daughter and co-heiress of Thomas Wriothesley, fourth and last Earl of Southampton. When lots were cast between the three sisters, she drew for her share, besides certain estates in Hampshire, 'Southampton House and the manors of Bloomsbury and St. Giles in Middlesex.' Here she came to live with her 'dear Lord,' here a son was born in

[1] Gladys Scott Thomson, *The Russells in Bloomsbury, 1669–1771* (Cape).

1680, and from here, three years later, Lord Russell was taken to prison, to die for the cause of English freedom. When in 1694 his father was created a duke, the patent recounted the 'great merit' of the son. After Lord Russell's death the widow administered the domain which she had brought into the Russell family—the first of several strong women who, through a queer fatality, were to rule over it, leaving their mark on the family and the estate. The second Duke married Elizabeth Howland, a granddaughter of Sir Josia Child of East India fame, who brought into the Russell family the Streatham and Rotherhithe estates, and energy and ability inherited from her City ancestors with which to administer the family property through another long minority; for her husband died at the age of thirty, when their son Wriothesley, the third Duke, was three, and John, subsequently fourth Duke of Bedford, was one year old. Wriothesley married a granddaughter of Sarah, Duchess of Marlborough, and died childless in 1732, aged twenty-four, having come very near to squandering the family fortune and to disposing of the Bloomsbury estate. John married Diana Spencer, also a granddaughter—the favourite—of the great Sarah, whose powerful personality impressed itself on Bedford House during Diana's short life; she died in 1735. Two years later, the Duke married Gertrude Leveson-Gower, another great character; well-informed contemporaries allege that, more than the Duke himself, she determined the policy of his very important following in Parliament, the so-called 'Bloomsbury gang.' 'I acquit His Grace . . . . of malice,' wrote Horace Walpole, 'but his Duchess, her sister Waldegrave, and Rigby, seldom acquainted the Duke with the true grounds on which he acted.' Their only son died in 1767, at the age of twenty-seven, and his wife a year later; when the fourth Duke died in 1771, his eldest grandson was six years old. A further chapter opened in the Bloomsbury matriarchy; and the work of Gertrude, Duchess of Bedford, an able administrator, on the development of the great urban estate is commemorated in the name of Gower Street.

A few years ago I went in search of an important eighteenth-century correspondence. In the Muniment Room of the Castle we opened box after box, and bundle after bundle: and we found nothing but bills. I said to my friend: 'I have heard that when one goes up in a balloon, the last sound which reaches one from the earth is the barking of dogs; apparently bills play that part on our final journey.' Bills, accounts, rent and pay-rolls, etc., abound in almost every old mansion or estate office; but naturally they are fullest and most explicit where there was a ramified administration, and especially during minorities. Of such material Miss Scott Thomson has made remarkable use; it is difficult to praise too highly the skill and scholarship of her work, the care with which she has pursued various trails in her material, and her sureness of touch in tracing them: such as only knowledge and untiring research can give. What a number of things can be read from household and estate accounts! You can see how the people dressed and how they furnished their rooms, and what they ate and drank; what they paid for their purchases; where these were made (and this opens up the subject of London shops, their character and location); who served in the household, and for what remuneration; how the people travelled, and how they educated their children; what books they had, what pictures and music. The estate accounts deal with a great variety of transactions: the history of Bloomsbury and of its planned development can be read in the rent-rolls; so can the history of the Rotherhithe docks; of the Devonshire estates round Tavistock—from these in the eighteenth century cloth was still sent to Bedford House, not for household use only, but even for sale and export. Even the history of banking and of money remittances can be studied in the accounts of Bedford House. Lastly, the heirs of Josia Child and owners of Rotherhithe engaged also in distant ventures, in Greenland whaling and East Indian trade.

For any part of London such a book, compiled with so much skill and quiet enthusiasm, would be of great value. But there is something unique about the London estate of the Russells. There is hardly a district with a more varied residential and business history than that area adjoining the Inns of Court and the City, containing the British Museum and Covent Garden Market, the oldest theatres and quarters of publishers not abandoned even now. There are few intellectuals of standing in English-speaking, or even in European, countries who do not know, frequent, and remember Bloomsbury. But much as it changes in every generation, of practically all its developments the origins are in the century covered by Miss Scott Thomson's book.

GEORGE III AND BUTE

'There was no one from whom I received so just accounts of the various factions,' writes the Duke of Grafton referring to 1767 when he was First Lord of the Treasury, '. . . than from Mr. Horace Walpole . . . no person had so good means of getting to the knowledge of what was passing, as himself.' But another purpose, besides that of political intrigue, was served by Walpole's researches: in secret from his contemporaries he was writing memoirs of those years. He took infinite pains over the work. When quoting a surprising document, he says:

> Should the original ever appear, as is not impossible, it will corroborate the truth of the rest that I have related. I trust much to collateral evidence for confirming the veracity of these Memoires.

I have found that original, and many others which bear out Walpole's claim to veracity.

Still, there is a central theme about which he does not write but romances: the story of George III, Bute, and the Princess of Wales. This was one of Walpole's 'Gothic fancies,' a tale rendered mysterious and sinister by his imagination, a pattern unconsciously derived from his own young years, which he stamped upon a historical canvas.

> Ilion! Ilion
> Fatalis incestusque judex
> Et mulier peregrina vertit
> In pulverem! . . .

This motto, deleted by the editor of the *Memoires*, was placed by Walpole on their front page; and they are filled with the idea of a great and mischievous influence exercised over George III, during many years of his reign, by his mother and the 'favourite.' The writing of the work was concluded in 1772, but Walpole continued adding to it and, looking upon it as 'memoires, not history,' he deliberately refrained from rendering it 'uniform by correction.' One of the latest additions, made after 1783, reads:

> I have changed my opinion, I confess, various times on the subject of Lord Bute's favour with the King—but this I take to have been the truth. From the death of her husband the Princess Dowager had the sole influence over her son, and introduced Lord Bute into his confidence—but I believe that even before his accession the King was weary of both his mother and of her favourite, and wanted to, and did early shake off much of that influence. After Lord Bute's resignation, his credit declined still more, and Lord Bute certainly grew disgusted, though he still retained authority enough over the King to be consulted, or to force himself into a share of the counsels that changed so many Ministries till after Lord Chatham's last Administration.

This, though it ante-dates the King's 'weariness' of Bute, is a truer account than any yet given of the subject. It is also a confession: Walpole obviously had no evidence for his innumerable statements, and even detailed stories, about the King, Bute, and the Princess; and his ignorance was shared by his contemporaries. They invented and believed tales which have ever since been uncritically reproduced by generations of historians.

Only George III's letters to Bute could determine the truth about their relations, and about these letters, in spite of published evidence to the contrary, a legend became firmly established: that they had perished in one of the two fires at Luton Hoo. I was instrumental in their re-discovery in 1926, and used them in my own work; and subsequently Mr. Sedgwick was entrusted with the task of editing them.[1] But the editing of these letters was not easy: of 339, only five are dated (one of them 31 June 1756!). On the others the hour is usually marked but not the day, month, or year—'¼ before 10,' 'past 12,' '35 m.pt. 3,' etc. W. B. Donne, the editor of George III's letters to Lord North, apparently meant to publish them, but gave up the plan, probably because unable to date them. Sedgwick has done so from internal evidence—

---

[1] *Letters from George III to Lord Bute, 1756-1766,* edited with an introduction by Romney Sedgwick (Macmillan).

a *tour de force* the equal of which I hardly know in work on modern records.

Similarly his introduction is a masterpiece: a gem of research and writing. The historical interest of the King's letters, says Sedgwick,

> is mainly derived from their bearing on the fictions which in his case have till recently done duty for the facts. In his own time George III was accused by his opponents of attempting to subvert the system of government established by the Revolution. By subsequent historians this charge was translated into that of attempting to subvert the system of responsible government. Thus by a double distortion he has been represented as having endeavoured to imitate the Stuarts when he ought to have anticipated Queen Victoria.

'In reality George III carried on, to the best of his more than limited ability, the system of government which he had inherited from his predecessors.'

It was obvious to me, on going through George III's papers, that the long-accepted and oft-repeated story about 'reactionary' notions having been 'instilled' into him in his young years was arrant nonsense; still, to destroy a 'deep-rooted delusion it is necessary to show not only its absurdity but its origin,' and Sedgwick is the first to trace how 'certain misrepresentations of incidents connected with George III's education' have given rise to this unfounded tale. Nor is any trace

> to be found in the letters of any political project more sinister than the vague idea, common to all oppositions of the period, that a 'reformation in government' was needed, with a view to 'purging out corruption' and combating 'the venality of the age.'

As for the story about the Princess Dowager and Bute, for which there never was any evidence,

> George III's letters dispose of the only justification for inventing it. They show that the key to the situation was not that the Princess but that her eldest son was infatuated with Bute.

They start with 'idolatrous adoration' and 'abject self-abasement,' and even after George III's accession remain on the whole 'otiose from the point of view of the efficient conduct of public business,' his role being confined to approving Bute's proposals, seeking Bute's advice, echoing Bute's opinions, giving 'puts off' to other ministers until he had ascertained Bute's views, and generally acting as Bute's rubber-stamp. If there is any period in the eighteenth century when there was a substantial element of truth in the stock opposition clichés that the King was a 'prisoner who had mistaken his gaoler' and that his minister was a *maire du palais*, that period is to be found in the two and a half years between the accession of George III and the resignation of Bute.

Of the letters in this collection, sixty are prior to the King's accession, some ninety cover the first seven months of his reign, about 140 Bute's term at the Treasury, and about fifty the formation of the Grenville Administration in March–April 1763. For more than two years of that Administration only six letters survive, though it is clear that the correspondence continued—but a clandestine correspondence, which, unless there were reasons to the contrary, was destroyed. For the term of the Rockingham Administration three letters are extant, of 10 January, 3 May, and 12 July 1766; but the contents of each cover about three months, and they prove moreover that the King did not see Bute during that time. These three letters, which I consider the most important single documents ever published for that period, throw a new light on the King's attitude towards the Rockingham Administration; and they show that a break, clear and final, occurred between the King and Bute in August 1766.

Should, however, a new 'standard work' on this period appear or a book 'revaluating' our knowledge of it, or a biography of George III, I shall not be surprised to read that his letters to Bute have perished, that he was brought up on *The Patriot King*, that he was eminently independent, able, and sane, that in 1766 he daily conspired with Bute against the Rockinghams, and that Lord North was Bute's nominee.

THE DUCHESS OF DEVONSHIRE

'GEORGIANA'S LIFE was now as full as only an empty life can be'—this sentence, well-turned and discerning, applies to more than a single period in her life. The Duchess of Devonshire (1757–1806) who 'kissed a butcher and wore a large hat,' and 'since then . . . is the beautiful Duchess of a million chocolate boxes,' who 'seldom wore and never met a frown,' wrote about herself in her early thirties: 'I can only add, Dearest Mother, that I am born to a most complicated misery. . . .' The age was reflected in her, its glitter and glory, its pleasures and prodigality, its passions and conventions, and its shallow, eager versatility. A distinct picture emerges from the material which the late Iris Leveson Gower, a descendant of hers, gathered with a *pietas* of modern directness, wove into a narrative akin to a historical novel, and yet preserved intact in numerous quotations from letters, diaries, etc.[1]

Georgiana was a daughter of the first Earl Spencer and of a formidably wise mother, and the wife of the fifth Duke of Devonshire, a rather dull, pompous, insignificant man. He gave her high rank, splendid circumstances, and paid her gambling debts, in so far as she dared to confess them; she bore him two daughters and a son, accepted his mistress for her closest friend, and received his illegitimate children into her home—but when she herself slipped in her one and only love affair, she had to go for two years into an expiatory exile, leaving behind all she loved and valued. Basically the couple were ill-assorted and meant little to each other.

She was a woman of good intelligence and understanding,

[1] Iris Leveson Gower, *The Face Without a Frown—Georgiana Duchess of Devonshire* (Muller).

versatile and gifted, quick, witty, and vivacious, but without perseverance, poise, or depth. She wrote pleasing verse and painted pretty pictures; but such was her appreciation of art that she could write from Rome: 'There is nothing in England gives a better idea of the buildings and villas of Italy than dear Chiswick as there is nothing here in better taste.' She admired Rousseau's *Confessions*, their 'romantick sincerity and candour,' their 'language and sentiments that inchant,' and clinched the argument for reading the book by saying that 'everybody I saw was talking of it.' She even tried reading serious history, but her enthusiasms, quickly stirred, gave out with equal ease:

It is my misfortune that every turn I take towards anything like study is by such starts that it is of no use to me—I am too eager at the moment and too easily disgusted, and you may observe I only succeed in what is to be obtained in a short time. . . .

In politics she embraced and professed with charming zeal the views held by her set of friends. She responded to outside impulses without integrating them. She was unstable, in thought as much as in emotions. 'Poor Lady Spencer,' writes the biographer, 'what was she to make of her chameleon child?'

The basic fact about Georgiana, concealed by her exuberance, her brilliance, and her 'insensate indulgence in a life of pleasure,' was that she was weak. 'Her small stock of moral courage,' 'her resolutions repeatedly made only to be broken again,' her inability 'to take what appeared to her as an unfriendly attitude,' sprang from a lack of emotional depth and strength. On one occasion she wrote to her mother:

. . . in spite of disliking the thing, I have done it because I was desired and have pretended to believe every word that was said to me, so that I actually have taken more pains to appear a dupe than most people do to show they cannot be outwitted. In things of consequence I hope I should be strong, but in common events I have so great an antipathy to the word *no* that I expose myself to many inconveniences not to pronounce it. It seems almost as if the activity of my nature spent itself in my mind, and gave me force to feel and reason, but that tir'd with the effort, it yielded to indolence the moment I was to perform.

She had insight and sincerity, was modest and uncertain of herself, not arrogant but simple, not condescending but human.

I

There was in her no real pride of class. If she attached weight to social rank or plunged into social life, it was once more from lack of self-confidence and from need of outward supports. It is this which made her, who seemed to break all conventions, fundamentally conventional. She was 'naturally religious and *pratiquante*,' but averse to excessive enthusiasms or religious asceticism. She wrote in a letter to her daughter:

> . . . it would perhaps be happier to lead a retir'd life. But your lot is cast in another line; and to do your duty in the world and be an example of it, is my ardent wish.
>
> Public entertainments have at least this good, that they support a number of poor and give cause to employ and exercise industry.
>
> I would not wish any young person to arrogate themselves as a judge, or to blame those amusements that the wisest and best allow themselves temperately. . . .
>
> . . . We have no right to arrogate ourselves against custom. . . .

She composed a moving epitaph for herself, and 'to this she added a short, conventional prayer.'

During the best part of her life she was oppressed by gambling debts; in the words of Lady Spencer, by 'the old and hopeless story of money difficulties.' With a whimsical humour she gave her husband the nickname of 'Canis,' or 'Ca' for short; and wore gold bracelets like dog collars with 'The Duke of Devonshire, Devonshire House,' engraved on them. Perhaps the much admired and much envied woman led a dog's life.

THE TREASURE ISLANDS

In the Caribbean Islands the wealth of the Indies, fabulous, real, and multiform, came within the grasp of Restoration England. The introduction of the sugar cane made them into the Rand of the century that followed. To North America Englishmen went in search of new homes, to the West Indies they went in search of treasure. Fortunes, big and blatant, were acquired, to be spent in England. The Sugar Islands loomed large in the public eye, and the West Indian cut a figure in eighteenth-century English society. When in 1757 the creation was mooted of a Secretary for the Colonies, the Duke of Newcastle referred to him as 'Secretary for the Indies,' or for 'both Indies'; and when the Seven Years War was drawing to a close the question which conquest it was preferable to retain, Canada or Guadeloupe, was seriously argued in Government circles and widely canvassed in print. The repatriation of men and money was a dominant concern in the colonial policy of the age. In 1698 Charles Davenant estimated the yearly emigration from England to the West Indies at about 1,800—but then

> for these last 20 years the West Indies have sent us back annually
> about 300 persons of their offspring, with this advantage that their
> fathers went out poor and the children come home rich.

In 1778 an anonymous West Indian wrote about the Sugar Islands: 'Few proprietors continue to live in them who think themselves able to remove to Britain.' And Charles Townshend, when pleading in 1760 for the retention of Guadeloupe, favourably contrasted the West Indians with the Continental settlers, firmly rooted in their American lands:

125

The inhabitants of the West Indian islands never consider themselves at home there; they send their children to the Mother Country for education; they themselves make many trips to the Mother Country to recover their health or enjoy their fortunes; if they have ambition, 'tis hither they come to gratify it. I need not, I suppose, observe to you, how many gentlemen of the West Indies have seats in the British House of Commons.

They have 'a very formidable number of votes in the House of Commons,' wrote Israel Mauduit, agent for Massachusetts, in 1764, when over the Sugar Act their economic interests clashed with those of New England.

Important, prominent, and exotic, the West Indians flash across the eighteenth-century scene leaving an impression which survives in vague statistical exaggerations, reproduced even by some of the best modern historians. Among recent books on the West Indies that are of outstanding merit are the works of two American scholars, Professor F. W. Pitman and Professor L. J. Ragatz, which, complementing each other, supply a comprehensive picture and a thorough analysis of the history of the British Caribbean in its growth and decline. Yet even they, observing the network of the West Indian interest, and seeing eighteenth-century England along its lines, tend to over-emphasize its importance. Thus Ragatz writes in the preface to his book on *The Fall of the Planter Class in the British Caribbean, 1763-83*:

The sugar planters were the conspicuously rich men of Great Britain in the middle of the seventeen hundreds. . . . Firmly entrenched in Parliament, they exercised a preponderant influence on the course of events. Sugar was king, they who produced it constituted the power behind the throne, and the islands, on which their opulence and commanding position had been reared, were regarded by all as the most valued of oversea possessions.

'Conspicuously rich' some of the sugar planters undoubtedly were, but 'the conspicuously rich men of Great Britain' is saying far too much. Home agriculture was the massive mountain-range against which any single interest stood out as a minor peak: and cloth, coal, and iron, shipping, brewing, and banking, each produced its conspicuously rich men and its interest in Parliament, although this, as a rule, did not become apparent till a disturbance brought it into the open. Thus, an ill-considered tax in 1763 proved how 'firmly entrenched' even cider was in Parliament—expressions such as 'the cyder-counties,' 'cyder-members,' and even 'the cyder Lords,' are current in contemporary correspondence.

Pitman, in his book on *The Development of the British West Indies, 1700–1763*, seeks to illustrate the power of the West Indians in Parliament by a debate on sugar in 1744, opened by Colonel Martin Bladen, whose wife owned a great West Indian estate; the speakers mentioned on the planters' side were: Sir Henry Liddell, S. Jenyns, William Pitt, G. Heathcote, Sir J. H. Cotton, W. Calvert, and Sir John Barnard: every name in this list signifies a great deal to the parliamentary historian, but none of them except Heathcote had any marked personal interest in the West Indies, and the debate demonstrates the attention paid to an important economic interest, but hardly its own 'power' in Parliament. In fact, the number of Members whose 'opulence and position' was based on West Indian plantations, and who, strictly speaking, can be classified as West Indians, did not as a rule exceed fifteen in a House of 558; with an outer ring of some fifteen to twenty who had an important, though not preponderant, interest in sugar plantations or the sugar trade. Far more numerous became, towards the turn of the century, the East India 'lobby'; yet even they can hardly be said to have had 'a preponderant influence on the course of events.'

From wider surveys, however excellent, it is necessary to pass back to case-history and explore the general in its individual setting, of a man or a family, combined with estate or business; and thus to perceive it in its complex, concrete incidence. Only a rich literature of that type, exploring the various interlocking 'interests,' will yield a well-balanced, three-dimensional presentation, in which every element is embodied in plastic, human figures—not a biographical approach in the old sense, but through the numbers involved and the features observed much rather a demographic approach to history. The idea of such a technique has occupied Professor Pares for some time past, and in his new book, *A West-India Fortune*,[1] he has carried it through with regard to the Dorset family of Pinney and its West India interests: he was enabled to do so by the truly wonderful collection of business records and family correspondence preserved by them, and willingly placed at his disposal. Collections of this kind are rare,

[1] Richard Pares, *A West-India Fortune* (Longmans).

especially for the West Indies. Very few have survived in the islands: estates have changed hands, families have left, the European community has shrunk to a mere remnant, and papers exposed to hurricanes, fires, and the extremely rich insect life of the islands, have perished at a rate exceeding the normal. It is therefore mainly in this country that material for the family and business history of the West Indies has to be sought; and even here one of the richest known collections, that relating to the West Indian interests and estates of the Lascelles family, went up in smoke during the *blitz* in a City office, in which it had been carefully preserved for generations. Moreover, the Pinney records present one peculiar feature; the Pinneys, half-way through their West Indian career, after having for a century been Nevis planters, turned into Bristol sugar factors, plantation financiers, and shippers, thus continuing the game from the opposite end; and so far this side of the game had not been given the full and expert treatment which, on the basis of the Pinney records, it now receives in Pares's book.

The West Indian story of the family opens with Azariah Pinney, son of a Nonconformist minister in Dorset, ejected from his living at the Restoration and turned lace-dealer. In 1685, Azariah, aged 23, having become involved in Monmouth's Rebellion, had to clear out to the West Indies; landed in Nevis, the smallest of the Leeward Islands, with £15 in his pocket; started as a commission agent; prospered, and in 1696 was returned to the House of Assembly, 'an august body of ten men'; became treasurer of the island, receiving eight per cent of the taxes collected; and died in 1720, owner of several plantations: 'the founder of a great colonial fortune.' His son, John, born in England and educated at Oxford and the Middle Temple, 'a harmless if ostentatious youth' who, to his father's annoyance, lorded it in London, and took 'his fortune a little too much for granted,' finally settled in Nevis, was returned to the Assembly, and next became Chief Justice of the island: 'a post of honour and not of emolument,' stated a report of the Board of Trade in 1782, 'seldom if ever . . . held by a person versed in the knowledge or practice of the law.' He survived his father by only a few months, and his son John Frederick, born in 1718 and educated in England, hardly regarded himself as a West Indian; still, when in 1739 he made his appearance on the island, to put his plantations in order so that he could resume the life of an absentee in

England, he, too, was 'elected, as of right, a member of the
Assembly'; but left in 1742, returning only once more in 1749.
He sat in the British Parliament for Bridport, 1747–61, and died,
unmarried, in 1762. At his death the Pinney plantations were
worth about £23,000, but were heavily burdened with debt, and
the story might have closed with that proverbial 'third generation' but for a young man, John Pretor, second cousin once
removed, to whom both John Frederick and another cousin, a
Dorset squire, left their estates on condition that he assumed
the name and arms of Pinney.

This John Pinney, 'one of the most successful planters and
West Indian merchants of his time,' became the second founder
of the fortune, which at his death in 1818 amounted to some
£340,000. But irretrievable decline had now set in for the
plantation economy of the West Indies: 'the price of sugar
plunged downwards after 1815,' and the days of slave labour were
numbered. The problem which faced John Pinney's sons, settled
in England, was how to 'repatriate their capital, more or less
intact, from the doomed islands.' The ablest and most active of
them, Charles, in 1831 Mayor of Bristol, wrote from Nevis in
1828: 'The expense and vexation in this detestable country is
tremendous. I wish we were well quit of it.' This they managed
to achieve in the next twenty years, though not without heavy
losses; by 1850 the story of their West Indian fortune had run its
course and reached its term. To Charles's nephew, William
Pinney, M.P. for Lyme Regis in 1832–41 and 1852–65 (when
the borough was disfranchised), and for Somerset in 1847–52,
'the West Indies were at most a troublesome source of income,
and long before the end of his career they were nothing more
than a memory.'

John (Pretor) Pinney is the central figure of Pares's story. He
arrived in Nevis in 1764 with no intenton to stay there very long:
like his cousin, he thought of the plantations merely 'as a con-
venient source of income for a Dorset country gentleman.' But
it was July 1783 before he at last left the West Indies, having by
almost twenty years of hard work greatly enlarged and improved
his plantations, without himself striking roots in the island: his
greatest pride, he told a friend in 1778, was 'to be considered a
private country gentleman,' and he was resolved to 'avoid even
the name of a West Indian.' When returning home he wished to
transfer most of his fortune to England; wherein he did not succeed.

For he now settled as sugar-factor at Bristol, sending out the planters' stores and selling their sugars, providing ships for the trade between Bristol and Nevis, and—which was to prove the most troublesome but also the most profitable part of his business— financing his West Indian correspondents by money advanced on their produce. But balances on chronically overdrawn current accounts tended to change into loans and mortgages, and mounting mortgages to finish in foreclosures, resulting in, not always wel- come, additions to the West Indian estate. Thus John Pinney's trans- actions as planter, merchant, shipowner, and financier cover almost every aspect of West Indian business, and that with a wealth of documentation illustrative of the mind and style of the man: the trader or early capitalist glorified by writers from Defoe to Samuel Smiles. John Pinney's letters to his sons, relatives, or employees, which enjoin 'a strict application to business united to an unexceptional conduct,' warn against idleness and dissipa- tion, and speak with a 'shudder' about debts ('interest money is like a moth in a man's garment, never asleep'), are but the frigid commonplaces of his class and time. But what distinguished John Pinney was, in Pares's words, 'the emotional intensity with which he felt and lived them.' Precise rather than mean, 'he made a religion of his accounts'; in them he expressed his most passionate feelings . . . in long vehement comments on particular items, or in marginal rubrics.' He was cautious and timorous; and it is the fears of men, at least as much as their vanity, which supply the historian with rich materials: the men who anxiously fix things in writing, and preserve every receipted bill or scrap of paper for their own reassurance or 'justification.' Indeed, some of John Pinney's book-keeping bordered on the pathological; or, as Pares considerately expresses it, must have given him 'purely intellectual or emotional' satisfaction—for instance, 'he opened an account with each of his children from the moment of its birth,' charging it with its midwife, christening fee, its share of the nurse, etc. But what a treasure such a man's papers, carefully preserved by his descendants, are for the economic historian!

John Pinney's success as a planter [writes Pares] is best judged from a summary of his accounts—that, indeed, is how he would have wished to be judged. . . . The result of his twenty years in Nevis can be summed up by saying that his fortune in money was at least £35,000 better than he found it.

He had settled one estate, improved his most important (the Lowland) plantation, and bought some more land. In his own words, 'the completest and best single estate in Nevis' had come into being. The Lowland Plantation comprised only about 400 acres, but half of it was caneland—the crop that counted; Pinney's other land, less than 300 acres in all, was largely mountain and pasture. (Comparison between different estates is difficult, especially if on different islands: on some of the large Jamaica estates of 10,000 and 20,000 acres, one-fifth or less was caneland, whereas in Barbados the best part of the acreage.) The average yearly production, 1768–83, of the Lowland Plantation exceeded 100 hogsheads of sugar, of a value of £2,000 to £4,000. The fascination which the story—of how the crop was grown, cut, ground, and boiled—had for Pares he has succeeded in communicating to the reader, who shares the life and concerns of the planter, to the last stage of production and shipment, and to this, by no means surprising, conclusion:

> With all their experience, there was something in the manufacture of sugar which neither planters nor merchants could explain or predict. . . . Some sugars would look well in the curing-house and arrive in England much drained and the worse for wear. . . . All that John Pinney could say about these mysteries was that 'Gentlemen in the West Indies are often deceived in the quality of their sugars, as some will mend on the voyage and others will turn out much worse.'

A husbandry so elaborate, a crop so delicate, variable, and costly, and a manufacture so full of surprises, naturally gave rise to a variety of theories and views; and John Pinney, after having left the island, would expound his own to his managers in letters and instructions which, in their entirety, form a remarkable treatise on plantation management. 'It is not the quantity of land that makes the sugar,' he wrote, 'but the number of acres under proper cultivation. . . . Half the quantity of land well dunged and properly worked will make more sugar than the whole planted in a slovenly manner and suffered to be overrun by weeds.' 'A sugar estate must be cultivated more like a *garden*, than like a *farm*.' But what he had still to learn to his cost was, in Pares's words, that not every manager could figure, in return for a salary of £200 and his keep, as the perfect agriculturist, manufacturer, disciplinarian, accountant, and business man.

John Pinney had to undergo the usual 'torments of the absentee,' who in the long run was left with 'the choice between eternal friction . . . and a gentle decline into bankruptcy.' Here is his rubric on the plantation accounts for 1792:

> Thank God! This is the last crop put in by my late miserable manager . . . or rather, by my late mismanager.

And here is the epitaph of the successor, written in the account-book in red ink:

> The enormous expenses and injudicious conduct of my present manager . . . cannot be submitted to any longer. He is too bad! My losses under him has been very great, one crop in four! . . .

Inefficiency and injustice were the common lot of absentees.

> Whatever vows of fidelity managers, attorneys, friends, even brothers might make [writes Pares], it was almost a law of nature that every month a planter stayed away from the islands, he was treated more and more as a stranger whose interests went to the wall.

And local public opinion was always against the absentee—'nobody helped him and many protected the culprit.' It became obvious that the changing of managers would lead nowhere; Pinney decided to sell his plantations; and at last succeeded in doing so in 1808. But even this did not end the Pinneys' connexion with West Indian land: new estates came to them as Bristol merchants.

Part II of Pares's book includes chapters on the Bristol sugar-market and on West India shipping and finance: once more, things of general import and occurrence appear in the concrete form of individual experience. Those acquainted with commodity markets will find in the story familiar features of the extension to which a factor's or broker's business is liable, and of risks taken for the sake of retaining or acquiring customers.

The sugar-factor's 'main business in life was to sell sugar, and his main revenue—or so he thought—was the commission upon these sales,' a 2½ per cent for work which required judgment, experience, and constant attention. In the sugar-market he had to face the grocers, refiners, re-exporters, distillers, and speculators, and know their requirements or habits. There was a seasonal rhythm in prices, 'as well as irregular fluctuations brought on by the weather, politics, war, economic development and fiscal policy.' Hurricanes and slave troubles were endemic to the West Indies, and war was very nearly so—considerably more than half of the period 1739–1815 consists of war years; and in the nine-teenth century abolitionist agitation, free-trade propaganda, and the general economic and financial rhythm of business added to the troubles of a highly sensitive market. But this is a bird's-eye view of the sugar trade.

In everyday practice,

the sugar-factor . . . was the planters' factotum in England, and executed all their commissions, of whatever kind. He made what sense he could of their (often tardy or inaccurate) orders for planta-tion stores or personal luxuries; bought, packed, and shipped these supplies, and listened to complaints about quality, the price, and the terms of payment.

His reward again consisted of a 2½ per cent commission, and interest on the debit balance of the current account. Besides, he attended to the personal affairs of his correspondents: would procure for them white employees, manage their law business, help them to obtain seats on the council, or executive office, etc. —'for the sake of the commission on the homeward cargoes of sugar.'

And even this was not all. The sugar-factor could only hope to get business if he could help the planter to ship his sugars to England; and so he had to own or control shipping—a new chap-ter in his transactions and in Pares's book. And last but not least the factor had to finance his West Indian correspondents—lend them money for the sake of consignments, advancing sums even in excess of their probable value.

Planters slid inexplicably but surely into debt to their factors. . . . Debts on account current continued to increase even in the years of high prices.

It might have been hoped that the debit balances of some planters would be offset by the credit balances of others. But there were four or five planters with debit balances for every one with a credit balance. . . .

In the last year of John Pinney's life (1818), his loans converted into mortgages on West India property exceeded £127,000, besides one small estate taken into possession, and some £45,000 in mortgages owing to the firm as distinct from Pinney himself.

Pares seems puzzled by 'the natural history of that malignant organism, a West-India debt'; and having adduced various reasons for its growth, concludes:

> All these encumbrances which the planters and merchants themselves created—personal extravagances. excessive endowments of families and high interest—do not explain the whole increase of West-Indian indebtedness. Much of that increase could not be explained and never was explained at all.

He quotes a case where neither extravagance nor persistent mismanagement, nor absenteeism could be alleged, and yet a good plantation sank deeper and deeper into debt. And he comes near to one basic reason of this wellnigh universal tendency in rural economy:

> The truth was that one could not put much trust in the planter's estimates of their financial position and prospects. They were always over-sanguine. Next crop was always to be a bumper crop and the sugars were sure to arrive at an improved market.

Whoever has grown up in a community of 'green squires'—so-called because they invariably had to sell their crops when they were still green—will feel at home in that financially embarrassed West Indian milieu. Behind the chronic miscalculations loom unconscious moral postulates: that he who sows should reap, and that the worker is worthy of his hire. Hence a good year is accepted as normal, while a bad one is an 'act of God' within the meaning of English Common Law: 'what no reasonable person can foresee'; and the standard of life is based on what is considered normal. Further even a surplus will not, as a rule, render the position of the farmer more liquid: farmers who will keep it in cash are far fewer than those who will sink it into improvements or new land. Indeed, in that way good years, by encouraging investments, are apt to add to the farmers' indebtedness. But when luck turns, they have to contract debts. And interest money, in John Pinney's words, is like 'a moth in a man's garment,' or in Pares's more modern simile, 'ticks up like a taxi.'

On the other hand, here is the question put from the creditor's point of view:

It is easy . . . to see many reasons why the planters borrowed so much and repaid so little; but why had the Pinneys ever lent them the money?
. . . [they] did not always know what they were doing, nor proceed upon any plan. Still less had they any conception of the lengths to which they were fated to go, nor could they always explain afterwards how they had been brought to advance so far. . . .

On one occasion John Pinney was accused of deliberately lending money in order to get his debtor's estate; this he sincerely and indignantly disclaimed; but he did get the estate, against his own wish.

Why then did he lend so much? There were three reasons: . . . out of personal friendship, for the sake of consignments in his business as a sugar-factor, and finally for the sake of the interest upon these investments, which he recognized, more and more clearly, as the chief source of his income.

And this is perhaps the most surprising conclusion from Pares's close study of the Pinney accounts: that in spite of endless trouble, sometimes severe losses, and the final liquidation of the West Indian business under the highly adverse conditions of 1830–50, the interest upon the Pinneys' loans was the greatest source of their West India fortune, whose main growth falls into the Bristol period; commissions, profits from shipping (if any), and plantation income contribute far less to it. Interest in Nevis in John Pinney's time was up to 8 per cent., at which rate even, with minor setbacks, capital might double in ten years; and a five-fold increase in fifty years would allow for considerable losses.

When in 1833 Parliament voted twenty million pounds for compensating the West Indian owners of slaves, little of that money went into the pockets of the planters: most of it went to their creditors. Sugar production in the old islands had ceased to pay: its vast extension to other countries and climates had resulted in a catastrophic drop in the price of sugar, while exhaustion of soil had set in on the long-overcropped islands. 'The old plantation economy of Nevis was decaying fast,' writes Pares. 'Some planters could not raise the cash to pay wages to their former slaves; others could no longer keep the negroes on the plantation at all, or even in the island.' And by 1830 'nearly every educated white man had abandoned the colony.' One of the few remaining big planters wrote from Nevis to a son of John Pinney in 1852: 'I am sorry to say our crop will not bear the expense of labour and contingent expenses, and if the Government of Her Majesty do not take our deplorable condition into consideration, I see nothing but ruin. One third of the island is now out of cultivation. . . .'

By that time the Pinneys had completely cleared out of the doomed islands, cutting their losses where necessary, but still repatriating a good fortune to their old home. 'They had never lost touch with England, and even kept most of their original lands,' writes Pares. 'An excursion of a century or two is not very long in the history of a family. Once more there are Pinneys in Dorset, in the old houses, the old fields, and the old churchyards. It is as if they had never been out of the county.'

GEORGE IV AND HIS MINISTERS

FAR TOO much of modern British history is ensconced in biographies which dribble away their material without coming to grips with basic problems. Letters, documents, and diaries are cut up to make vestments for the more or less conventionalized figures of statesmen, while constitutional and administrative developments, which transcend their lives but moulded their work, remain unexplored. The growth of the Cabinet system or the rise of party in the nineteenth century, to give but two examples, have not, so far, been made the subject of careful and incisive studies comparable with the work on medieval history. But then, integral publication of documents must precede analysis, and this is more easily contrived where the texts are few and obscure and there is little inducement to produce for a wider public.

Credit is therefore due to Professor Aspinall for his patient and systematic editing of materials relating to the first third of the nineteenth century, and for his scholarly monographs such as *The Grand Cabinet* 1800–1837,[1] *George IV and Sir William Knighton*, etc. *The Diary of Henry Hobhouse* falls into the framework of those publications. One section of it was previously published in part by the late Mr. Christopher Hobhouse in the *Cornhill Magazine* for 1938, and another by Aspinall in his *Formation of the Canning Administration*; it also was extensively used by him in the essay on George IV and Knighton. The Diary, which is now published in full, is not exactly what its title would suggest: the entries are of irregular incidence, and diminish in frequency till 1827 is reached, with its Cabinet-making on the retirement of Lord Liverpool in April, and on Canning's death in

[1] Arthur Aspinall (editor), *The Diary of Henry Hobhouse, 1820–1827* (Home and Van Thal).

August. A total of 112 entries is divided thus between the eight
years 1820–7: 33, 30, 17, 6, 5, 4, 3, 14.

Henry Hobhouse, whose family had been merchants, sailors,
barristers, and finally country gentlemen, entered the Civil
Service, and during the years covered by the Diary was Permanent
Under-Secretary of State for the Home Department. The Home
Office was acquiring a peculiar importance during those years when
government by patronage was gradually changing into government by party, and Hobhouse himself was one of those semi-
political Civil servants many of whom were—and indeed had to
be—Members of Parliament: thus it was with the Secretaries to
the Treasury from Lowndes to Arbuthnot, and the Secretaries
of the Admiralty from Pepys to Croker, while with regard to
Under-Secretaries of State there was no rule, and Hobhouse, for
one, never sat in Parliament. From that, as yet unapportioned,
borderland between government and administration he observed
transactions which touched him closely without directly concerning him: foremost the relations between the King and his
Ministers, and the relations of these with one another. And as the
growth of Cabinet government has at all times been empiric—
full of tentative, and often ephemeral, starts and advances, and of
theories strangely erroneous in retrospect but not so at the time—
its record, even in its fully developed form, will retain the character of a case-history.

Looking at the transactions recorded by Hobhouse, we may
well wonder how, within the memory of men who had witnessed
them, the legend could have been started of modern 'constitutional government' under George II, or of George III's 'un-
constitutional' claim to choose his Ministers; and further, how
during the next twenty or thirty years the new system could have
acquired a complete sway and a theoretical validity, coupled with
amnesia of what had preceded. George IV's accession on 29
January 1820 rendered acute the question of his Queen's position;
and on 12 February the King sent a message to the Lord Chancellor 'insisting on a divorce as the condition of his retaining his
confidential servants' (the Cabinet). Lord Liverpool in reply
'delivered to his Majesty the Minute of Cabinet' (again a thing
long forgotten and whose extinction is shrouded in darkness),
and 'received his pleasure to see the Lord Chancellor, Lord
Liverpool, and Lord Sidmouth'; to them the King gave 'a paper
containing some observations on the Cabinet Minute, probably

drawn by Sir J. Leach' (one of his semi-official advisers). Two days later he saw Castlereagh in an audience lasting five hours; 'for the first three the King delivered a speech' which Hobhouse supposes to have been originally intended for the three Ministers. But when at a further audience, on 16 February, Castlereagh 'apologised to the King for having discussed with him matters which were more fit for deliberation with the Prime Minister,' the King 'said it was impossible for him to hold such a discussion with Lord Liverpool, so deficient is he both in manner and temper.'

In fact, the King would have liked to retain some of his Ministers and change others, and when, at the end of April, he was forced to accept a Speech which was displeasing to him and of which he suspected Liverpool to have been the author, he remarked to Lord Sidmouth 'that it was time to determine whether the Ministers were the servants of the King or the servants of Lord Liverpool.'

In reality a new Cabinet practice was growing up without those concerned as yet fully realizing it or avowing it in theory— a circumstance which left room for deviations. Thus in July 1820 the King very strongly urged Lord Sidmouth, then Home Secretary, to accept the Premiership, and when he declined, 'asked him to whom else he could look, and suggested the Duke of Wellington, but Lord Sidmouth begged to be excused from offering any opinion on that subject, and pressed on his Majesty the expediency of continuing to confide in Lord Liverpool.' Still, this was an expression of Sidmouth's views and of his personal loyalty to Liverpool, but not as yet a part of a binding constitutional etiquette. The King in retaining the Tory Government was much moved by considerations of foreign policy and by the prestige which Wellington and Castlereagh enjoyed on the Continent—'the King,' writes Hobhouse, 'who cares little about home affairs, but is fond of mixing in the intrigues going on in Europe, felt the advantage resulting to himself from Lord Londonderry's influence in the Continental Courts.' Nevertheless, when in June 1821 the Ministers tried to make him re-admit Canning to the Cabinet, after Canning had offended him over the affair with the Queen, the King declared himself ready to treat Canning

as a gentleman wherever he fell in with him, and to gratify him in any way he wished, except by a seat in the Cabinet . . .; but even

K

> if his exclusion from the Cabinet were to lead to a change of the
> Administration . . . and consequently to a cessation of the pre-
> dominance of British influence in the Continental Courts, he was
> prepared to submit to all those consequences, rather than to take into
> his favour a man from whom he had received a personal affront. . . .

And Sidmouth told Liverpool that 'as on the one hand he would
not lend himself to the King to effect an undue exclusion of
Canning, so on the other he would not lend himself to any other
party to enforce undue dictation on the King'; in fact, it was
agreed between Londonderry, Wellington, Bathurst, and Sidmouth, 'to carry on the Government without Lord Liverpool if
he should determine to resign for the sake of Canning.'

It is naturally difficult to determine to what extent personal
inclinations or views entered into the Ministers' decision; but that,
in spite of growing cohesion within the Cabinet, the King could
still discuss its composition with different Ministers, offer places
in the Cabinet, and insist on certain men being appointed or
omitted, appears also from other transactions during the period;
and whether the King carried his point depended on circumstances.
The theory of 'the King's independency,' that is, of his right to
choose his Ministers, was still alive, and it was hardly realized
that it was dying. Thus in July 1821, 'the Duke . . . after hearing
the King's complaints, said in his brusque manner, "if you do not
like us, why do you not turn us out?"' And a month later he
expatiated, in the best eighteenth-century style, to Arbuthnot and
Sir Benjamin Bloomfield, the King's secretary, on 'the unpleasant
relation existing between the King and his Ministers'; he stated

> that himself and several other members of the Cabinet had no wish
> to retain their offices but for the sake of promoting the welfare of the
> Kingdom, wch. it wod. be impossible for them to do unless they
> enjoyed the confidence of the King; that if the King weakened the
> Govt. by dividing his confidence, they must resign their places.

But what followed was different and more modern (and wrong):

> . . . that if the Opposition came in, they must necessarily dissolve
> the Parliament; that the new Parlt. wod. be a radical one, and wod.
> soon turn out the new Govt., and oblige the King to form another
> of more popular materials, which wod. overset the Monarchy.

In August 1822, after Londonderry's death, the King offered
Peel, who had held the Home Office since January, and was with

the King in Scotland, the leadership of the House of Commons and the Chancellorship of the Exchequer; but Peel 'begged to decline saying a word on the subject.' Most of the Ministers urged that 'it was necessary to place Canning in Lord Londonderry's position,' and the Duke of Buckingham and his friends insisted on this being done. Finally the King acquiesced, and Wellington wrote a letter to Buckingham

> in wch. he stated that the King had surrendered his private feelings to the public good, that Canning ought in entering upon office to estimate the magnitude of this sacrifice; and the Duke of B. was authorized to impart this letter to Canning.

And so well did Canning learn the lesson that a few weeks later he made Lord Francis Conyngham, a son of the King's mistress, his Under-Secretary.

Again, when in January 1824 there were several candidates for the office of Solicitor-General, the King 'laid his commands' upon Liverpool 'that Wetherell should be the man.'

In time Canning became the King's favourite Minister, and when in April 1827 a successor had to be found to Liverpool, it was the King who finally decided in favour of Canning (the King had 'at first proposed that the Cabinet should elect their own head,' but Peel 'objected upon principle to the delegation by the King of this act of royalty'). And so much did the King resent Peel's refusal to serve under Canning that when in September a successor had to be designated to Canning, and everyone expected Peel's appointment, George IV called on Goderich to step into Canning's place. He, however, as a peer, could not hold the Chancellorship of the Exchequer with the Treasury as commoners did. 'For this the King named Mr. Herries, one of the Secrs. of the Treasury, originally a clerk in that Dept. and private secretary to Mr. Perceval.' But when Herries was to be sworn in at Windsor, some of the Ministers raised strong personal objections to him. 'The eleven Cabinet Ministers present divided 6 to 5 agt. Herries, Ld. Goderich (as it is understood) being one of the majority.' The ultimate decision was postponed; but the King 'peremptorily insisted on Herries's appointment,' and it took effect.

It was only the rise of organized, stongly disciplined parties which gradually deprived the Crown of the choice of 'the servants' to be consulted on its 'confidential business.'

PRINCESS LIEVEN

PRINCESS LIEVEN was the wife of a Russian Ambassador, a companion of the Imperial Family, and the intimate friend first of Metternich, next of Lord Grey, and finally of Guizot. 'I quite like Prime Ministers,' she wrote to Metternich in 1820. Prussia was the only Great Power whose policy she never tried to run.

She is often cited as a 'Russian.' But her father, Baron Bencken-dorff, was of a Prussian family settled in Estonia, and her mother, Baroness Charlotte Schilling, came from Württemberg: Princess Lieven had not a drop of Russian blood, nor had her husband; and both were Lutherans. They were of a Court which moved between St. Petersburg and Peterhof: Tsarism and its power-politics were their home and realm. There was no feeling in her for real Russia nor understanding of its Slav, Greek-Orthodox people. She thought of the world in terms of her own small circle. And if the German Nesselrode, the Greek Capo d'Istria, or the Corsican Pozzo di Borgo ('his presence lent great distinction to Russian politics,' she wrote to Lady Palmerston in 1842) could speak for Russia, and the Rhinelander Metternich personify Austria, why should not the Lievens play a part in Hanoverian London? She boasted: 'I am treated so much as an Englishwoman . . . that nobody minds talking in front of me.' She advised Wellington and patronized Palmerston ('Lord Grey praised Palmerston to me yesterday,' she wrote on 27 October 1831 to Lady Cowper, an intimate friend and subsequently the wife of Palmerston; 'an excellent Secretary of State'). When Grey had become Prime Minister she wrote to Lady Cowper:

> I see Lord Grey every day—I try to give him courage—he must feel himself strong. One must assume a certain pomposity when one is in power—it inspires confidence in other people.

And a fortnight later:

Lord Grey . . . has responded nicely to my constant repetitions that he must be and show himself proud. . . . I endeavour to instil as much pride as possible into you.

But there were things touching her person and position which that quasi-Russian, acclimatized in England, did not fathom. Wellington wrote about the Lievens on 24 August 1829: 'They have played an English party game instead of doing the business of their Sovereign. . . .'; and, later on, expressed surprise that, 'so long employed in public office in this country,' should they 'have committed the extraordinary indiscretions of which they have been guilty.' Palmerston, in 1834, managed to rid himself of them. 'Lord P. found my husband a stumbling block,' wrote the Princess to Lady Cowper on 7 October 1834. The husband?

Many friends preferred Princess Lieven at a distance. She seldom met Metternich even while she was his mistress. They corresponded: 'Some day, if our letters are read,' wrote Princess Lieven, 'people will wonder what they were about—love or politics. . . . In fact, I don't know myself . . .' Because her love affairs were so political. 'Personally I prefer weakness to strength in women. It is more feminine.' She herself was masculine and pursued a man's career in the only way open to her: a peculiar career, successively identifying herself with statesmen of different countries. Yet there was in her a deeper sense of frustration: her adjustments were superficial, and she venomously turned against husband and lovers whenever a rift opened. She had great social culture and vulgarity underneath. Even her normal correspondence is rendered unpleasant by a strain of irritable disparagement. The Duchess of Wellington is 'stupid,' Lady Grey 'a horrible woman, passionate, bitter, Jacobin, everything that is most detestable,' Lady Conyngham 'a malicious fool,' Countess Esterhazy 'a mediocre person . . . and what pretences to airs and graces!'; and the Duchesse de Berry 'a hopeless nonentity' whom 'nothing but the assassination of her husband before her very eyes could make . . . an object of interest'; etc. ('How much better the world would be,' she wrote to Metternich, 'if people were kinder.') Men escaped it, so long as they served her purpose. But her interest was in situations and schemings, not in human beings.

'Some day, if our letters are read . . .' Hers, half-diary, were literature. She wrote to Lady Cowper, from Petersburg, on 8/20 February 1835:

> I remain alone in my room writing, for I have strange tales to tell. I have seen much in my life. I have all my papers with me—it is a way of passing the time.

And to Lord Grey, on 6 October 1834:

> . . . as to my mental occupations, do you know what is the greatest source of my pleasure? It is putting in order of all my voluminous correspondence with my friends and among them all, the first place is taken by your letters. . . . Your letters are the history of the times we have lived through. . . .

Grey protested that they were meant for her only: 'I have no desire that they should be preserved as materials for history.' Now her correspondence appears one lot after another, and people are apt to overrate the historical value of such letters if they are spicy and 'high-lifey.'

Of the correspondence with Lady Cowper-Palmerston[1] five-sixths are subsequent to Princess Lieven's expulsion from the English paradise (which was drab and dull and cold and 'frankly depressing' while she inhabited it). 'Oh God! How I love everything that I have left behind!' '. . . . not a day passes but I bemoan my separation from England'; 'England is always in my thoughts . . . never fails to interest me. . . .' 'Everyone around me is enjoying life. I alone lie ill, sad, deserted.' 'Dearest, letters and again letters, these are what I need' (23 October 1834). 'My only joy is to read letters from England. And you know what a joy your letters are in particular' (6 January 1835). 'Dearest, how good you are to write to me so regularly. I beg you will continue to do so' (12 February 1836). And she repeats a dozen times throughout the years: 'Your letters are my greatest pleasure.' But to Grey on 9/21 November 1834:

> Lady Cowper writes to me very often, but then she is so hand in glove with the present Ministry that I do not learn much from her letters. I prefer hearing from outsiders, for they at least do not try to mislead. It is astounding how like bad faith this Ministerial prudence too often becomes.

And on 6 December 1834: 'Pray take pity on me and write, for it is only on you that I can count for getting at the truth.'

On the straight hedonistic view of life and of human pursuits one could truly wonder why these two women continued their

---

[1] *The Lieven-Palmerston Correspondence, 1826-1856*, edited by Lord Sudley (John Murray).

correspondence; it is sometimes like cats screaming at each other in the night—rising in pitch or dropping into a hostile purring. When Princess Lieven in July 1835, having lost two sons ('there has never been a greater grief than mine'), wanted to seek comfort in England ('your politics still interest me more than any others'), Lady Cowper replied:

I really believe that I should choose Paris . . . you need to live where there is constant news and political activity—and in Paris there are more travellers than anywhere else—and more owners of country houses; I do not think that England would suit you at all . . . you would be dreadfully bored here. . . . It is much better to keep England in your mind's eye as a place to return to when your grief has abated. The Duke of Wellington, my brother, all your friends advise you to go to Paris. . . .

And when the Princess dropped into (temporary) silence: '. . . can it be possible that you are offended . . . you could not be so unjust towards me . . . thus misinterpret my friendship and devotion.' And on another occasion: 'I love everyone who is kind to you.'

Princess Lieven would express fears of revolution in England, decry the Whigs (Lady Cowper was Lord Melbourne's sister), assure her (from Paris) that the Tories were firmly established in office, and greatly respected abroad, or tell her how much the English were disliked in France. Lady Cowper would, in reply, beg her 'not to worry about the peerage,' which was 'stable and deeply rooted'; assure her that Peel was 'embracing liberal ideas . . . to gain popularity,' and losing credit with his own party; that the Whigs were grand when in office, and happy when out of it; and that the things which made Palmerston unpopular in France 'made him popular in England,' etc. She demurred: 'You can always count on my affection, although you certainly are a *trifle* unkind towards my friends.' The Princess retorted: 'I deny absolutely your accusation . . . with one exception I like them all'—the exception being Palmerston! And Lady Palmerston, when sending her congratulations on a Parliamentary success of Guizot's, regretted 'that a Minister who is usually so dignified should have lost his dignity to the extent of confessing such petty motives. . . .'

'I agree with you, dearest, that our friendship should be able to withstand all political changes. . . .' No matter which of the two said it.

PALMERSTON

'PARLONS UN peu de l'Empereur, ça nous fera du bien,' said Victor Hugo under the July Monarchy. After Munich and Abadan let us talk of Palmerston. In foreign politics, to this day the man in charge counts for more than where masses are engaged: on the diplomatic chess-board States are the pieces, and it is in the nature of the game that it should be played by individuals. Yet such are the stakes that no Foreign Secretary can take exception to interference by colleagues co-responsible for the nation's affairs and inclined, as they often are from lack of knowledge, to shun risks or to act on preconceived ideas: 'people who do not follow up questions,' wrote Palmerston in 1836, '... are generally for the doubting line'[1]; and in 1838: 'There are very few public men in England who follow up foreign affairs sufficiently to foresee the consequences of events which have not happened.' A Foreign Secretary with a mind and policy of his own must fight on the domestic no less than on the foreign front, and becomes a con-tested person—hardly any nineteenth-century British Foreign Minister met with more opposition in the Cabinet than Palmer-ston. In a Foreign Secretary it is therefore no excuse for failure that he has to deal with a 'divided Cabinet,' an undecided public opinion, or unwilling allies: these are ordinary ingredients of a diplomatic situation, and so many occasions for his exertions. Nor are adverse circumstances an excuse: every hand can be played well or badly, and incapacity to use one's advantages accounts for failure more often than their absence. The change which Palmerston wrought in Great Britain's international position during the years 1830–41 shows what the skill and determination of a Foreign Secretary can achieve.

[1] Sir Charles Webster, *The Foreign Policy of Palmerston. 1830–1841. Britain, the Liberal Movement, and the Eastern Question.* 2 vols. (G. Bell).

European alignments during those years were determined by the intersecting of ideologies and historical memories with national interests, real or presumed: again very usual components of diplomatic situations. The Whig Government and the July Monarchy were drawn together by their domestic systems based on representative government, and still more by the dislike and hostility which these evoked in the three Powers of the Holy Alliance. The question was at times whether constitutionalism and absolutism could exist side by side without producing a European war. Palmerston's reply was that the only security against war was 'that England and France should be prepared and able to meet it, if threatened'—he wanted 'to form a Western confederacy of free States as a counterpoise to the Eastern league of arbitrary Governments'; and he thought it 'of great importance to us, not only to be well with the French Government but to appear to all Europe to be so': England could not 'carry her points on the Continent' without allies. He once said to the French Ambassador that 'the Anglo-French alliance should embrace the globe as it was founded on the essential interests of the two countries.' Yet no one knew better the complexities of the situation: national ambitions do not necessarily tally with 'essential interests.' Anglo-French co-operation staved off intervention by the Eastern Powers in Belgium, Spain, and Portugal; but whereas Palmerston wished these countries truly independent, and thus free to co-operate with Britain, the French, haunted by memories of pre-eminent greatness, aimed at gaining satellites or even territory. Palmerston vetoed the Duc de Nemours's election to the Belgian throne, his proposed marriage to the Queen of Portugal, and frontier rectifications for France in Belgium, and tried to check her by imposing 'self-denying ordinances' on the Great Powers. In September 1833 he assured the King that he was 'fully alive to the propriety of keeping a watchful eye upon the proceedings' of France. In November 1835 he wrote about Louis Philippe and Talleyrand that

> they both look on the changes from despotism to free institutions as unfavourable to French ascendancy at Madrid. . . . They see Spain fast slipping out of their hands and becoming instead of a satellite of France an independent ally of England.

And in 1840:

. . . to draw Spain into political connexion with France . . . is the fixed policy of France and not an unnatural one. . . . But our business is to endeavour to thwart and counteract such policy, and . . . our Minister at Madrid . . . should proportion his salutary influence to the mischievous interference of the French Agent.

No wonder then if the French representatives, in turn, were doing their best to thwart British policy. For some time attempts were made to keep up 'the façade of special relations between the two Governments,' but 'in reality there was constant jealousy and suspicion on both sides.' The age-long world-wide rivalry could not be extinguished until the ambitions which had given rise to it were themselves extinct.

And this was Palmerston's declaration of faith and policy:

The system of England ought to be to maintain the liberties and independence of all other nations; out of the conflicting interests of all other countries to secure her own independence; to throw her moral weight into the scale of any people who are spontaneously striving for freedom, by which I mean rational government, and to extend as far and as fast as possible civilization all over the world.

Nor was there greater harmony in the opposite camp. Russia, Austria, and Prussia were agreed in upholding autocratic monarchy, dynastic property in States, and 'legitimacy,' and in denying popular sovereignty and rights. But while the maintenance of the territorial *status quo* was essential for Austria's survival, Russia and Prussia were military Powers bent on expansion. Prussia was as yet too weak to be daringly aggressive without a Frederick II or a Bismarck at her head; and her weakness made her a lukewarm partner in the Eastern alliance (in a conflict between east and west she would have been its most exposed member); moreover, the struggle for leadership in Germany between her and Austria was never altogether in abeyance. The lurking conflict between Austria and Russia was even nearer the surface: Russia was out to transform Turkey into a satellite or to partition her, two developments equally repugnant to Austria. In 1833 Metternich, when asked by the British Ambassador

if he had any views of compensation should the Ottoman Empire be dissolved . . . declared . . . 'that he should consider the day when this system should be entered upon as the last of the Austrian Empire.'

Was here a basis for an Anglo-Austrian *rapprochement*? At times Metternich would express 'a desire to be the most intimate ally of England,' and his conviction that such an alliance was 'the best and most useful for Austria'; but at other times he would argue that Britain was in an even worse way than France who had now stabilized her revolution, while Britain 'had not yet made her national bankruptcy.' Palmerston was to Metternich the *Chef de Propagande* of Liberalism; Metternich was to Palmerston a monomaniac possessed of 'all the cunning which accompanies such affections [? afflictions.]' Austria's political principles and economic system were obnoxious to Palmerston, and he saw no advantage in an alliance with her. If Britain abandoned France for Austria, he argued in 1835, France would turn to Russia—

> and what . . . should we gain, if while we exchange active, powerful and neighbouring France for sluggish and temporizing and distant Austria, Russia, . . . instead of being united with Austria, who, though subservient, acts as a clog, . . . were to strike up an intimacy with France, and gain a more active ambitious and a *naval* ally?

Theoretically an accurate perception: Russia and France could have best pursued a policy of conquest together—but for Tsar Nicholas's obsessionist hatred of France. When after France's humiliation in 1840 the British Ambassador in Paris was alarmed by talk of a Franco-Russian alliance, Palmerston himself replied that this 'was a quite natural development, but would not come yet awhile.' Indeed, so strong were on the Continent ideological divisions and historical memories that the most expedient combination of all was never considered: a Franco-Austrian alliance which, by safeguarding Habsburg predominance in Germany and Italy, and hence their disunion, would have equally secured the pre-eminence of France—such an alliance was, indeed, impossible so long as France was haunted by Napoleonic memories and Austria by fear of revolutionary France. Most difficult and least probable of all, in view both of ideological divisions and conflicting interests, seemed an Anglo-Russian understanding; and yet it came about and worked successfully in the crisis of 1839-40: Britain had shown strength, and consequently Tsar Nicholas felt respect for her.

Palmerston was neither an appeaser, nor (in spite of pet ideas and bias) a doctrinaire. He believed in representative government; considered 'no set of men . . . too ignorant to understand their own interests and to manage their own affairs,' and 'all nations . . . ripe for a representative assembly who have interests with respect to which it is necessary to make laws'; and he wished to believe that constitutional governments would be more friendly to this country, and 'more likely than arbitrary ones to admit British goods.' For if forced to choose, he was 'concerned with British interests rather than the protection of constitutional government,' and ready to co-operate be it with arbitrary rulers —Metternich, Tsar, or Sultan. He was convinced 'that British interests could only be maintained by a strong and determined policy,' and should be asserted with vigour. He had clear vision, immense energy and courage, and he spoke his mind with un-diplomatic frankness; he was the most industrious and 'the toughest Foreign Minister of the century'; he had 'complete mastery over all the complicated problems with which he had to deal'; and he himself wrote the drafts of important dispatches. Pursuing no acquisitive aims and morally committed to no foreign power (he trusted none), he could strike out his own line. In a letter to the King, on 8 October 1832, he described the course which he had followed with regard to Belgium (and was to follow in 1838-40 over the Eastern Question):

Your Majesty will remember in the earlier period of the trans-action, France was unreasonable and encroaching. She wanted Philippeville and Marienbourg as a beginning of the dismember-ment of Belgium; she wanted to put the Duke of Nemours on the Throne; she wanted to continue indefinitely to occupy Belgium . . . Upon the occasion of all these pretensions the British Govern-ment brought the three Powers to bear upon France, and France was upon all compelled to yield; latterly the three Powers have in their turn been unreasonable and deficient in good faith. . . . The British Government then brought France to bear upon the three Powers, and it is to be hoped with ultimate success. . . . France will not venture to attack the three Powers, if she is also to be opposed by England; and the three Powers will pause before they attack France, if they think that France could in that case reckon upon the support of England. Thus . . . by throwing the moral influence of Great Britain into one scale or the other, according as the opposite side may manifest a spirit of encroachment or injustice, Your Majesty may . . . become on many occasions the arbiter of events in Europe.

Nor would it be necessary to send an army to the Continent; 'on most occasions the moral influence of Great Britain would probably be effectual'; or else, a 'prompt and vigorous employment' of naval forces would suffice.

Palmerston may have been self-conscious or even self-righteous; but he did not flinch or prevaricate, and he never disgraced his country. When in 1833 Turkey concluded with Russia the Treaty of Unkiar Skelessi which threatened to establish a Russian protectorate over her, the British Government protested at Constantinople; but when next some of Palmerston's colleagues hesitated to protest at St. Petersburg, he wrote to the Prime Minister:

> ... if knowing, as we do, that the treaty ... was forced by Russia upon Turkey ... we should hold a high tone to Turkey, the weaker Power and the tool, and not dare even to whisper our dissatisfaction to Russia, the stronger Power and the plotter, it would have been far better for our national honour ...to have held our tongue to Turkey as well as to Russia. If we were to quail before Russia on the question of protest ... Russia would henceforth treat England as a Power from whom no serious resistance need ever be apprehended. She would be mistaken, but ... she might be tempted by her reliance on our acquiescence, to do things, which ... might draw us into a situation in which public opinion would force us to go to war. ...

Mutatis mutandis, a singularly accurate forecast of 1938–9.

The Treaty of Unkiar Skelessi was itself the result of timid inertia on the part of Britain. In 1832 the Sultan, threatened by his rebellious vassal Mehemet Ali, Pasha of Egypt, had applied to Britain for help. Palmerston favoured action, but the Cabinet, preoccupied with Belgium and home affairs, was for delay, which meant refusal. Then the Sultan turned to Russia. After the conflict with the Pasha had reopened in 1838, Palmerston wrote, thinking back of 1832:

> Our refusal at that time has been the cause of more danger to the peace of Europe, to the balance of power and to the interest of England than perhaps any one determination ever before produced.

He was resolved that this 'tremendous blunder' should not be repeated. He refused to admit 'the single independent and self-regulated interference of any one Power'; a European conference

and treaty was to settle the problem; and while he would have
wished personally to direct that conference, in order to conciliate
others he agreed to its meeting in Vienna. Vanity and historical
memories and passions, perhaps more than interests, determined
Continental policies in the crisis of 1839–40: Metternich saw
Vienna once more as the centre, and himself as the dominating
figure, of European diplomacy; while the French delighted in a
Concert of Europe used for once as a strait-jacket on Russia and
not on France. The Tsar was isolated and thwarted; and his anger
turned not against his legitimate opponent, Palmerston, but
against Metternich and the French: he refused to accept Vienna
for centre of discussion—a shattering blow to Metternich's pride;
and when a rift opened between Britain and France, he was willing,
from sheer hatred of France and a wish to isolate her, to accept
almost anything that Britain offered. Napoleonic memories and
Egyptian dreams made the French into warm partisans of
Mehemet Ali, while Palmerston was determined to maintain the
territorial *status quo* between the Sultan and his vassal, whose
strength and importance he for one did not overrate. Russia was
playing into his hand, and Austria and Prussia followed suit; and
by the London Convention of 15 July 1840, the four Powers,
without consulting France, decided against Mehemet Ali. But
Palmerston and the Tsar alone relished the *coup*; anxious colleagues
in the Cabinet, and still more the Germanic Powers, frightened
of what the French might do in their exasperation, pressed for
reparation to French feelings. The well-known technique of
threatened 'vapours' was applied: Louis Philippe would fall—
and then . . . But Palmerston was not moved by 'predicted
dangers.' He wrote on 26 October 1840:

> The French have on every occasion since 1830, when they wanted
> to drive us to make some concession to them, used this same
> argument; . . . but we were hard-hearted, and yet L. Philippe con-
> tinued to reign.

He stuck to his guns and gains, and had his way.

Types and situations endure, only the unquestioning trust in a
better future has vanished. The very men 'who most applauded
Palmerston's support of the Liberal cause in Europe,' insisted on
a reduction in British naval and military establishments; they
'who were making the loudest outcry about Poland,' remarked
William IV in 1832, 'would have refused to grant the supplies

necessary to support her cause.' 'Non-intervention' in Spain was planned in 1836 by the French, as a century later it was to be practised by others: the African Legion 'was to be increased by recruits from the French army, nominally volunteers, to such an extent that it would settle the issue of the war.' The Austrian Ambassador in London, writing about the tribulations of his Russian colleague, commented on 'the miserable life of a Russian agent who must always be afraid of the anger of the Tsar if he makes a false move.' Palmerston spoke with contempt of men who thought 'that the whole art of government consists in the application of military force,' and of those who had not yet reached

> that point of civilization at which the Government of a powerful country discovers that there are other subjects deserving of attention . . . besides augmentation of territory and foreign conquest.

Like all believers in progress, he expected a more enlightened age to free humanity of such rulers and errors. But if wrong in his forecasts, was he also in his contentions? He wrote in 1841 to the British Ambassador in Vienna:

> You say that a constitution is but a means to an end and the end is good government; but the experience of mankind shows that this is the only road by which the goal can be reached and that it is impossible without a constitution fully to develop the natural resources of a country and to ensure for the nation security for life, liberty, and property.

Nor was he perhaps mistaken when he declared that as long as England

> sympathizes with right and justice she will never find herself altogether alone. She is sure to find some other State of sufficient power, influence, and weight to support and aid her.

With vigour in action Palmerston combined a sincere, humane idealism; and men felt that 'England was herself again.'

Yet even in this country a distorted picture of the man has been widely accepted. He had, writes Sir Charles Webster, 'made enemies of some of the most active and influential individuals of this time'—for instance, of Talleyrand and Princess Lieven, 'attractive personalities' and 'deliberate liars,' whose

> assertions have often been accepted by historians of repute and become part of the stock of text-book makers. The legends of the

nineteenth century have done more to obscure the truth than those
of the Middle Ages, because they have not been examined with the
same scepticism and historical technique.

This applies to all periods for which there is abundant material:
it is easier to quote Horace Walpole or Charles Greville (mostly
without having studied either) than to work on original sources;
and to 're-assess our knowledge' (or show one's lack of it) than
to add to it. To go through the extant material for the eleven
years of Webster's monumental monograph, and to digest
and marshal it, required scholarship, experience of diplomacy,
judgment, and even wisdom, and great perseverance. But will
the book uproot legends? It is highly readable, and its gist and conclusions are given in brilliant introductions and summaries; they
will be quoted—probably along with the legends which the
author has tried to destroy.

PART III

THE END OF THE 'OLD GANG' AT PRINTING HOUSE SQUARE

WHEN IN January 1908, Lord Northcliffe entered into negotiations with the Manager of *The Times*, C. F. Moberly Bell, for the purchase of its control, his name was withheld from the other parties concerned, and even the chief proprietor, Arthur Walter, the fourth of his line, was only let into the secret two months later, to stop him from assuring people that Northcliffe was not the person in question. *The Times* was a partnership-at-will, and the agreement had to pass the Court of Chancery: even then the identity of the new proprietary remained undisclosed. 'The most obstinately anonymous newspaper in the world' was secured by 'X': Northcliffe's designation in *The Times* office for more than a year after the sale.

Alfred Harmsworth had started in 'the *Tit-Bits* school' of journalism; his first venture as newspaper proprietor was, in 1888, a weekly called *Answers*, followed by *Comic Cuts* and *Home Chat*; in 1891 he acquired the *Evening News*, and in 1896 founded the *Daily Mail*. Two years later, one of the smaller proprietors of *The Times*, in bitter opposition to 'Mr. Walter's autocractic powers of management' wished to enlist effective support and offered to sell to Harmsworth a share in the newspaper. 'In March 1898 Harmsworth came for the first time to Printing House Square and learnt there from Walter's lips that the sale to him of any share or portion would not be admitted.' 'There is nothing I would like better in all the world,' wrote Harmsworth to a friend in 1900, 'than to obtain control of *The Times*.' In 1908 he acquired it in a manner which averted a public outcry and opposition; and he became 'infatuated with his new connexion as he had never been before with a newspaper property,' but protested 'his irrevocable

L

determination never to "interfere with the paper" ': he would 'keep *The Times* as it had been,' and merely reorganize it technically. Talking to a member of the Walter family, in January 1909,

> 'X' . . . said that . . . he had been reading the files, had taken the trouble to make notes on the history of the paper and had gone deeply into the period when it first earned its prestige. He recalled the careers and achievements of John Walter II and Thomas Barnes —which that generation had utterly forgotten. The history of the paper as a whole, said 'X,' had been lost. The name of Delane was well enough known, but the earlier and formative enterprise . . . was submerged beneath a stream of loyalty to the Walter family as such.

And on 20 March 1909 Northcliffe wrote to the Manager:

> I wish I could find a good history of *The Times*. I do not believe there is one. If that is so, one ought to be written by a very able man —a very good one, full of pictures, caricatures, etc., a work that would take two or three years. My idea is that the volume should be a very handsome one and not on the barest margin of paper. It would constitute a great advertisement of *The Times*.

By 1912 Northcliffe had lost interest in the history of *The Times* and had grown contemptuous of its tradition. He himself had to pass away before his idea was realized. The first volume of *The History of 'The Times'* appeared in 1935, the second in 1939; and now the work is continued,[1] 'a very good one,' handsome in its attire of pre-war design. The production of each volume takes normally several years, and a fourth is still to come. But the concern for advertisement is nowhere traceable, and even this volume, so near to the present day and covering the Northcliffe interlude, adheres to the undertaking to reveal the work and character of those directly concerned with the production of *The Times* 'to the utmost extent that research has rendered possible.'

More than one hundred years ago *The Times* outgrew the mould and functions of the conventional newspaper. John Walter I had run it as an appendage to his printing works, in Printing House Square, and his politics and practice were, like so much in eighteenth-century England, 'private and pecuniary.' The transition to Victorian austerity was anticipated by John Walter II, who, having renounced Treasury favours and private payments

---

[1] *The History of The Times*. Vol. iii, *The Twentieth-century Test, 1884–1912*
The Times Publishing Company).

for 'suppressions' and 'corrections,' secured the independence and integrity of The Times. Under his father's will only a partner in the copyright of the newspaper, but Chief Proprietor with practically autocratic hereditary powers, and sole owner of the premises and the printing works, he added to the complexities of the situation when, having turned country gentleman with Parliamentary ambitions, he handed over The Times to an editor, while the ultimate indefeasible 'prerogative' remained vested in his family.

The Walters changed into a dynasty—detached, revered, and not always effective; while the editor, anonymous, completely identified with the newspaper, without ambition other than 'to place The Times at the head of the Press,' was their employee rendering devoted service. In time a conception arose, realized before it was formulated: the proprietor and his executives became joint trustees in a great national institution with a particular function in English life. In Barnes's conscious thinking The Times was still 'a privately owned political instrument and newspaper, conducted for private profit, and expressing his private judgment.' But in practice he consulted, first, the public interest, and, secondly, public opinion. This tradition was firmly established and developed under Delane, 1841–77. It was his 'passionate determination to be independent of every influence but that of instructed public opinion.' Yet the position and circulation of The Times entailed a further responsibility: 'to form aright the public opinion of this nation,' to stimulate, to anticipate, and on occasion to organize it. As 'a national repository of history to which intelligent people would willingly go for the authentic day-to-day account,' The Times had 'to find out the true state of facts,' and to report them with fidelity. Reproached for a premature disclosure,

> We hold ourselves responsible [wrote The Times on 18 March 1854] not to Lord Derby or the House of Lords, but to the people of England, for the accuracy and fitness of that which we think proper to publish. Whatever we conceive to be injurious to the public interests, it is our duty to withhold. . .

This was a high claim which even in that self-reliant and self-righteous age few would have uttered in their own name; it was rendered possible by the 'impersonality' of The Times, the resultant of one of those complex constitutional situations which this country develops, welding 'apparent anomalies into consistent principles.' But a structure of that kind is often slow in admitting the developments and readjustments imposed by a changed situation, and is therefore ill-adjusted to its strain and stress. There came for *The Times* 'The Twentieth-Century Test,' the theme of the present volume.

There is inherent history. The past is in us and with us, in the pattern of our lives, in habits and reactions, and in dim traditions —an incalculable force and an uncertain guide. Habits long survive, while their meaning and initial purpose are quickly forgotten; the present is projected into the past, and early origins are often ascribed to things of comparatively recent growth; as the shadows lengthen, the sense of distance becomes uncertain. A routine requires no guidance, but when change is upon us, the living past needs to be known and understood: to harness it is the primary task of history. The newcomer may be the first to inquire; but all who live within a tradition need to have it rendered conscious. This is the recovery of our lawful heritage. This is why contemporary and near-contemporary history has to be written: the history of *The Times* for the direction of those who conduct it; for the much wider circle of its occasional contributors; and, last but not least, for the great constituency of its readers, that public opinion with which its life is a constant interaction.

There are three aspects to the life of a newspaper: its history as a business enterprise; as an organization for the performance of its specific functions; and the record of that organization in action. Twelve out of twenty-four chapters in the present volume deal with ownership, management, and organization: with the financial difficulties brought on by the competition of the 'New Journalism' and the 'popular' Press, and by the crippling expense of the Special Commission which inquired into the charges raised by *The Times* against Parnell; with the attempts to create subsidiary resources through subordinate publications and activities when it seemed impossible 'to make *The Times* pay'—the *Encyclopedia Britannica*, *The Times Atlas*, the Book Club, etc.; with the internal discords caused by some smaller shareholders whom adversity and falling dividends had rendered acutely critical of the autocratic rule of the Chief Proprietor and hereditary printer; with schemes for reorganization hampered by the cumbersome partnership-at-will: the Hooper and Jackson scheme, and the

Pearson draft agreement; and, lastly, with the sale to Northcliffe and his gradual emergence as effective controller of the newspaper, out to break up the 'Old Gang'—the 'Black Friars' of Printing House Square, as he called them. The story of these business transactions, told in a terse, crisp style, with a wealth of factual data, but with human insight and a pervasive, unobtrusive humour, reads like a novel by R. L. Stevenson, seasoned with an admixture of Dreiser, Galsworthy, and Bennett.

Of the twelve chapters which treat of *The Times* in action three are on what may be described roughly as Imperial affairs: the first deals with General Gordon in the Sudan and *The Times*, represented there by a brilliant young journalist, Frank Power, who perished in an attempt to carry to Kitchener information of Gordon's desperate plight; the second with Ireland, the Pigott letters and their sequel; and the third with the Jameson Raid. The remaining nine chapters are all on international affairs, a dominant concern while 'the shadow of Germany falls more and more across the course of world politics.' Students of any period of European history during the last hundred years turn to *The Times* for a day-to-day record of foreign affairs; but it was during the years preceding the First World War that a most remarkable array of experts worked for it in its Foreign Department or as correspondents, and helped to shape British opinion and policy—Mackenzie Wallace, Valentine Chirol, Henri Stefan de Blowitz, William Lavino, George Saunders, Henry Wickham Steed, 'Chinese' Morrison, David D. Braham, James D. Bourchier, etc. What appeared then in the columns of *The Times* is now for the first time supplemented by the confidential correspondence of Printing House Square with its representatives abroad: they were at both ends well informed, eager and yet detached observers of national policies in the making. These letters, including reports of private talks with statesmen, politicians, and diplomatists, are first-rate historical material, and are blended with the contents of *The Times* into a coherent survey which will make this volume rank high among works on international relations. 'The book is essentially a history of *The Times*, not of contemporary events as seen from Printing House Square,' protests the introduction to the second volume. But for European history, 1890–1912, it has become such a record—and occasionally the writer very nearly forgets even Printing House Square over the events which rivet his attention.

Another criticism of this excellent production concerns its almost complete neglect of home politics: there is not a chapter about them. With this goes a lopsided treatment of *The Times* personnel. 'Buckle . . . whose long reign must loom large in the third volume,' was the forecast in the second; but although the period covered by the third is made to coincide with his editorship, it is *Hamlet* with the Prince mostly in the wings or off the stage. The first chapter describes Buckle's personality and methods of work, and he is seen once more in the foreground when Northcliffe forces his way into the editorial department; otherwise he is overshadowed by the Manager, the Foreign Editor, and the leading correspondents. Some responsibility for this disparity rests with Buckle himself: he was not a great letter-writer; he wrote in his own hand and kept no copies; and, both in the office and at home, he was an inveterate destroyer of papers. With a distressing scarcity of material, a deliberate effort would have been required to drag him and his work into the limelight; and even then both might have remained rather pale. But with the stage already crowded by two great dramas proceeding simultaneously —the domestic history of *The Times* and that of European politics —the effort has not been made.

Pigott's cross-examination and his collapse when confronted with a misspelling which he repeated in court in writing down some selected words, has a perennial interest. But while the proceedings of the Special Commission have been retold repeatedly, it is now for the first time that the story appears as seen and experienced at Printing House Square, and aspects emerge which have been hitherto obscured by the sensational element. In March 1887 *The Times*, in a series of articles on 'Parnellism and Crime,' made out a formidable list of charges and accused Parnell himself 'in no ambiguous language of direct complicity in conspiracy and murder'; after a while it challenged him to take legal action; and only a month later, on 18 April, it solemnly published what is known as 'Letter No. 2,' which over Parnell's signature excused his denunciation of the Phoenix Park murders as a tactical move and, while regretting 'the accident of Lord F. Cavendish's death,' 'admitted' that Burke 'got no more than his deserts.' Parnell, prodded by friends, denounced the letter in Parliament as 'an audacious and unblushing fabrication,' though even then he merely asked the Government to have it examined by a Select Committee. The Government declined, but offered to set up a Special Commission to examine the whole body of charges contained in *The Times* articles. This put the newspaper at a very serious disadvantage: while in a libel case the plaintiff has to indicate the passages of which he complains, the newspaper had now to act the public prosecutor, proceed 'as if the Irish members were being charged on an indictment containing all the matters alleged in the articles,' and substantiate facts, repeated after Irish newspapers, by direct evidence: 393 witnesses were called, and the case cost it £200,000; this, and not the £5,000 damages ultimately paid to Parnell, was a shattering financial blow. But though the Commission sat on 129 days, the question of the letters was not probed as thoroughly as it would have been in a libel court; a rule of procedure, peculiar to that quasi-prosecution, forced the newspaper to assume the disastrous course of summoning Pigott as its witness—which it would not have done otherwise. That 'squalidly dishonest' Irish journalist had no sooner sold the letters to *The Times*, through a respectable but misguided intermediary, than he tried to get money from the Irish for declaring them forgeries; next, attempted to extort £5,000 from Printing House Square for giving evidence; then approached the other side through Labouchère; and after the collapse in court, presented Labouchère with 'a full confession in writing that he had forged all the letters,' followed by a statement to a solicitor acting for Walter that only some were forged. And here the matter rests, with certain points concerning the letters not cleared up even now. People have a passion for clinching a defensible argument by an 'irrefutable' piece of evidence and, in that mood, develop a credulity which makes them an easy prey for forgers: a recurrent phenomenon in history.

The Jameson Raid was the other *cause célèbre* of the period in which Printing House Square was involved; and though it soon became known that '*The Times* was "in it," ' who, if any, of its leading figures had been privy to the Raid remained a secret till now. By 1890 the newspaper was strongly Imperialist, and a friend and admirer of Cecil Rhodes, Miss Flora Shaw (the later Lady Lugard), a woman of outstanding ability and character, was in charge of its Colonial Department. 'Her views were definite; her influence was considerable.' She knew of the preparations for the Raid: 'Can you advise when will you commence the plans,' she cabled in code to Rhodes on 10 December 1895; 'we wish to send at earliest opportunity sealed instruction representatives of the London *Times* European capitals. It is most important using their influence in your favour.' On the 12th she cabled that 'delay dangerous'; and on the 17th, that she had 'special reason to believe' that Chamberlain 'wishes you must do it immediately.' No wonder that *The Times* was the first with the news of the Raid and with the text of the letter which Jameson had extracted from the Johannesburg leaders about the terrible dangers which threatened 'thousands of unarmed men, women, and children of our race'; it was by Miss Shaw that the Colonial Office was first told that the Raid had occurred and Chamberlain shown the 'letter.' Meanwhile *The Times* preserved a judicial view of Jameson's action and, though it stood by Rhodes who had 'secured for the British race an Empire in South Africa,' 'it did not uphold his connexion with the fostering of a revolt in a friendly State': the Editor had been neither consulted nor informed by Flora Shaw, only the powerful Manager, Moberly Bell, whose contacts with the Foreign and Colonial Departments and with correspondents of *The Times* were closer than Buckle's. The drafts of those three cablegrams, sent by Miss Shaw from her private address, are all in Bell's handwriting and were press-copied into his official letter-book. Before the Select Committee, set up to inquire into the origin and circumstances of the Raid, Flora Shaw was examined by Harcourt, Labouchère, Campbell-Bannerman, and others, and claimed to answer questions 'freely and frankly, in order to clear up once and for all the so-called mystery.' But she succeeded in adroitly screening Bell—'neither the precise details of the part played by *The Times*, nor the identity of the "person" at the office . . . with whom Miss Shaw was in regular consultation, were made public.'

Moberly Bell, rather than Buckle, stands out as the central figure in this volume; it was he who 'played the paramount part in the conduct of the paper's imperial and foreign affairs.' This was not due solely to his personality and antecedents (he had been *The Times* correspondent in Egypt). Under his predecessors also, the control, appointment, and dismissal of foreign correspondents rested largely with the Manager, who made the financial arrangements, and, 'charged in a special sense with the personal interests of the Proprietor . . . was regarded more definitely as his agent than the Editor.' In 1852 Mowbray Morris wrote when dismissing a correspondent: 'The Editor . . . had been driven to other sources and means of information than the responsible ones

which it was the duty of the Manager to provide.' It was Bell
who in 1891 took the initiative in creating a separate department
to deal with foreign affairs; Buckle agreed on condition that he
approved of the man for the new appointment and 'that the
editorial control over the leading articles was not diminished.'
Bell's choice was Donald Mackenzie Wallace, previously *The
Times* correspondent in Turkey and Russia, and a member of
Lord Dufferin's staff in India: 'it was a formidable figure that
Bell sought to bring into Printing House Square.' Wallace was
'a diplomat rather than a journalist; and a student rather than
either.' His task was to create the department and train its staff.
From the correspondents

> he wanted news, facts and ideas, not essays on everything in
> general and nothing in particular. . . . He insisted that they should
> adopt towards the Governments . . . the attitude of diplomatic
> envoys. Their duty was not to obtain news for sensational publica-
> tion but to put themselves into intimate relations with ministers, to
> ascertain the policy of Governments and the opinions of influential
> persons, and to report, as much confidentially for his own private
> guidance, as publicly for the benefit of the readers of *The Times*. In
> the use of material he took into account, first, the diplomatic effect
> of a telegram and, secondly, its value as news. Wallace, nevertheless,
> would instantly rebuke a correspondent who sought to rise from
> the position of passive chronicler to that of actor in events. . . .

He wrote in one of his letters of guidance:

> A correspondent should listen to all prominent politicians and
> attach himself to none; he should always be in the orchestra stalls,
> but never jump on the stage.

Wallace 'resisted any attempt . . . to use the organization of *The
Times* as a supplement or substitute for diplomatic negotiation,'
and considered that the sole correct medium for exercising its
influence 'was through the columns of the paper.' A conservative
in foreign policy, he 'supported combinations which tended to
stabilize the world and made for peace.' He 'was an early
supporter of friendship with Russia and with France'; and 'as
time went on he became increasingly suspicious of Germany,
but, at the same time, acted as a brake upon the growing hostility
to German policy.'

Between 1896 and 1914, repeated complaints against *The Times*
were made by German official circles. In November 1899 Bülow

had his Ambassador explain to Chamberlain that 'a not un-important obstacle to the improvement of Anglo-German feeling is the present *Times* correspondent, Saunders.' And in 1907 Bülow said to W. T. Stead:

> There's Mr. Saunders. I wonder that *The Times* keep a man like that here, who so entirely misrepresents Germany to its readers. Mr. Saunders creates a Germany which does not exist. . . .

In June 1902, the German Ambassador, Count Metternich, having presented to Edward VII the Kaiser's congratulations on the Peace of Vereeniging, named *The Times* 'as the chief obstacle to good Anglo-German relations.' In December 1905 the Kaiser, speaking to Alfred Beit, 'reverted to his favourite topic that the real cause of all the trouble between the two countries, was the Press; he meant the British Press, above all, *The Times*.' And a few months earlier he had informed the British Ambassador, Sir Frank Lascelles, that he

> had at last found out who it was who was doing all the mischief. It had taken him two years to find out, the Kaiser said; now he knew. He had taken a lot of trouble to discover the ultimate source of this trouble. . . . It had hitherto been alleged that the soul of the anti-Germanism in the Press was either Chirol or Saunders, or both. When Lascelles asked the miscreant's name, now at last dis-covered, the Emperor answered: 'Moberly Bell.'

But Bülow had written from London, in November 1899, to Hohenlohe, then German Chancellor:

> The British politicians know little of the Continent. . . . They are . . . rather naive in their artless egoism. . . . They find difficulty in believing in really evil intentions in others. . . . In general, there is no question that the feeling in Britain is much less anti-German than the feeling in Germany is anti-British. For that reason those English-men who, like Chirol and Saunders, know from personal observa-tion the acuteness and depth of Germany's unfortunate dislike of Britain are the most dangerous to us. If the British public clearly realized the anti-British feeling which dominates Germany just now, a great revulsion would occur in its conception of the relations between Britain and Germany.

Hence the wrath.

In reality most Englishmen of that generation started as pro-Germans, and most of the men who served Printing House Square were no exception. In 1902, neither Buckle nor Bell regarded the Germans as Britain's enemy, actual or potential. Bell had all his life preferred the Germans to Frenchmen.... He might almost be ranked with the pro-Germans. ...

Even after the Kruger telegram he believed 'that any anti-German feeling here was a passing phase and could never ... become a basis of policy'; and on a visit to Berlin he enjoined on the newspaper's correspondent 'that no unnecessary friction between official Germany and *The Times* was to be risked.'

'As you know I have always advocated and, as far as I possibly could, assisted a policy of friendship towards Germany,' wrote Chirol, then correspondent in Berlin, to Wallace on 4 January 1896. And Cecil Spring Rice, about a fortnight later, in a private letter to a friend, said that Chirol was 'the most ardent advocate of a good understanding with Germany and always has been so.' Indeed, Chirol, preoccupied with Asiatic problems and 'haunted by Russian intrigues,' in the days of Fashoda reverted to a policy of cultivating Germany; and it required a good deal more of Germany's devious, obscure, but aggressive policy finally to convince him that a conflict with her was inevitable. For Chirol, as for many Englishmen, the Kruger telegram, that 'intentionally unfriendly act,' had been the first eye-opener. It was, as Marschall von Bieberstein, then German State Secretary, explained to him, a *Staatsaktion*, part of a matured German policy. Seeing the gulf which divided Britain from France and Russia, Germany seems to have hoped for their support. During the next decades a Continental bloc against this country was a constantly recurring aim of German diplomacy which tried to frighten England into a sense of her dangerous isolation, and thus to 'kick her into friendliness.'

But such 'enforced love' would have meant close collaboration with Germany on her own terms: concessions to begin with, and next subserviency to a ruthless policy of aggression and aggrandisement; for any understanding with a Germany bent on conquering *Lebensraum* is bound to be directed against a third party. There was in Germany intense jealousy of the great British Empire: 'because it was great and was British'; but as Germany's naval armaments were passing through a danger zone comparable with that through which Hitler's rearmament passed in 1933–7, 'an atmosphere of good will in Britain' had to be maintained.

Once a navy equal or superior to that of Britain was added to Germany's pre-eminent military strength, a new language could be adopted, especially if Britain was by that time 'up to the neck' in conflicts with France and Russia: and that the three could never make up their differences was an axiom of German diplomacy.

The Times correspondents in Central Europe were among the first to see through Germany's policy and to perceive its danger.

None of the qualified observers that *The Times* appointed to its Continental service in the nineties was destined to be permanently agreeable to the German Government: Chirol became a deep disappointment; Steed an occasion of fear; Saunders an object of hatred.

'We shall have to reckon with these people long before anything like a decisive reckoning with Russia comes,' wrote Saunders to Wallace in 1897. And in 1899 to Chirol, who had succeeded Wallace as Foreign Editor: 'We shall soon enough have to come to close quarters. In thirty years . . . we shall perhaps be at each other's throats' (time is a most difficult factor to gauge accurately). And in November 1900: the Germans 'are the only nation which intelligently and of set purpose contemplates a struggle with Great Britain for commercial and colonial predominance.' The best *exposé* of Saunders's position is contained in a statement which he wrote for Bell during the night of 14–15 June 1902 (negotiations for an Anglo-German alliance were by then suspended but the idea was not discarded). After Metternich had complained to Edward VII about *The Times* and Saunders, the King (again one of those taxed with inveterate hostility to Germany) 'spoke to Alfred Rothschild . . . and Rothschild promised to see what he could do for Metternich.' He turned to Bell, who wrote to Saunders 'and asked for an expression of views which he could incorporate in a letter of his own, since Rothschild wished for something in writing.' Saunders's statement, jotted down in a hurry and with passion, is none the less 'monumental.' There is vision in it.

The moment is one for a decision which is of decisive importance for the future of the British Empire. The question is: 'Are we to ignore the whole tendency of German policy during the present reign . . . and to range ourselves definitely on the German side, accepting for ever the lead of the Foreign Office in Berlin . . . which will take us in tow?'

This would mean to alienate France, a country whose ideas, ambitions, and ideals 'we can understand and know the *limits* of.'

Germany the British public does *not* know. . . . Can you consent to place British policy in German leading-strings? . . . Look at Austria chafing under the yoke . . . ! Look at Italy . . . ! These Powers I do not blame. They can hardly do anything else. England does not *need* to enter into this bondage. . . .

It means permanent separation from Russia with the cunning, assiduous German broker ever between. . . . War to the knife with Russia is far better, if it be on an *independent* basis, than subordination of Anglo-Russian relations to the Wilhelmstrasse. . . .

. . . I have sat for fourten years watching every sign of the heavens here—my heart at home in England; and my . . . firm verdict is: —Any arrangement . . . which caused England to make a final choice for Germany against Russia and France, would be a *fatal*, *irrevocable* step. . . .

Germany is a *new*, crude, ambitious, radically *unsound* Power. . . . The artificial Army system, the pampered commerce and shipping, the Agrarian-industrial cleavage, the unfamiliarity with the perils of civilization—a thousand things convince me that Germany, with all her phenomenal development, is radically unsound and unhealthy. . . .

. . . one of the greatest objects of German endeavours is to detach us from America. . . . This was put to me with singular imprudence at the German Foreign Office some months ago. . . . They said: (literally)—'It is the interest of Germany and England to combine as against Powers which, like Russia and America, are economically dangerous owing to their vast undeveloped resources.'—A perilous fallacy! It is *Germany's* interest to drag England into such a combination. It is not at all *our* interest to enter into it. . . .

I summarize my essentials of British Foreign policy as follows:—

(1)   Absolute independence of Germany. No closer relations with Germany than with France. Friendliness, politeness, where friendliness is impossible, but above all alertness and political aloofness. . . .

(2) Friendly, neighbourly relations with France. . . .

(3) *Above all* we must go hand in hand with America in good and in evil fortune. This is absolutely essential. . . .

(4) A *steady* object . . . ought to be the ultimate settlement of our relations, territorial and political, with Russia. . . .

Here are just a few salient points from a memorandum, written at speed, of nearly 2,500 words: some of them so prophetic as to be commonplace after a lapse of fifty years.

The Triple Entente having been formed, the question remained, could it endure? The Germans were out to prove to Britain's partners that her support counted for little; to France over Morocco in 1904, to Russia over Bosnia in 1908. Were it not for the heavy-handedness of the Germans and the delight they take in humiliating men and nations, they might have succeeded; especially as this country, safe behind the Channel—even in 1940 a remarkable anti-tank ditch—was slow, or even unwilling, to realize that an army would have to be sent across the water; still less that adequate military help would have to be given. It is to the credit of Steed and Repington, on the staff of *The Times*, that they early came to see it. Steed became a strong supporter of Clemenceau's ardent plea 'for the creation of a British Army fit to help France in case France were attacked by Germany in consequence of an Anglo-German quarrel.' 'As things are to-day,' said Clemenceau to Steed in August 1908,

> you are hopelessly unprepared. Even if you could find the men you would have neither the arms nor the ammunition for them to use. You could smash the German fleet, et vous feriez ainsi un beau trou dans l'eau. En 1870 la flotte allemande n'existait pas—ce qui n'a pas empêché aux Prussiens d'entrer à Paris.

And in fact Edward VII, who five years earlier had worried 'about *The Times* and Saunders,' now sympathized with the demand for prompt British aid to a hard-pressed France. And this is Steed's rendering of the argument:

> Were England to remain impotent to help France on land, France might be compelled to detach herself from us; or, if she stuck to us, to face a constant risk of defeat. . . . By the detachment of France we should be not only isolated, but discredited . . . as a nation ready to take but not to give; and ready to expose our friends to risks, but to accept none ourselves.

A redeeming feature of Northcliffe's acquiring the control of *The Times* was that otherwise it might possibly have passed to pro-Germans. When in November 1911, Steed reported to him expressions of concern by a French lady, she need not worry herself as to the *entente* [replied Northcliffe], because I am a firm adherent and am always working privately and publicly for it.

The dictum of a megalomaniac: yet sound in sense and sentiment.

Whatever Northcliffe may originally have promised himself or others, his ambition of many years could not be satisfied by anything less than direct and effective control of *The Times*, both on its business and its editorial side. By the end of 1908 he was sending Bell daily notes on the current issues of paper; and these communications soon 'became less advisory and more supervisory in character.' At first Bell was 'grateful'; by March 1909 'he expressed his view that neither he nor the office needed "persistent urging"'; and by the end of the month, 'that less criticism and more encouragement would . . . produce a better paper.' Bell had brought in Northcliffe: now, in his own words, he tried to 'keep Northcliffe in order.' It was a hopelessly uneven struggle, and Bell's basic idea was 'to maintain *The Times* by maintaining the editorial staff and himself in their positions.' But

> in truth 'X' was henceforth to be master of his own paper; he was going to stand no more 'obstinacy' from Bell. He was to be 'X' no longer; he was to be Northcliffe; to be the 'Chief.'

Still, he had to proceed warily and not upset political circles and the public by sudden changes at Printing House Square. He started with the managerial department, that is by attacking Bell. He wrote to Buckle on 10 August 1909:

> I am sure you realize as well as I do that the old man is one of the most difficult characters with which to deal: He is perfectly straight, and yet most elusive; most amiable and gentle, and, on the other hand, inordinately vain and obstinate; most industrious, yet doing little real work; and, above all things, tactless. . . . It might not be wise to show him this letter, but you are quite at liberty to do so. . . .

Northcliffe concluded with remarks flattering to Buckle. But 'Buckle, who had so frequently in the past protested against Bell's invasion of the editorial province, was not the man to desert his colleague now that he was unfairly attacked.' He wrote to Northcliffe on 15 December 1909, in reply to another outburst about 'the obstinate incapacity and the ignorance of Bell':

You have absolutely lost confidence, and for half a year have not hesitated to say so in decided language, in the Managing Director, the pivot on whom turned the whole negotiation by which you acquired your commanding interest in *The Times*. In these circumstances nothing but duty to the Paper, to which he is wholly devoted, can keep him at his post. Your entire disbelief in him is in itself a serious matter . . . especially for Chirol and me, his friends, who realize all that he has done for the Paper.

But Bell, Northcliffe's original sponsor, still tried to argue that the position was not hopeless:

The one thing I attached importance to [he wrote to Chirol in January 1910] was that there should be no interference with the political line of the paper—that the paper should be independent of his opinions.

A year later that very point was brought to a test over the Declaration of London. Buckle, Chirol, and Thursfield, the naval correspondent, favoured ratification; but Northcliffe wrote to Bell on 3 March 1911:

As far as the Declaration of London is concerned I have made up my mind what I am going to do about it and I shall act very definitely. I do not propose to allow one farthing of my fortune to be used in connection with that which would injure this country. I trust these words to the wise will be sufficient.

Buckle and Chirol took a serious view of this stark exertion of proprietary authority; Bell continued to preach appeasement: he thought that 'there was no point in forcing a quarrel and getting ejected over a matter in which, he said, not editorial conscience, but only the editorial dignity, was touched.' They remained. But within a month Bell fell by the roadside; worn out by the struggle he died of heart failure on 5 April 1911. And by January 1912 Northcliffe decided 'that if I wish to make *The Times* what I mean to I must begin to act. . . .' Chirol was forced to resign on 28 February 1912, and Buckle on 31 July. The 'Old Gang' was broken up.

THREE CONTEMPORARIES

1 JOS WEDGWOOD

'I am a philosophic anarchist.' 'I . . . judge degrees of excellence in Government by how far Government enables the governed to do without them. . . .' 'Teach them to think, not *what* to think.' These are a few characteristic dicta from Lord Wedgwood's *Testament to Democracy*.[1] 'The Leader of the House accused me the other day of "inciting violence." I admit it. In a sense my whole life has been an incitement to think, to see, and then to act. Every idea is incitement. . . . The only difference between the expression of opinion and an incitement is the speaker's enthusiasm for the result.' A weekly paper charged Wedgwood with 'arrogance and intolerance.' He replied: 'Toleration, in these later days, approximates to cowardice; and I hope I may die still utterly intolerant of cruelty, injustice, and error.'

Such was 'Jos,' perhaps the most lovable and the most eccentric figure in British politics during the last half-century. English to the core, he was imbued with the finest tradition of England, proud of that tradition, a passionate lover of his country, jealous of its honour and moral integrity, a knight-errant of Englishry. Wrong-headed the man could be who, 'intolerant of error,' proclaimed himself possessed of the truth; but never could one who had his courage, his passion for freedom, and his flaming hatred of cruelty and injustice be insignificant or ignoble. He was sometimes inconsistent in argument, confused in thought, inaccurate in his 'facts'—not a painstaking historian; but a light burnt in him, a fire, more valuable than logic and precision, and far more sacred than mere intellectual achievements. Well-

[1] Lord Wedgwood, *Testament to Democracy* (Hutchinson).

framed argument, carefully tested and marshalled facts, and fool-proof statement can provide the hard shell for truth, but truth itself springs from the human heart, from the depth of human emotions. Jos's truth often lacked the shell which should protect the kernel; but how much superior was he to those whose hard, polished shells encompass a void or cover a shrivelled decaying core!

His *Testament to Democracy* is a discourse on the virtues of Parliamentary government ('our form of democracy'), on the dangers which beset it at this juncture, and on how they should be avoided. Having, after thirty-six years spent in the House of Commons, entered the Lords, he surveyed the experiences of his public life; and that this lonely fighter, this self-confessed anarchist, who so often championed unpopular causes, should have been able to do so without a tinge of bitterness or despondency was in itself high tribute to the community and system, and especially to that representative body and governmental organization within which, and with which, he battled. The basic problem of government is to Wedgwood 'how best to help forward the virtue and conscience and character of the governed,' and the answer is through democracy which is 'government by reason and persuasion,' by trial and error. But there is another thing which Wedgwood never mentions, though it suffuses every page of his book: democracy means respect for the human being. Does this spring from mere 'reason'? Is there not something deeper and greater behind it? Jos was a Victorian and thought himself a rationalist. But he understood the affinity which there is between all believers. 'I may have no faith save in freedom, but there is much in common between all faiths which demand courage and self-sacrifice, . . .'

About the House of Commons, its inner life, the 'family feel-ing' which unites nearly all its members and 'provides consola-tion for failure and encouragement to sacrifice,' Wedgwood writes with warm affection. Fascists rant about 'corruption' in Parliament. 'Emphasis may rightly be laid,' replies Wedgwood, 'on the futility of joining it in order to get rich'; ' . . . our com-munity existence and wide interests and enthusiasms spoil the market for corruption.' Is Parliamentary government 'inefficient'? 'The more spotlight of publicity is thrown upon any Govern-ment the less inefficiency there is and the more inefficiency is seen.' But there is no free criticism and no free press without a free

Parliament. Social misfits form everywhere 'the grievance gang' which 'is the backbone (or tool) of every anti-democratic movement.' But one of the chief and oldest functions of Parliament has always been to secure the redress of genuine grievances. Parliament is the greatest check on administration. Is Parliament 'a machine for making laws'? Wedgwood denies it. 'A free Parliament ... is a machine for *preventing* Government from making laws. It is the only check upon the departments. . . .'

But will Parliament remain truly free? Wedgwood felt apprehensive. The power of parties is growing; he believed that the party system has destroyed Continental Parliaments and endangers it in this country. Party control has even 'to some extent increased the unavoidable humiliations of a political career.' And therefore, though one of the freest members of the Commons, he felt a certain relief at his translation to the Lords. He recites an old indictment in a new version: 'The power of the Cabinet has increased, is increasing, and ought to be diminished.' There are too many 'placemen,' too many 'junior Ministers.' 'They continue indefinitely in their particular office; they are forgotten, and tend to forget that they are members of Parliament; they tend to think of themselves as part of the bureaucracy they were deputed to control.' A revival of the 'King's Friends'? Wedgwood also disliked the hold which the Premier's power of dissolution gives him over the House (but next he admitted that the lack of such power prevented the Popular Front Government in France from obtaining the necessary electoral support for their policy in 1936).

These anxieties are as old as the Executive in Parliament. Wedgwood postulates an independent House of Commons. But some 160 years ago Soame Jenyns, after almost forty years spent in the Commons, wrote: 'An independent Parliament is no part of the English Constitution. . . . A numerous assembly uninfluenced is as much a creature of imagination as a griffin or a dragon.' And yet Parliament has always been the victorious host in what Wedgwood calls 'our ever-successful fight for freedom.'

And this is the note on which the book concludes: 'Liberty is the crusade of all brave and conscientious men, the new religion, the chivalry of all gentlemen. For that crusade this testament is written.'

2 WYNDHAM DEEDES

Some time in 1913, somewhere in Anatolia, a small boy of fifteen came up to Deedes, 'very wretched-looking,' and starved.

> I was told [wrote Deedes] to talk English to him, and, indeed, it turned out that he knew English, French, Italian, Russian, Arabic, Turkish. Very sharp and clever. A Cretan Moslem by race.

The child was homeless and friendless, a grain of dust in the wreckage of Turkish disaster and disruption. Deedes had him fed, cleaned, and properly dressed, and he placed the boy, at his own expense, in a school at Smyrna. 'To see this little black child, all in rags, talking away to me in French . . . was very strange.' But he asked the boy no questions—so nothing more is known or recorded. The man is seen in that incident: active and gentle, never indifferent yet aloof, not willing to speak, still less to inquire, where it serves no practical purpose.

How, then, ask idle questions of one who never asks them himself? Many who have known him for years, know next to nothing about the first part of his life. Of squirearchy by birth and a soldier by training, Brigadier-General Sir Wyndham Deedes, C.M.G., D.S.O., in 1923, at the age of forty, left the Army, resigned the post of Chief Secretary of Palestine, and settled in Bethnal Green to do work which he had long wished to undertake: on behalf of the poor, depressed, dispossessed, and brutalized. 'It's not money that's wanted,' he wrote in 1913 from Turkey, 'it's personal service and courage.' He did not consider the change a renunciation, and divested it of all such appearance. Nor did he discard his previous interests and associations—he would still go on a Zionist tour to Poland or South Africa, on a salvation errand to Nazi Germany, or on a relief mission to Turkey after the earthquake of 1939; but having 'done so many strange things and mixed with so many queer people,' he now settled down to a different life. There are points of resemblance between him and Lawrence: the same ascetic superiority of mind over body, and a courage which knows no danger; a self-abnegation and a detached spiritual existence which isolate a man, but secure other men's trust and allegiance. John Presland writes about Deedes:[1] 'He once

[1] John Presland, *Deedes Bey. A Study of Sir Wyndham Deedes, 1883–1923* (Macmillan).

said that ideas have always meant more to him than human beings, and ideas have in a manner always been more alive to him than human beings'; and Lawrence says in the *Seven Pillars of Wisdom*: '. . . in all my life objects have been gladder to me than persons, and ideas than objects.'

But Lawrence defines his attitude in a carefully constructed phrase; Deedes's personality does not reveal itself 'in the written word'—'he lives in some ways uniquely, he writes like hundreds of others.' Lawrence, in spite of his nihilist attitude towards life and its values, was essentially an artist striving for self-expression: this was bound to destroy the balance into which an active purpose had, for a time, welded dangerous contradictions. Deedes, a sincere Christian, has a lasting purpose. 'He never rests; there is nothing to rest for; only life to be filled with its insistent duties. . . .' Dynamic and austere, he has a supreme capacity both for concentration and for detachment. He has moved 'through innumerable scenes of violence,' and 'has never committed an act of violence in his life.' He has dispassionate judgment, 'a remarkable sang-froid, and, when he chooses, an inscrutable countenance', and is 'a rare example of an idealist who is very difficult to take in.' And how much there is in this casual remark of his biographer: 'It is no use being dramatic with Deedes.' Lastly, he has 'an overpowering reluctance to go back on the past,' and a faculty to shut out completely all that has become irrelevant to him. He therefore could never write reminiscences, still less an autobiography. But for many years he had written letters to his mother, and during part of the 1914–18 war he kept a diary; these, with his permission, his mother, who died in 1940, turned over to a friend of theirs, Mrs. Gladys Skelton, who writes under the *nom de plume* of John Presland. And mainly on these materials her book is based.

From 1909 to 1914 Deedes was engaged on the reorganization of the Turkish gendarmerie in Tripoli and Anatolia, and, after the Balkan Wars, also on schemes for resettling refugees from the lost provinces. Possessed of a thorough knowledge of Turkey and and the Turkish language, he served with the Intelligence Department in the Dardanelles Campaign, closely collaborating with George Lloyd, Captain Guy Dawnay, and Captain Aspinall, then in their early thirties. The chapters on the Dardanelles, the most interesting and important in the book—they contain material of first-class historical importance—make sad reading: a story of commanders not comprehending the problems which

faced them, and of lackadaisical 'optimism' which let opportunities slip. At Suvla Bay, on 6 August, General Stopford had
25,000 men, and only 1,800 Turks facing him. But after a successful landing had been effected, Dawnay reported, 'with a
mixture of cold anger and hot despair, "The troops are on the
beach, washing their clothes!" ' Sir Ian Hamilton thereupon sent
General Stopford

> a gentlemanly cable saying: '. . . Chief glad to hear enemy
> opposition weakening and knows you will take advantage of this
> to push on rapidly'

—and Stopford ordered the troops to dig in. On the morning of
8 August, Aspinall reported: 'Feel confident that golden opportunities are being lost and look upon the situation as serious.'
And at 11 a.m. Sir Ian pointed out to Stopford the importance
of forestalling the enemy on the high ground, if this is 'lightly
held,' but, being short of artillery, he should not attack an entrenched position. The same afternoon Sir Ian found Stopford
'tired but happy.' But by that time Liman von Sanders had, by
forced marches, brought up two divisions, and placed them under
Mustapha Kemal, the later Ataturk. The best chance of forcing
the Dardanelles was lost. And here are two passages from Deedes's
diary:

> (May 8) . . . We are such good improvisers, one is told, but we
> carry that to such an extent that we for ever improvise and never
> organize. . . . A hundred times a day I find myself saying, as I used
> to at the War Office: How do we come to possess such an Empire
> and how have we kept it?
>
> (Aug. 24) When criticizing the whole war I always come back to
> the before-the-war days and lay the whole blame for *all our* mis-
> fortunes on the country itself, for refusing to be woken, and on those
> in power in particular for refusing to try and wake them. All our
> errors now have their root in our pre-war unpreparedness. *You can't
> run an Empire on gallantry.*

By the middle of August it was obvious to the four young men
that the Expedition would have to be withdrawn, though

> the knowledge that in a withdrawal like that *some* troops have
> to be *last* and then to be sacrificed is, I think, a terrible idea—and it
> must be many years since British troops had to *withdraw* from any-
> where.

But dispatches and telegrams from those in charge were

all written in the sanguine, optimistic vein—which is again due to nothing but, on the one hand, we firmly believe, ignorance and inability to grasp the truth and, on the other, the desire to keep up the semblance of a rosy situation to enable certain people to keep their seats!

Finally, the young men managed to have Dawnay sent to the War Cabinet, and, though he was at first snubbed by Kitchener, his mission bore fruit. Hearing Dawnay's account of his interviews in London, Deedes remarked: 'And I bet the best you found was Winston after all!'

From 1916–18 Deedes served with the Military Intelligence in Egypt and Palestine. There is a note by him, dated 8 April 1916, setting out the terms 'which he thought would be acceptable to the main Turkish parties and to the majority of the Arabs,' and containing the following points:

(iv) Autonomous rule for the vilayets of Damascus, Aleppo, and Jerusalem, but under Moslem Governments appointed by the Entente, all the Governments to be under the guarantee of the Entente Powers.

(v) For the remainder of the Ottoman Empire, the provisions of the agreement entered into by the High Commissioner (MacMahon) and the Arab Bureau with the Shereef of Mecca (Hussein).

Thus Deedes, in the closest touch with MacMahon, Clayton, Hogarth, etc., and fully acquainted both with the text of the documents and the intentions of those concerned, clearly considered that 'the agreement entered into' in the MacMahon-Hussein correspondence did not cover the vilayet of Jerusalem.

Deedes was one of the officers who, in December 1917, entered Jerusalem with Allenby; and he was, 1920–3, under Sir Herbert Samuel, the first Chief Secretary in Palestine. As such, he gained the confidence and respect of both Jews and Arabs, and struggled hard against the anti-Jewish bias of many of his colleagues. He has remained a friend of Israel to this day.

3 ORDE WINGATE

William Wingate, Orde's grandfather, was the eldest son of a well-known Glasgow merchant. At the age of twenty-one he entered his father's business. His prospects in life were brilliant, and he joined with zest in social pursuits. 'Yet, when the call came to his soul, he gave up everything which had hitherto represented pleasure to follow the word of Christ.'[1] He engaged in social work in Glasgow, and next turned to 'God's ancient people.' He learnt Hebrew and joined the Church of Scotland Mission in Budapest. His father, disapprovingly, left his wealth to the second son—a loss never regretted by William or his descendants.

Orde's father, Colonel George Wingate, was a musketry instructor, a dead shot, and like William Wingate, a brilliant horseman. He served in seven frontier campaigns in India, and was the founder of the Central Asian Mission for evangelization and medical work among the Pathans (he was of the Plymouth Brethren). When in 1895 the Kafiris were handed over by the British Government 'to the merciless hands of the Ameer of Afghanistan' (on their invoking British protection, 'the unexpected and ominous answer came over the field telegraph wires "Tell them they are now *subjects* of the Ameer"'),[2] their fate deeply moved George Wingate, as that of the Abyssinians and of the Palestine Jews moved Orde some forty years later. On the death of Colonel Wingate in 1936, *The Times* described him as 'one of the last survivors of a generation of soldiers which united the service of the State with that of the Christian faith.' They counted without his son.

Orde's maternal grandfather, Captain Orde Browne, was a gunnery expert, a well-known specialist on armour-plates, and Captain-Inspector at the Royal Laboratory, Woolwich. He was an Evangelical, and an intimate friend of General Gordon, together with whom he engaged in Ragged Schools work. 'When Gordon went to the Sudan for the first time, he asked Orde Browne to go with him. Orde Browne refused to leave the

[1] Rev. Gavin Carlyle, *Life and Work of the Rev. William Wingate, Missionary to the Jews.*

[2] George Wingate, *Across our Indian Frontier*, pp. 6–8.

school work.'[1] In a female line the Brownes were descended from Archbishop Sharp, and collaterally from Granville Sharp, the prison reformer. Through the Chapmans, they had Anglo-Irish blood. For generations they had been soldiers.

Orde's mother, to whom he was much devoted, inherited her father's faith (and having acted as his secretary, some of his expert knowledge). In September 1943, shortly after her death, I saw Orde for the last time: he talked to me about her, and what she had taught her children; that Biblical precepts enjoined Christians and Jews to be friends, and Biblical prophecy declared that the Jews shall return to Palestine.

Orde Wingate was born on 26 February 1903, the third child and the eldest boy—there were three sons and four daughters. They received a careful, even expensive, education—seven, on the pay of a retired colonel. 'We were brought up,' the eldest daughter said to me, 'on "the Scots régime of porridge, bread and dripping, and the sincere milk of the word." ' Strict discipline, frugality, and hard work: Orde grew up physically tough, and spiritually a rebel; and yet he assumed the full inheritance of his family. He was a Protestant, a Puritan to the core; a searcher after the inner light; a man with a tortured conscience, and with the certainties of a believer; therefore often intolerant and impatient. An individualist and a lonely man, he showed a preference for what he could do on his own—for instance, for swimming, shooting, and riding (he had a collection of cups won in point-to-point races) as against organized team-games. In deeper opposition against authority, he was not a good learner. He had to do everything his own way: in things big and small, he consequently would head for collisions, but at the last moment, by a swerve, escape a smash. He taught himself to drive a car: 'We arrived,' reported his youngest sister, 'without what Orde would describe as "undue delay," but I as "accidents." ' Writing about his trek across the Libyan Desert 'In Search of Zerzura'[2] he gives excellent reasons for having used camels and not a car; not mentioned is his preference for animals. He studied and understood them: the birds he watched, the animals he rode or hunted.

His daring was not the courage of one who did not see danger, nor was it based on the intoxication which team-spirit and mass action are apt to produce. He knew terrors, physical and spiritual,

[1] 'Charles Orde Browne,' in the *Engineer*, 14 September 1900.
[2] *Geographical Journal*, April 1934.

but he was hard, had high standards of honour, and the completest disregard for his own safety or interest. He could not be stopped nor scared; nor pleased nor bribed by things which others fall for. He was a closed book to strangers: his pale, drawn face with its joyless smile, his drooping head, his eyes, shy yet sharp and determined, with a piercing concentration in them. That concentration, born of spiritual struggles, was his strength. From those struggles were also born simplifications, sometimes bordering on the naive, yet impressive. Moshe Sharett, later Israel's first Foreign Secretary, once asked him: 'Tell me, Orde, when you call one man "good" and another "bad," what exactly do you mean?' Wingate looked astonished: 'Why, of course, I use the words in their Biblical sense: when I say a man is "good," I mean he is one who lives to fulfil the purposes of God; when I say he is "bad," I mean he lives to frustrate the purposes of God. I believe you and I are good men.'

In the course of the last three centuries Englishmen have come to look upon evil as a mere (regrettable) deviation from good: they have dethroned Satan. To Orde Wingate, good and evil, and the constant struggle between light and darkness in the world and in the heart of man, were as real as they were to Milton or to Dostoyevsky and Tolstoy. From the torment strength can arise and a drive of supreme intensity. These were in him. He could not have translated them into words. He could only express himself in action. It was his release.

Life was not easy for him, or with him. Intense, passionate, efficient, and wholly absorbed in his work, he made the highest demands on himself and on others; and was a severe, aggressive critic. Though irritable, often contemptuous of men, and sometimes touchy, yet in reality he was affectionate, generous, and harboured no personal rancours. When he returned from Burma, I mentioned a man who had wronged him, but could no longer hurt either him or what he stood for: the name evoked neither bitterness nor triumph, but was dismissed with lenient indifference. Orde was not concerned with men but with causes. His passionate pursuit of them was his search for God, and surrender to God's purpose.

Zionism was the cause nearest his heart. The thoughts and prayers of his ancestors, the faith and teachings of his parents, religious traditions neglected by most of his own generation, led him to Zion; by spiritual adoption he became one of Israel in the fight for the Return and Redemption. He was a missionary no less than a soldier, and there had to be moral content in what he fought for. He wanted to command men imbued with the same spirit and found them among a tortured nation, devoid of the easy joyful graces of life, but which after thousands of years still followed the Pillar of Fire.

Orde Wingate came to Palestine in 1936, during the Arab Rebellion. Things were going from bad to worse: the British Administration governed by day, and the Arab bands by night. He realized that measures were required of a new and unorthodox character: that guerrillas had to be met and defeated by guerrilla tactics. He decided to try the Jewish settlers. Keeping his own counsel, he took a few weeks' leave from the army, went to Tirat Zwi, a village of religiously most strict settlers, and demanded ten men for an urgent night operation (without bothering whether their rifles were 'legal' or not); next he went to other settlements. Supported by the Jewish Agency, he was obeyed. At first, however, there was a touch of suspicion and doubt: this British officer may successfully carry off an operation, and then go his way: they, the settlers, will remain, burdened by a blood-feud with their Arab neighbours. But when, on talking to Wingate, they found that he was not just a soldier on his job, their attitude changed completely.

Meantime he had tested his men, and proved to them what could be achieved by training and forethought and by un-relenting effort. He then went to his brigadier, a man free of anti-Jewish prejudice, and was given the chance of forming his 'Special Night Squads,' composed of Jewish boys from the settlements, with a stiffening of British troops: they were all trained and led by Wingate himself. In these operations he learnt a great deal which he later put to use in more famous guerrilla operations; in his men he implanted the self-confidence of efficient fighters. He inspired in them a devotion which would have made them follow him anywhere. But the Palestine Administration at no time desired to see military qualities develop in the Jews, least of all when a Palestine Munich was being prepared. Orde Wingate was recalled in 1938.

The bond between him and his men never broke. In October 1939 forty-three Jews were caught drilling with 'illegal' arms in the Beisan; some of them had served with distinction under Wingate. The existence of the Jewish self-defence organization was known, and even acknowledged, by the authorities; there was no suggestion of these men planning to attack anyone; they pleaded that they meant to enlist in the British Army as soon as given the chance. The military court condemned one man to imprisonment for life, and forty-two to ten years each. Orde sent them, through a Jewish friend, a message of confidence and cheer; they replied that they would always remain true to him. When, after eighteen months, they were released from prison, most of them enlisted; three were killed in an expedition commanded by a British officer, from which not a man returned, nor ever had much chance of returning; others distinguished themselves in the Syrian campaign and in various theatres of war. But a Jewish Force was not allowed to arise till late in 1944, a few months after Orde Wingate's death.

Wingate was unorthodox and unconventional as a soldier. But his unorthodoxy was of a man who having been trained to his craft goes beyond it. He knew every weapon, and was an expert in search of new ways and means, with no regard for entrenched prejudices. He did not suffer fools gladly, least of all among his superiors. It was said of him that before the end of the war he would either have to face a court martial or be a field-marshal.

His familiar terrain was the deserts and hills of the Near East. Even more remarkable therefore was the success which he achieved in the Burma jungle, completely strange to him, both with regard to country and men. Only once in the last war did he fight in country of which he had previous experience. The victory of Debra Markos, where at the head of 1,000 Sudanese and 800 Abyssinians he defeated and captured more than 12,000 regular Italian soldiers, was the result. It was never given to him to command that Jewish Army of which he had laid the foundations.

TWO GENERAL ELECTIONS; 1945 AND 1950

I

GENERAL ELECTIONS are the locks on the stream of British democracy, controlling the flow of the river and its traffic. Britain knows no direct democracy: neither through elections of executive or judicial officers, nor by means of a referendum. National self-government is practised through the House of Commons. But Parliament is no longer the self-contained arena which, in the absence of organized and disciplined parties, it was under George III, when in the course of seven years the House returned in 1761 gave its support to at least five different administrations. Now, barring the widening in a crisis of a party Government into a Coalition, changes of government in this country are invariably linked up with general elections, the decisive factor in the political life of the nation. Their circumstances, nature, technique, course, and results deserve therefore close study and analysis: this the general election of 1945 received in the book by Mr R. B. McCallum and Miss Alison Readman,[1] which in simple and lucid narrative systematically surveys the various aspects of that election, whether of a permanent or an incidental character.

A short and useful account of the 'electoral machinery,' its structure and working, is given in an early chapter; alongside of it emerges an electoral routine, of a quasi-ritualistic character—the candidates go through a series of motions of indeterminate value, perhaps equally uninteresting to all concerned, yet not to be dispensed with: they are of historic growth and of a traditional character. The performance starts with the election address, replacing 'the actual spoken appeal which used to be made by the

[1] R. B. McCallum and Alison Readman, *The British General Election of 1945* (London: Cumberlege).

183

candidates at the "hustings," ' and ends, after the result has been announced, with short speeches from the candidates; convention bids the defeated to declare with a cheerful smile that he has 'enjoyed every moment of the contest,' that he looks forward to the next election, and meantime wishes his rival all strength in representing the constituency.

However insipid the average election address may be, the aggregate of such addresses acquires a new meaning and value. If all the addresses of 1945 had been obtained, they would probably have amounted 'to over 1,600,000 words or more than three times the length of the Old Testament'; but in spite of support received from the party organizations, the authors were able to secure only 77 per cent of the addresses issued by the Conservatives, 69 per cent of the Labour addresses, and about one-quarter of those of the Liberals. (A similar analysis, based on four times the number of addresses but limited to one single aspect, was made in France by M. Henri Moysset when he traced the problem of *l'organisation du travail* in some 4,000 *professions de foi* issued by Parliamentary candidates at the general election of 1848.) In this, as in several other directions, the book marks an advance along lines of inquiry which have been previously pursued, and their ingathering into one comprehensive study. Still, the questions which the average man asks after a general election bear on its practical lessons: what were the factors which determined its result? Is their effect likely to endure, or to rebound against their present beneficiaries? What changes has the election made in Parliamentary representation? How much of a swing in the vote has produced this degree of dislocation?

In 1945 the Labour Party was better prepared for the general election than were the Conservatives, who had held no party conference during the war until 1943, while the Labour Party held one every year. 'The Conservatives interpreted the electoral truce to mean a political truce, while the Labour party . . . drew a sharp distinction between the two,' and, though supporting the Government in Parliament, freely engaged in the country in party propaganda, mainly concerned with post-war problems. In the constituencies the Conservatives and Liberals allowed their 'organizations to run down farther than had the Labour party,' which moreover had the advantage of its associations being 'more corporate' through their connexion with trade unions and co-operatives.

Labour went to the country with a fully developed program, the Conservative party presented Mr Churchill. 'For the Labour party the centre of interest . . . lay in domestic affairs'; for Mr Churchill, 'and perforce for his party, in foreign affairs, including the Japanese war.' Conservatism at all times places the emphasis on a practical approach to problems as they arise, rather than on doctrinal programs and blue-prints for the future; therefore the man to be put in charge of affairs invariably appears more important than theoretical disquisitions. And in Churchill the Conservative party had a leader who had proved himself 'to be among the greatest statesmen in British history,' and it seemed inconceivable that the country should reject him: his party and its candidates naturally tried to put his popularity to account—and perhaps overdid it, for a one-man show does not as a rule appeal to the British public. About half of the Conservative election addresses displayed Churchill's photograph, and 95 per cent contained a eulogy of him; Labour mentioned its leaders 'very little indeed.' In apportioning broadcasting time among speakers, the Conservative party 'concentrated nearly half their time on Mr Churchill' who spoke four times; the Labour party ran a team of ten, and none spoke more than once, while 'the policy of the Labour party as expounded in these broadcasts was more compact, concrete, and co-ordinated than that of the Conservative party.' But the past attitude of the Conservative party to Churchill was perhaps the weakest point in their approach: Labour was able to retort that the Conservatives were 'seeking to get a new lease of power by sheltering behind the prestige of a man who was distrusted and rejected by them before the war.'

By 1945 the thoughts of the electors naturally turned to problems of reconstruction: and here the memories of the previous post-war period, and of the twenty inter-war years, with their disappointments and frustrations, their unemployment and insecurity, their apparent sterility at home and ultimate failure abroad, worked heavily against the party which had been in power almost all that time. Nor did Mr Churchill's personality and popularity supply a fully effective antidote to such propaganda: it was widely believed that the qualites required in a great war leader differ so much from those of a peace-time Prime Minister, that the same man could hardly succeed in both roles. Nor did the 'Laski incident' prove a clear gain in the Conservative election campaign. Whatever the merits of the constitutional issue, 'it left the great mass of the electorate surprisingly un-interested' and, when pressed too far, gave an opening to the Labour party's 'anti-stunt propaganda.' Recalling the Zinoviev letter of 1924 and the Savings Scare of 1931, they had from the outset been foretelling 'a shameless Tory stunt.'

> Through all their propaganda, in the press, in speeches, and in election literature, there ran a constant note of warning to the electors to beware of tricks, frauds, and stunts. This part of the Labour party's campaign is perhaps the most brilliant piece of prophylactic political medicine ever achieved in electoral history.

In general, there seems to have been more bitter invective on the Labour than on the Conservative side: 'While the Con-servatives accused their opponents of trying to apply doctrinaire, or academic theories to politics,' Conservative failures were attributed by Labour 'not to incompetence but to self-interested-ness amounting to dishonesty.' And such accusations, if believed, mattered a good deal, for reconstruction problems seem to have overshadowed everything else in the minds of the electors. No less than 97 per cent of the Labour candidates and 94 per cent of the Conservatives raised the question of housing, and when on 11 June the *News Chronicle* tried a 'Gallup' poll concerning the principal issue of the election, 41 per cent answered 'housing,' while on 16 June, to an inquiry 'as to which party would handle housing best,' 42 per cent answered Labour, 25 per cent Con-servative, and 13 per cent Liberal. Next in importance in the addresses ranked Social Security, discussed by 77 per cent of the Labour candidates, and 81½ per cent of the Conservatives, and Full Employment (79 and 73 per cent). Reduction of taxation was scarcely mentioned in Labour addresses, and by only one-fifth of the Conservatives; 'more attention was paid to benefits than to burdens.' 'Local problems and industries make little show in the English addresses,' much more in the Scottish and Welsh. 'When one considers the addresses as a whole, one is left to surmise that most foreigners would be impressed by the degree of national integration which they show.' The country expects to be saved or ruined as a whole. The treatment to be given to Germany was discussed in only 8 per cent of the addresses.

'The electorate were in earnest, sober mood.' 'Political debate has fallen from the heroic to the conversational level,' wrote a correspondent in a Liverpool paper. The campaign was 'very

decorous; some might even say dull.' There was a fair amount
of general vituperation ('less in doubtful than in safe seats,' with
women candidates tending to be 'more vituperative than men'),
but 'little personal invective'—'the electors were markedly bored
and irritated by "personalities" . . .' There was no mass excitement: 'the quietness of the election and the comparatively thin
attendance at meetings' is largely accounted for by the part played
by broadcasts. According to an estimate of the B.B.C., 44·9 per
cent of the adult population listened in; and 'where the greater
part of the electors are . . . in their own homes beside the wire-
less . . . the element of mass emotion . . . is entirely absent.' 'It
may well be that this method of radio campaigning has revolu-
tionized the nature of British elections.' But then also the bond
which an election forges between the electors and the successful
candidate will tend to disappear; the 'sense of constituency,'
which was the foundation of the British representative system
and has grown dim in the modern amorphous electoral divisions,
is in danger of being eclipsed still further.

It is hardly possible to say to what extent the election campaign
influenced the voting—the evidence is, in its very nature, too uncertain. But 'a "Gallup" poll taken by the *News Chronicle*
between 6 and 13 June stated that before nomination day as many
as 84 per cent of the persons questioned in the poll declared that
they had already made up their minds how to vote'; and the
authors aver that 'when it came to voting the electors appeared
to have been little influenced by the actual record and occupations
of the candidates and voted more for the party.' But what determined their choice of party? The authors do not stress the class
element; still, in a passage which may refer to one particular
district or may be of wider application, they say: 'It was in-
dubitable that the majority supported the Labour party because
they looked upon it as the working-class party. Their allegiance
was for the most part unquestioning and uncritical.' In the
1860's men like Lord Salisbury carefully calculated the relative
numerical strength which an extension of the suffrage would
give to the have's and have-not's: they expected class-voting.
The experience of the next seventy-five years seemed to disprove
such forecasts—has now the majority of the working population
turned to exercising their political rights and influence, if not
exclusively through men of their own class, at least through a
party bearing their name?

N

Still, even now a comparatively small turn-over can reverse the position: at the general election of 1945 nearly 12 million votes were given for Labour, nearly 10 million for the Conservatives and their allies, and over 2,200,000 for the Liberals. Having made some minor corrections because of unopposed returns and two-member constituencies, and then grouped all the classifiable votes into a pro- and an anti-Socialist bloc, the authors find that there was a Socialist majority of 66,000 (12,008,000 against 11,942,000); and even that tiny margin of a quarter of a per cent would be cancelled out if the votes of certain unclassified Independents and of the Welsh Nationalists were added to the other side. On 48 per cent of the votes Labour secured 393 seats in a House of 640 members, that is 61 per cent of the total, giving them a clear majority of 146 over all the rest. The Conservative alliance, which in the previous Parliament had held 397 seats, was reduced to 213 (the nearest to an exact one-third of 640). The authors put the swing-over in votes at 12 per cent; thus the loss by the Conservatives 'of a quarter of their supporters . . . more than doubled the Labour representation in Parliament and almost halved the Conservative strength.' Still, the system under which these disproportionate turn-overs are bound to occur has for a long time past been quite consciously and deliberately maintained in its present form 'without serious criticism or anxiety being evident in any large mass of the population.' The authors do not enter upon a discussion of the problem: but it is obvious that the system, besides usually securing good working majorities in the House, vastly enhances the weight of the voters who are apt to fluctuate between the two leading parties; and that this forces sensible leaders on either side to steer a middle course. It is perhaps a deeper, instinctive understanding of the British Parliamentary system which makes the nation put up with the apparent paradoxes of such election results.

A careful and, what is more, a critical analysis is supplied of the occupational and educational antecedents of the candidates—statistics of that kind call for a good deal of common sense and discrimination. It would be easy but hardly profitable to plank down material obtained from almanachs, etc.: it has to be sifted, interpreted, and classified, and it is this work which determines the value of such statistics. As for age, an analysis of the available (incomplete) data yields for both Conservatives and Labour an average age of forty-six. In the Parliaments of George III it was about forty-three; in the Frankfurt Parliament of 1848, about forty-four and a half. But is this not perhaps also the average age of the entire adult population with a slight addition for longer life in the classes and groups from which the members or candidates were, or are, drawn? In 1851, the average age of males in England and Wales of twenty years and above was forty, and in mid-1938 the average age of the population of twenty-one and above was forty-four. The age structure of Parliament is always like a vase, very narrow at its base—members below thirty —and bulging in the regions between thirty and sixty; while for a normal population that structure is like a pyramid. And yet apparently a very similar average is reached in both. Among the particular age-groups, those of 30–40, 40–50, and 50–60 yield the following percentages: with the Conservatives 21, 36, and 19 per cent; with Labour candidates, 26, 31, and 24. The authors do not attempt to explain this more even distribution, and one wonders what the results would be if the Labour intelligentsia was separated from the trade unionists; possibly the intellectuals are responsible for the disproportionate strength of the group 30–40, and the trade-union leaders of that of 50–60.

One other, significant, lacuna in this extremely thorough and painstaking work concerns the regional extraction of the candidates; to what extent were they 'local men'? It is mentioned that about one-third in both parties claimed in their election addresses 'that they are local men, not necessarily living in the actual division, but brought up or working in the district' (and their wives sometimes say in their supporting letters 'that they want to come and live in the constituency, but are often careful to add "if elected" '). But then it would be an almost impossible task, as far as England is concerned, to define a 'local man': the country is too thoroughly integrated. In France M. Chaboseau analysing the Parliament of 1848 found that out of its 876 members exactly 676 were natives of the *départements* for which they were returned, and that of the remaining 200 the overwhelming majority were closely connected with their constituencies. No such high figures could ever in modern times have been produced for England: there is probably no other country in the world where the choice of members is so little bound up with their local origin—one of the many blessings for which England has to thank that admirable, and so much maligned, institution, the rotten boroughs of the Unreformed Parliament. The authors rightly remark: 'If . . .

membership were limited to local men, then the House of Commons would be more representative in the sense of being more average; but it would be less distinguished and less effective.'

2

The general election of February 1950 came when the Parliament of 1945 was approaching its statutory end. The parties were fully prepared, and out of a total of 625 seats, 623 were contested; the Conservatives ran 620 candidates, and Labour 617; 28,772,671 valid votes were cast, making 83·96 per cent of the registered electorate; a close finish was expected. Yet the campaign was eminently quiet; Mr Churchill called it 'demure'; in restraint and decorum it surpassed even that of 1945. 'The election oratory ... was becalmed,' writes one observer; election meetings, 'sober, well-conducted, inquiring, and rather dull,' listened to lectures on economic subjects, mostly flat and 'jargon-loaded.' Yet 'each side felt that the stakes were great,' and 'expended all the pent-up effort' it could command. 'The public took the issue of this election seriously,' writes another observer. 'The mood of seriousness that prevailed was averse to display,' writes a third.

Also the election literature was, to say the least, unexciting, and probably held the attention of few besides those who had to retail its argument in speeches and writing. Are election campaigns indeed changing into a ritual gone through to satisfy the demands of conscience, of habit and tradition, and of courtesy towards the voters? Even the canvass is losing its character of house-to-house propaganda, and now primarily aims at ascertaining where the candidate's support lies, so as to get it out on polling day—canvassing teams are told by organizers not to 'waste time arguing.' Still, there is the floating vote, and not all of it was fixed before the campaign of 1950 had started. But perhaps advertence to that vote actually helped to damp down the

---

H. G. Nicholas, *The British General Election of 1950* (Macmillan).

The General Election in Glasgow, February 1950. General Editor: S. B. Chrimes (Glasgow: Jackson).

The British Journal of Sociology, vol. i, September 1950.

The Manchester School of Economic and Social Studies, vol. xviii, No. 3, September 1950.

campaign: both in 1945 and in 1950 feelings tended to rise less 'in constituencies where the parties were running neck to neck than in areas where one enjoyed a secure majority'—obviously party fervour was thought more likely to put off than to attract voters not wedded to either of the two major parties. There is much that calls for explanation.

Mr. H. G. Nicholas, in his study of *The British General Election of 1950*, consciously follows the example of Mr R. B. McCallum and Miss Alison Readman. Both surveys, undertaken under the auspices of Nuffield College, received active outside assistance; but it is the workmanship at the centre that gives shape, and Nicholas's is not equal to that of his two predecessors. Fear of being overtaken by another general election may have accounted for some of its shortcomings—his work was completed in half the time they took over theirs. But there are inherent weaknesses: the keen, inquisitive spirit is lacking which through the accumulated rubble of the top layers would penetrate to the core of the matter; the planning of the book is inert, and the execution often inept; the attention which subjects receive is out of proportion to their intrinsic interest, and essential aspects are left out altogether. In the very first pages, the account of party losses through the redistribution of seats is confused. In the next chapter, the growing 'concentration of power in the hands of the central offices' is noted, but the discussion of the party organizations is limited to the election agents. The age, education, profession, etc., of the candidates are analysed, but not of the members returned. Statistical tables are often defective, and questions arising from their contents are left unasked and unanswered. The chapters on the campaign traverse in excessive detail ground very similar to that covered by McCallum and Readman, and even were the performance equal to theirs, the repetition would render it wearisome. If nation-wide surveys of general elections are to be repeated at comparatively short intervals, it might suffice to deal in brief with things fully treated or points established previously, while concentrating on what is new or has not received adequate attention. The work of predecessors should serve as starting-point rather than as frame for further studies.

Perhaps the time has come for a different approach: for a more intensive study of smaller geographical units. Several such monographs were published in 1950. An electoral survey of Glasgow, the second largest city in the United Kingdom, returning fifteen

members, was carried out by a team of lecturers and students
from its University; a survey of 'Politics in the North-West'
(Lancashire, Cheshire, and the High Peak division of Derbyshire:
eighty members) was made by two lecturers of Manchester
University: the same two assisted by students from the Department of Government and Administration, undertook an inquiry
into 'voting behaviour' in the Lancashire constituency of Stretford; lastly, an inquiry into the 1950 election at Greenwich was
made by the British Institute of Public Opinion in conjunction
with the London School of Economics.

While limiting the area of surveys it would seem advisable to
extend the periods covered by them. The greater part of the
electorate forms solid *blocs*, voting consistently for one party; and
swings in the 'floating vote' mostly set in between the elections
—even successful election campaigns merely reinforce existing
trends. But there is nothing in this country to compare with M.
André Siegfried's extensive studies in electoral history, based on
searching sociological analysis: his *Tableau Politique de la France
de l'Ouest sous la IIIᵉ République*, and his *Géographie Electorale de
l'Ardèche* covering the same period. Below a seemingly changing
surface he has traced remarkable continuity in the politics of the
regions examined; a similar persistence of attitudes could probably
be shown in this country, and that not in obvious regions only,
such as Ulster or the 'Celtic fringe.' Thus Mr Birch and Mr
Campbell, in their essay on 'Politics in the North-west,' speaking
of its Conservatism greater than in the country as a whole,
observe that this

> has been a feature of English politics since the enfranchisement of
> the urban artisan householder in 1867; only in the few years of
> Liberal supremacy just before the First World War did this rule
> not hold good.

Indeed, the peculiar Conservatism of the North-west goes back
far beyond 1867: to the Reformation and the Civil Wars, to the
Non-Jurors and Jacobites, and to the eighteenth-century Tories.

But while attempting a study in Siegfried's style, Birch and
Campbell argue that it is difficult in this country to correlate
'local variations of economic activity and social structure . . .
with variations in participation and political allegiance' because
British constituencies are mostly arbitrary units for which no
social or economic statistics are available; nor is it possible to draw

up satisfactory comparative tables of elections, say, since 1867, in view of the many changes in the area of constituencies and of the number of uncontested seats in earlier elections, etc. That lack of serviceable statistics, they conclude, may force studies of voting in this country 'to pass earlier than their foreign counterparts from statistical methods to case-study.' It is through such studies that a deeper insight can be obtained into the habits and reactions of the electorate, and a safer judgment formed about our present election campaigns.

The Representation of the People Act of 1948 greatly affected the 1950 campaign by cutting down permitted expenditure at a time of steeply rising prices, and still further by a clause (or 'joker') it contained forbidding outside persons to incur expense on behalf of the candidates. An interpretation, undisclosed while the Bill was before Parliament, was put forward by Mr. Herbert Morrison on 26 November 1949: for instance, propaganda against nationalization, such as that of 'Mr. Cube,' might have to be included in election expenditure. However strained the argument, it put all parties on their guard—he warned 'everybody' if the law were in doubt 'to err on the side of keeping it'; while Central Offices and most constituency associations were holding their fire for fear of expending their ammunition too soon.

A paradoxical situation ensued [writes Nicholas] in which an election which was on every man's lips positively receded from public view, disappeared from the hoardings, was less debated on the hustings than three months before, and soon went off the front page of the newspapers. A 'phoney war' had supervened.

One had to search for the posters that used to brighten up elections; nor were the few produced equal to those of 1910, or even of 1945. A blanket of boredom seemed to have fallen on the land.

When, on 6 February, Mr Attlee set off on his 1,000-mile propaganda tour through Great Britain, it was undoubtedly

a *tour de force* of unassuming advertisement. The family car, pre-war and far from *de luxe*, Mrs. Attlee at the wheel, no entourage beyond the indispensable detective, the roadside stops when, ahead of schedule, Mrs. Attlee would catch up with her knitting and Mr. Attlee would do a cross-word puzzle—this was the very stuff of honest, uninvidious, unpretentious, non-queue-jumping, post-war

Britain. . . . However worked upon by hostile critics, it could not be presented . . . as a curtain-raiser to . . . class-war. . . .

Attlee reported on his 'four and a half years of stewardship.' His function, writes Nicholas, 'was to personify the quiet reasonableness of Labour.' What they seemed to fear was Churchill's 'flamboyancy'—his putting some life into the campaign. When on 7 February he declared that it ought to be possible to abolish petrol rationing he was branded as a stunt-monger; and when on the 15th he urged 'another talk with Soviet Russia upon the highest level' this was again, to Bevin and Morrison, 'electoral stunting.' Churchill replied:

> Why should it be wrong for the British nation to think about these supreme questions of life and death, perhaps for the whole world, at a time when there is a General Election? Is that not the one time of all others when they should think about them? What a reflection it would be upon our national dignity and moral elevation, and indeed, upon the whole status of British democracy, if at this time of choice, this turning-point in world history, we found nothing to talk about but material issues and nice calculations about personal gain or loss. . . .

The Labour leaders winced at what between men of equal stature would have resulted in give and take. They relied, foremost, on the stodgy solidarity of organized Labour, shunned excitement, and practised once more their 'prophylactic political medicine' of 1945: on 17 February Morrison referred to 'rumours' that a 'scare' was being prepared; and on the 18th Attlee

> warned his audience that if any new issues were 'developed' between now and polling day it would be 'neither honest nor genuine. It will be a mere election stunt.'

All along it was again conveniently forgotten that the 'Red Letter' was an extraneous incident bungled by Ramsay MacDonald, while the scare about the Post Office Savings Bank was the work of Philip Snowden.

The Government were on the defensive; pointed to their record and asked to be allowed to continue; contrasted full employment in their own time with pre-war unemployment; defended nationalization; and talked of 'fair shares for all.' But Sir Stafford Cripps, writes Mr. D. D. Raphael in the Glasgow survey, 'denied explicitly that fair shares meant equal shares'; and a Labour candidate, when asked what it did mean, referred the questioner to St. Mark, vi, 38–42—the loaves and fishes—but did not explain

whether Labour policy was supposed to depend on miracles, or whether the point was after all that loaves were equally divided. But presumably the candidate meant simply that food was to be made available for all. For most Labour election addresses treated 'fair shares' as meaning 'fair shares of food' ensured by the system of rationing.

Did anyone dispute that program? It was not a 'basic standard' for all to which the Conservatives objected, but the cramping of individual initiative and the killing of incentive to work. Raphael notes a passage in the Conservative election manifesto treated by Churchill 'as the hub of his policy':

We are determined to give a solid base of social security below which none shall fall and above which each must be encouraged to rise to the utmost limit of his ability.

The Conservatives pointed to 'the creeping paralysis of State monopoly' and the mismanagement of nationalized industries; the unfulfilled housing program, the depreciation of the pound and the rise in the cost of living, the crushing burden of taxation, etc. Election propaganda disclosed differences in attitude and emphasis rather than in social philosophy; and as Nicholas points out, its issues were administrative rather than legislative— employment, housing, controls, taxation and expenditure, etc.

It is generally admitted that nationalization as an issue fell flat— in Glasgow 'the interest of voters who asked questions about it at meetings seemed to lie in the high price and poor quality of coal, and in the high salaries paid to officials.' Deep concern was shown about repayment of post-war credits and an increase of pensions —the poor and the old obviously felt 'very sharply the pinch of the current cost of living'; and Mr. Wright, in his essay on the election campaign in Glasgow, states that 'no more than 10 per cent of the audiences were of young people,' largely helpers drawn from party youth organizations. Was this a local or a nation-wide phenomenon? And if nationwide, does it mean that election meetings belong to a defunct period and a declining generation? Have broadcasts killed them? But even interest in party broadcasts seems to have decreased: in 1945 the average of the adult population listening to them during the weeks before the election was put by the B.B.C. at 45, 44, 47, and 41 per cent; in 1950, at 33, 37, and 39. 'Only Mr Churchill held audiences . . . as he had in 1945'—his figure was 51 per cent.; Attlee's, 44; and third came 'the Radio Doctor,' Charles Hill, with 42 per cent. Equally significant was Hill's success; his broadcast became 'a point of departure for opponents' arguments' and 'part of the cultural currency' of the campaign. It voiced 'the plain man's grouse,' and was 'recorded and distributed to the constituencies for use on loud-speaker vans.' Foreign affairs were not an issue; there was substantial agreement, and a consciousness of how little it was in our power to determine their course. There was also a 'prevailing sense of economic crisis' and no belief in a panacea for it. Concrete programs in either field were hardly possible. The voting had to be for parties and not for measures.

The struggle was for the floating vote, hence to a high degree for the Liberal vote, actual or potential. Labour claimed to be the heirs of the Liberal Governments of 1906 and 1910, the Conservatives spoke of the need of a common front against Socialism. The Liberals, in putting up 475 candidates, meant to offer 'the electorate the opportunity of returning a Liberal Government to office'; they 'displayed portraits of their leading parliamentarians . . . to present themselves as a party led by figures of national stature'; but they put up mainly young candidates (in Glasgow, of nine not one had previously stood for Parliament, two were undergraduates, and all lost their deposits). The Liberals harped on standing outside the 'class struggle' of the two major parties; demanded for labour a share in the management and profits of business; oscillated between 'individual liberty' and 'social justice,' a free economy and public control; exhumed Free Trade; displayed U.N.O., successor to the League of Nations; advocated separate Parliaments for Scotland and Wales; equal pay for women; etc. They tried to please, and cut no ice. The Liberal 'appeal was noble and idealistic enough,' remarks Wright, 'but it hardly seemed grounded on terra firma.'

By regulations strictly limiting contributions from candidates, the Conservative party seems to have put a stop to the buying of needy constituencies; although these regulations affected mainly new candidatures, it would appear [writes Nicholas] as if the great majority of candidates went into the election free of any considerable financial commitments to their constituency associations.

On the Labour side 'the problem has been how to prevent the union contributions . . . from swamping the initiative and independence of the divisional labour parties.' Of 441 candidates sponsored by constituency Labour organizations, 186 (42·2 per cent) were successful; of 140 trade-union candidates, 110 (78·6 per cent); but while the bigger unions carried 85 per cent of their elections, the smaller carried only 56 per cent. Geographical concentration accounts for the Mineworkers winning every single seat they contested; but when the Union of Shop, Distributive and Allied Workers won eight out of their nine contests, one is led to conclude that they had the pick of the constituencies. Of 241 Labour candidates with university education, 120 were successful—almost exactly half; but a more detailed analysis reveals significant differences: of 96 graduates of provincial universities, 53 were returned; of 84 Oxford and Cambridge men, 46; of 61 London graduates, excluding the School of Economics, 21; and of 22 graduates of the School of Economics, 4 (of 5 Etonians, also 4); of 14 men from Ruskin College, with its trade-union affiliations, 9. Of 146 Labour candidates who were Fabians, only 57 were successful; but Nicholas's conclusion that 'politically . . . membership of the Society might appear something of a doubtful asset,' seems unconvincing: it was probably a question of residence, occupation, and social setting, and not of politics. Most London School of Economics graduates and Fabians presumably stood for non-industrial districts.

Participation in the general election of 1950 (83·96 per cent) was '10½ per cent more than in 1945,' writes Mr. D. E. Butler in a statistical appendix to Nicholas's book, 'and 7½ per cent more than in any of the inter-war general elections'; and it varied little between one part of the country and another. It was highest in the two Ulster constituencies won by Irish Nationalists (92 per cent) and lowest in remote rural areas and in safe divisions of big cities—in three Labour strongholds of Glasgow it was less than 77 per cent and in Chelsea and South Kensington 71 per cent. (Generally the poll in big cities was below the national average: in London the mean was 79·3, in Glasgow 79·97, in Liverpool 80·1, and in Manchester 82·2). But Butler, by grouping constituencies according to the size of the majority, finds 'the very highest turnout . . . in the 48 seats where the Labour majority was more than 40 per cent of the poll'—33 were miners' seats, 23 of them held by majorities of over 20,000. Social cohesion and group solidarity counted for at least as much as political interest and uncertainty of the result.

Birch and Campbell, having divided the north-western region into eight areas, found that the coal-chemical area, which is solidly Labour, and west Lancashire and southern Cheshire, which are strongly Conservative, have invariably heavier polls than the Manchester area, where 'in each of the four elections from 1923 to 1931 between ten and fourteen of the area's [22] seats changed hands,' and twelve in 1945; and that this pattern of participation, subject to only very slight modifications, has continued since 1867, apparently 'unaffected by the extensions of the suffrage in 1884 and 1918.' (Similarly their inquiry into local elections at Stretford has shown that voting depends largely on the extent to which electors are socially rooted in the district.) In a mining or an industrially homogeneous area an election turnout is akin to a parade; not so in a residential or a nondescript urban district. In the country as a whole the average poll in constituencies returning Labour members was, in 1950, 1·2 per cent higher than in those returning Conservatives.

In 1950 Conservatives, Labour, and Liberals obtained 12,500,000 13,250,000, and 2,500,000 votes, and gained 298, 315, and 9 seats, the division of seats between the two major parties being in the exact ratio of their votes. In 1945 the poll was 10 million, 12 million, and 2,200,000 and the representation in the House 213, 393, and 12: a vote of six to five gave Labour nearly twice the number of Conservative seats. In representation this is felt as deviating from the proportional; in mathematics it must be accounted for as a deviation from a dead average, that is, from an absolutely even distribution of votes between the constituencies, which would give them all to the majority party. But the laws of chance would preclude such uniform distribution even were we dealing out red and blue balls from a box. And with regard to general elections, is it possible to offer any formula whereby to forecast the result? In 1909 the Right Hon. James Parker Smith, giving evidence before the Royal Commission on Electoral Systems, quoted one propounded by the distinguished mathematician, P. A. MacMahon: 'If the electors are in the ratio A to

B then the members would be at least in the ratio of A^3 to B^3.'
Therefore a poll of six to five should produce in the House a ratio
of 216 to 125: which closely corresponds to the 1945 figures of
393 and 213. That formula was recalled by *The Economist* in
January 1950, and has now been examined by Messrs. M. G.
Kendall and A. Stuart, who show it to be a mathematical consequence of the particular form taken by the distribution of the
vote-ratio of the two principal parties over the constituencies.
This form has been found remarkably constant over a number
of general elections, and those of 1931 and 1935, besides that of
1945, conformed to the MacMahon formula. But the circumstances in which it held true can easily change, and then the
formula is no longer valid. There can be a bias either in the size
of constituencies, or in the distribution of majorities: in 1945, the
average Labour seat contained 51,000 electors, and the average
Conservative seat 57,000, which bias was removed by the redistribution of 1948-9; and both in 1945 and in 1950 Labour
suffered from an excessive piling up of its electoral majorities in
certain areas (especially in the mining districts): Butler calculates
that in 1950, on a 50-50 vote 'the Conservatives would have had
35 more seats than Labour.' In 1945, the two biases seem to have
cancelled out each other; in 1950, the one surviving bias vitiated
the MacMahon formula.

In 1950 the swing from Labour to the Conservatives was 3.3
per cent for the whole country: 3·6. in England, 0·3 in Wales,
and 3·1 in Scotland. England returned 252 Conservatives, 251
Labour, and 2 Liberals; Wales, 4, 27, and 5; Scotland, 32, 37, and
2; Ulster, 10 Conservatives and 2 Irish Nationalists. The swing
was greatest in Essex (8·2 per cent), the Hampshire ports (7·6),
and the surburban London boroughs (7·2); altogether in the
dormitory areas of the big towns. A B.I.P.O. poll showed that
whereas in 1945 of the middle class voters 54 per cent intended
to vote Conservative, 21 Labour, and 11 Liberal, in 1950 the
figures were 63, 16, and 13. Another B.I.P.O. poll taken on the
eve of the election showed that 'in the absence of a Liberal candidate two-fifths of the Liberal supporters would have abstained,
two-fifths voted Conservative, and one-fifth Labour.' On that
basis, according to Birch and Campbell, the Liberal intervention
lost the Conservatives twelve seats. On the other hand, Butler
calculates that Communist intervention lost Labour four seats. If
both figures are correct, without either intervention Labour

would have secured a majority of one over the Conservatives! The Liberals put up 475 candidates, won 9 seats, and lost 319 deposits; the average poll of their candidates was even lower than in 1945. The Communists in 1945 put up 21 candidates, obtained 102,780 votes, and 2 seats; in 1950 the figures were, 100 candidates, 91,684 votes, and no seats. Another feature of the 1950 election was the entire extinction of Independents; the hold of parties over constituencies and members has been steadily growing for at least 120 years, and is now complete.

There undoubtedly is correlation between social class and party, but no clear class division. The Labour following among the middle classes is by no means negligible, and without working-class support the Conservatives could never win a general election; working men and women form about three-fourths of the British electorate, and, according to public opinion polls, vote Conservative and Labour in a proportion of roughly three to five. Hence, while almost every seat in the United Kingdom was contested in 1950 by the two major parties, the Conservatives lost only five deposits and Labour none. In Glasgow in only one of its 15 divisions the Labour poll dropped below 30 per cent of the votes, and in only three altogether below 40 per cent; in none was the Conservative poll less than 30 per cent, and in six less than 40 per cent—there was cross-voting between classes besides residential inter-mixture. 'Case studies' concerning the relation of social class to political attitude and behaviour have been attempted at Greenwich and Stretford by means of interviewing a substantial sample of electors drawn from the register. In both places a classification of electors was made by the investigators, but at Greenwich the elector was also asked about his social status, so that besides the 'attributed' there is a 'subjective' or 'self-rated' status.

Here are some of the results of the Stretford survey of Birch and Campbell. The percentages of middle-class electors voting Conservative, Labour, and Liberal were 61, 22, and 17; of working-class voters 39, 52, and 9. The percentage of working-class Conservatives was thus higher than in the country as a whole; and the Liberals had a more pronounced class basis than the Conservatives. Among the lower ranks of white-collared workers, rated as of the working class, Conservatism was found as strong as in the middle class; but middle-class industrial technicians (works managers, chemists, engineers, etc.), while predominantly Conservative were much less so than the non-industrial workers—evidence of the influence of occupational setting on political attitude. Of electors consistently voting Conservative, women formed 63 per cent, and among industrial workers and unskilled labourers 76 per cent; of consistent Labour voters 55 per cent were men. There was no Liberal candidate at Stretford in 1945, and in 1950 the Liberals obtained the largest share of the floating vote—probably consisting of Liberals now enabled to vote for their own candidate, or of middle- and lower-middle-class electors, disillusioned with Labour, 'but still reluctant to support the Conservative Party.' The loss of Stretford by Labour was due to the floating vote much more than to changes in the boundaries of the constituency.

And here are some of the results of the Greenwich survey, undertaken by the British Institute of Public Opinion and analysed by Mr. Mark Benney and Miss Phyllis Geiss. The Labour Party at Greenwich was found much more homogeneous in its social structure than the Conservative Party, and 'the social distance between its officers and its voters was much narrower.' It was further found, comparing 'attributed' with 'self-rated' social status, that although only 41 per cent of Conservative voters had white-collar occupations, 59 per cent claimed middle-class status, while adherents of the Labour Party seemed predisposed to declare themselves members of the working class. Of 215 electors of the self-rated middle class, 160 intended to vote Conservative, 42 Labour, and 13 Liberal; of 474 of the self-rated 'working class,' 105 Conservative, 356 Labour, and 13 Liberal. The electors when asked which party they thought 'would do the best job' for the upper, the middle, and the working class, showed

> a very pronounced tendency . . . to associate the Conservative Party with the interests of the 'upper class.' Not so pronounced but still unmistakable is the association of the Labour Party with the welfare of the working class. . . . But . . . Conservatives of both classes are more convinced than are the Labourites that their party will best serve the middle class.

And here is a significant detail: of the 105 self-rated working people who intended to vote Conservative 24 thought that the Labour Party was best for the working class without this changing their voting intentions.

Next, five propositions based on the Conservative program and five based on that of Labour were put before the electors.

The Conservative Party program seems to have been decidedly the more successful in appealing to *all* classes. That is, you could predict a person's class less readily from his response to Conservative items than from his response to Labour items.

But there was, on the whole, a clear division between the middle and lower middle class on the one hand and the working class on the other. And when the replies are grouped according to their response to the goals of socialism (greater equality of incomes, 'full employment,' more control of industry by workers, 'socialism') and to its methods (nationalization, State trading, building controls, closed shop),

the goals of socialism receive a generally high degree of approval from all classes, but highest among the groups which have most to gain from them; the means of socialism receive a generally low degree of approval. . . .

Among the middle class the percentage of informants approving of those means varied from 10 to 20 per cent; but even among the working men not one of the four 'methods' obtained a majority, while among working women the percentages approving of them were: 29, 18, 21, and 17—in short, there was marked disapproval.

In general the table suggests that, if voting behaviour were determined by attitudes to *published* policy statements alone, the Greenwich candidate for Labour might have lost his seat.

Briefly, the elector's conception of social class and his self-classification were found at Greenwich 'the chief determinant of political behaviour'; and voting was greatly influenced by the elector's social environment, and was more closely related to the image he formed of the parties than to the detailed policies propounded by them. Fleeting opinions do not make social groups 'float,' and the greatest part of the electorate is ensconced in such groups; yet the votes that do float are not to be gained by class appeals, and it is they that foremost decide the issue of general elections.